DATE DUE

DE 2 96			
MY 29 97			
SE 29 97			
OE 15 97			
MR 12 98			
MR 31 98			
JY 30 98			
OE 15 98			
MR 29 99			
AP 21 99			
MY 27 99			
OE 1 99			
FE 13			

DEMCO 38-296

Composers of the **Twentieth** *Century*

The Music of

YALE UNIVERSITY PRESS · New Haven and London

Gershwin

STEVEN E. GILBERT

Designed by Richard Hendel.
Set in Monotype Garamond type by
Tseng Information Systems, Inc.
Printed in the United States of America by
Thomson-Shore, Dexter, Michigan.

Library of Congress Cataloging-in-Publication Data
Gilbert, Steven E.
  The music of Gershwin / Steven E. Gilbert.
    p.   cm. — (Composers of the twentieth century)
  Includes bibliographical references and index.
  ISBN 0-300-06233-8
  1. Gershwin, George, 1898–1937 — Criticism and interpretation.
I. Series.
ML410.G288G55   1995   95-12086
780'.92 — dc20   CIP
                    MN

A catalogue record for this book is available from the
British Library.

The paper in this book meets the guidelines for
permanence and durability of the Committee on Production
Guidelines for Book Longevity of the Council on Library
Resources.

10 9 8 7 6 5 4 3 2 1

For Jonathan and Matthew

Contents

Preface

As Jake of Catfish Row might have put it, it has taken a long time to get there, and I still may not have reached the Promised Land. From inception to realization, this project has occupied more than a decade, encompassing a series of life passages which, if retold, could spawn another opera, albeit more soap than grand.

My acquaintance with the music of George Gershwin began in childhood, when, like just about every other kid in Brooklyn who took piano lessons, I viewed *Rhapsody in Blue* and the ability to play it as the zenith of musical achievement. Gershwin, after all, was one of our own.

My roots were left behind as my supposed sophistication grew, and I came to disdain this unschooled composer of semi-popular music. Schoenberg and his pupils were the order of the day; and despite the Schoenberg-Gershwin connection having been known at the time, no one I knew ever mentioned it. Yet the Gershwin presence was kept alive by the remarks of one of my most quotable former teachers, the late Ernst Levy. To Professor Levy, a pianist on a par with Schnabel and the composer of fifteen symphonies, I owe a repertoire of aphorisms that I repeat to students to this day. When I once casually dismissed Gershwin in a discussion with him (in the halls of the building at

Brooklyn College that bears Gershwin's name), he quickly replied, "Ah . . . but Gershwin had the gift of melody."

That he did. And it was this quality that eventually led me to suspect that Gershwin's tunes would bear up well—indeed, speak eloquently—under analytic scrutiny. Some initial sketches, used in a seminar in American music in 1983, formed the basis for an article completed during the next year. The suggestion that I build this material into a book came from Allen Forte, my teacher and friend for over a quarter-century, with whom I had written *Introduction to Schenkerian Analysis*. Neither of us, however, imagined that the project would take me as long as it did; for his patience, guidance, and continual positive reinforcement I shall be eternally grateful.

The comprehensive books on Gershwin by Edward Jablonski (1987) and Charles Schwartz (1973) both contain detailed, chronological work-lists. The present book seeks not to duplicate or improve upon these, and when biographical facts and assumptions do surface (as they occasionally must), its approach is to refer to pertinent sources for amplification. By design, its subject is not the life of George Gershwin but his music.

In discussing this music, I have tended to use the vocabulary in which I have been schooled. The analytic method of Heinrich Schenker (1868–1935), although not originally intended for music after Brahms, has proved useful in depicting basic melodic, contrapuntal, and harmonic structures and in showing why Gershwin's tunes work as well as they do. A Schenkerian graph will highlight the main melodic outline of a piece or song along with the large-scale progression of local key areas—such as, for example, the shift from I to III (that is, E♭ major to G major) in the refrain of "'S Wonderful" (ex. 11b). At the same time, it will point out certain details—melodies, parts of melodies—that relate to the larger picture in some significant way. Thus the refrain's main melodic figure, B♭–G, can be seen as a complement to the harmonic interval E♭–G; together, the two form the tonic E♭-major triad. The descending minor third that begins the refrain also dominates the verse (ex. 11a), thereby tying the two together in a very tangible way. Such features make for an organic piece of music and demonstrate that the composer lavished the same care on his songs as he did on his concert works. Gershwin's song manuscripts, by the way, tended to be fully notated, often down to the last detail of the piano accompaniment.

I close with profound thanks to those without whose guidance and support this project might not have come to fruition. Encouragement has come from no fewer than three successive editors at Yale University Press: Edward Tripp, Jeanne Ferris, and—the third being the charm—Harry Haskell, who finally saw the completed work. At California State University, Fresno, proposals relating to this book have passed through the administrations of two deans, Joseph Satin and Luis Costa, and two academic vice presidents, Judith Kuipers and Alexander Gonzalez, whose endorsements secured me two sabbatical leaves. My initial forays into Gershwiniana might well have run into dead ends were it not for the help of Wayne Shirley of the Music Division of the Library of Congress, who generously served as a sounding board for all these years and who has guided me, from a distance of three thousand miles, through the labyrinthine ways of the collection that he knows so well. Ray White, the collection's other steward, was of great assistance during the final stage of getting things together. Stephen Dydo's Noteprocessor program enabled me to produce a huge number of musical examples with relatively few compromises. I also owe a debt to Larry Starr, whose thoughtful and constructive reading of my manuscript went well beyond the call of duty and inspired some small but crucial changes that I like to think have helped make this a better book than it might otherwise have been.

Inevitably, there were those gaps that needed to be filled at the last minute. Marianne Kielian-Gilbert (no relation), responding to my query on the Internet, referred me to Gerardo Dirie of the Indiana University Latin-American Music Center, who gave me some background on the source material for *Cuban Overture*. Not least, as the manuscript editor, Mary Pasti has been helpful, enthusiastic—and, above all, patient.

1 The Music of Gershwin

George Gershwin died young, yet he accomplished much, as if he knew he had little time. His life, fast-paced and colored by worldly success, has been a source of fascination to many; his music, the subject of this book, is no less so. Although Gershwin sought greatness as a composer of concert music, he no doubt reached more people through his showtunes, his first line of endeavor, in which his and his brother Ira's mastery is acknowledged. The experts have been less agreed about the concert works, in which Gershwin's skill showed considerable growth with each new composition. Though similar progress can be traced in his songs, these have not been subjected to the same scrutiny.

From the perspective of a half-century after the composer's death, it is possible to see how a just appraisal of George Gershwin's work has thus far been difficult to achieve. American music has long been dichotomized into "high" and "low" cultures, and the tendency has been to put such uniquely American art forms as jazz and the musical show into the latter rather than the former category. As the son of immigrants, possessing little formal education and having first made his mark as a songwriter (and even worse, a song plugger), Gershwin understandably had difficulty finding a niche in the world of "serious" music. Although the best of his songs were as serious as anything he wrote for the concert hall, they have yet to be studied with a fitting degree of care.

Gershwin's career as a songwriter made its first great stride in 1919 with *La-La-Lucille!,* the first show containing only his music. It included "Nobody But You," whose impact was sufficient to merit its inclusion, a dozen years later, in *George Gershwin's Song Book.*[1] Also from 1919—and also among the tunes that were revisited in the *Song Book*—was "Swanee," which became immensely popular through its frequent performance by Al Jolson. Gershwin had written songs previously, including "Nobody But You," whose actual composition occurred during Gershwin's years as a song plugger for publisher Jerome Remick.[2] But what was performed or published during that earlier time gave little hint as to the greatness of what was to follow. The all-important collaboration with Ira Gershwin lay largely in the future, having thus far produced only one song, "The Real American Folk Song," one of two Gershwin numbers interpolated into the 1918 show *Ladies First.*[3]

In 1919, on the recommendation of his piano teacher Charles Hambitzer, Gershwin took his first theory lessons with Edward Kilenyi (1884–1968), a Hungarian-born composer, conductor, and arranger. These were to continue at least through September 1921, as substantiated in a notebook of twenty-eight unnumbered pages containing Gershwin's work and Kilenyi's annotations.[4] Gershwin worked on instrumentation and "free" composition, with the more traditional sort of harmony exercises playing a secondary role—that is, settings of hymn tunes or chorales for soprano, alto, tenor, and bass in the style of Bach and his contemporaries, here represented toward the end of the notebook by two versions of "Ein feste Burg," both incomplete, bearing the date September 28, 1921.[5] The essays in composition include fragmentary settings for string quintet (orchestra?), for two flutes and timpani, and for flute and strings. The latter, a *valse lente* dated September 15, 1919, comprises a pair of phrases in E♭ major. The first, about the lower third of the triad, is completely worked out; the second, of which only the melody is present, features the upper third and the alteration of A♭ to A♮, suggesting G minor. The first violin carries the tune, to which the flute part functions as an obbligato; the entire passage is shown in example 1.[6] Although it would be a mistake to overvalue this early fragment, it is interesting to note the prevalence of the third (Gershwin's favorite motivic interval, the minor variety in particular) and the composer's predilection, even at this embryonic stage, for contrapuntal layering.

The contents of the Kilenyi notebook give credence to the view that

Example 1. "Valse Lente" (September 15, 1919), *Kilenyi*, p. 15

Gershwin knew more about orchestration than some critics believe. In addition to the material summarized above, it contains notes about instrumental ranges, transpositions, timbres, and what to avoid. Page 13, for example, contains a summary on the flute followed by two cadenzas for the instrument; the date, September 13, 1919, precedes that of the flute-and-strings essay by just two days. Among the last entries in the notebook (p. 26) is a longer, more elaborate cadenza for two clarinets. Throughout, the reader gets a sense that Gershwin was eager to tie musical ideas to their instrumental settings, so that it would be difficult to imagine his writing an extended work without having an orchestration in mind.

The notes on harmony can also be seen to bear on Gershwin's later work, particularly in their emphasis on stepwise voice leading (Kilenyi's "law of propinquity" and *Stufenreichtum*)[7] and the use of sequences.[8] Less relevant, though of minor interest, is a hybrid system of superscripts and subscripts attached to Kilenyi's Roman numerals whereby, for example, what we would today normally label V_3^4 (the $_3^4$ coming from figured-bass notation) is represented by V_2^7, read as V^7, second inversion.

The one finished piece of concert music from the Kilenyi period—Gershwin's first, so far as we know—is the *Lullaby for String Quartet,* which Ira Gershwin dates from "sometime in 1919 or 1920."[9] Like the instrumental passages in the notebook, *Lullaby* is an essay in which Gershwin experimented with harmonics, mutes, and pizzicati, the staples of string effects. According to Jablonski, the piece "became a favorite among his string-playing friends, though he had no plans for its publication or public performance."[10]

The first theme of the string quartet reappears in part in "Has One of You Seen Joe?," the second of three arias in the one-act opera *Blue Monday* (1922), alternately called *Blue Monday Blues* (after its title song) and *One Hundred Thirty-Fifth Street.* With libretto and lyrics by B. G. DeSylva (Gershwin's main lyricist before Ira), *Blue Monday* was Gershwin's second completed concert work.[11] As *Lullaby,* in Ira Gershwin's words, "may not be the Gershwin of *Rhapsody in Blue, Concerto in F,* and his other concert works,"[12] so *Blue Monday* is hardly on a plane with the Gershwin of *Porgy and Bess.* It nonetheless deserves attention, if only as an early reflection of the interest in black folk opera that would eventually inspire Gershwin's masterpiece.

Gershwin's fame as a songwriter, first won with "Swanee," grew in the early 1920s, leading to the commissioning by Paul Whiteman of what was to be *Rhapsody in Blue.* Yet few songs from the period prior to 1924 are widely known today: only "Swanee," of course, and "Nobody But You," and, from

1922, "Do It Again" and "I'll Build a Stairway to Paradise." After *Rhapsody,* composed in January of that year, the number of Gershwin standards increased. From 1924 alone we have the following songs: "Somebody Loves Me" (from *George White's Scandals of 1924*), the title song from *Lady, Be Good,* and, from the same show, "Fascinating Rhythm." "The Man I Love" can also be traced to 1924, when it was initially written for *Lady, Be Good,* though not used. The following year, 1925, gave us *Concerto in F* and the songs "Looking for a Boy," "Sweet and Low-Down," and "That Certain Feeling" (from *Tip-Toes*); the year after that saw the piano preludes and *Oh, Kay!* The latter was by far Gershwin's most successful Broadway score to date and one of his best overall, comprising such stellar tunes as "Clap Yo' Hands," "Do, Do, Do," "Maybe," and "Someone to Watch over Me." The show's namesake Kay Swift, a talented and trained musician whom Gershwin met in 1925, would remain a prominent figure throughout his life.

Though no single score from the Gershwin musicals of the late twenties could match *Oh, Kay!,* there were notable individuals songs, among them "My One and Only," " 'S Wonderful," and the title song, all from *Funny Face* (1927); "How Long Has This Been Going On?" (initially written for *Funny Face,* then used in *Rosalie,* 1928); "I've Got a Crush on You" (*Treasure Girl,* 1928; later in *Strike Up the Band,* 1930); and "Liza" (*Show Girl,* 1929). The major concert work of the late twenties was, of course, *An American in Paris* (1928). The year 1930 yielded still more songs that remain standard repertoire today, in contexts that reflected contemporaneous advances in musical theater generally. There were two shows, *Strike Up the Band* and *Girl Crazy,* the former containing "Strike Up the Band" and "Soon," the latter "Bidin' My Time," "But Not for Me," "Embraceable You," and "I Got Rhythm." [13]

Based on the chronology presented thus far, it is possible to infer a pattern in which the concert works, few in number and steadily advancing technically, tend to signal a parallel advancement in the Gershwin songs. This seems certainly to be the case with *Rhapsody in Blue,* though it is less clear cut with *Concerto in F* and *An American in Paris.* The next large work, *Second Rhapsody* (1931, after material written for the film *Delicious*),[14] represents yet another plateau in the development of the composer's craft, as does the score to *Of Thee I Sing,* written immediately thereafter.

During 1932–36 Gershwin studied with Joseph Schillinger (1895–1943), the Russian-born composer and theorist whose quasi-mathematical methodology attracted several well-known, mainly popular, musicians, among them Glenn Miller and Vernon Duke.[15] This phase of Gershwin's work has been preserved in three notebooks, henceforth referred to as *Schillinger A, B*, and *C*, respectively. These contain exercises in species and imitative counterpoint, along with material that is recognizably from *The Schillinger System of Musical Composition:* special scales, interval expansion, additive rhythm, and an approach to harmony that stresses stepwise voice leading—the latter a source of strength for Gershwin ever since the Kilenyi days. During this period Gershwin wrote *Cuban Overture* (1932), the operettas *Pardon My English* (late 1932) and *Let 'Em Eat Cake* (1933), the *"I Got Rhythm" Variations* (1934), and *Porgy and Bess* (1935). The first of these, although maintaining the level of sophistication found in *Second Rhapsody,* shows no specific evidence of Schillinger's influence. This is not so with the *Variations,* a virtual case study in basic Schillinger, nor is it so with the operettas or with *Porgy.* Particularly in the last instance, Schillinger's role was pervasive.

The special place occupied by *Porgy and Bess* in Gershwin's output comes as no surprise. It was by far his most ambitious undertaking in both length and complexity, containing some of his most inspired writing, and it was his last major work. But it is also the point of departure for still another period: that of the last songs. These late songs constitute a stylistic unit in which the so-called popular or show tune was taken to new artistic heights. "By Strauss" (1936), the sole Gershwin contribution to the revue *The Show Is On* and the only late song not written for films, is a skillful and subtle parody of nineteenth-century cliché whose sophistication becomes increasingly evident in repeated hearings. The scores to the two Fred Astaire films, *Shall We Dance* and *A Damsel in Distress* (both 1937), contain hardly anything short of a masterpiece. Those songs that have remained standards—"A Foggy Day," "They All Laughed," "Nice Work If You Can Get It," "Let's Call the Whole Thing Off," "They Can't Take That Away from Me"—and those that are less well known but no less deserving, such as "(I've Got) Beginner's Luck," "Things Are Looking Up," and "Shall We Dance" (the title song from the film, not to be confused with the Rodgers and Hammerstein song of the same name)—are distinguished by their elegant texts, eloquent melodies, and accompaniments rich in motivic and contrapuntal interest.

The broad picture penned above is one of continuing evolution, with events occurring in rapid succession and frequently overlapping one another. Yet, although it is difficult to pinpoint any sharp breaks, one can discern four main periods. The first produced the songs and concert pieces before 1924, prior to *Rhapsody in Blue.* The second, 1924–30, covers the span from *Rhapsody in Blue* through *Girl Crazy.* It also includes the *Preludes for Piano,* which were premiered at the Hotel Roosevelt on December 24, 1926, by the composer.[16] The third period, 1931–35, begins with *Of Thee I Sing* and *Second Rhapsody* and culminates with *Porgy and Bess*. The fourth, resembling an epilogue, comprises the late songs of 1936–37. These four periods, which will be called "early," "developing," "mature," and "final," respectively, are discussed in detail beginning with chapter 4.

2 An Analytic Approach

Nobody dislikes a Gershwin tune. This fact, more than any other, is the motivation behind the attempts in this book to discern and delineate those structural traits that make the melodies of George Gershwin memorable. The main descriptive tool will be the analytic sketch, or graph, whose conceptual base is chiefly associated with Heinrich Schenker (1868–1935), an Austrian theorist who communicated his ideas through his writings and in private piano lessons.[1] But Schenker's field of interest, which extended from Bach to Brahms, plainly did not include Gershwin, and although Gershwin's and Schenker's lives overlapped in years, it is hardly likely that Gershwin even knew Schenker existed.

Caveats notwithstanding, there remain aspects central to Gershwin's music that make him a better subject for this analytic method than most twentieth-century composers. He was almost always tonal and an avid contrapuntalist. Above all, he wrote good tunes. A well-composed melody—indeed, a well-composed piece—will have a coherent profile overall and at the same time comprise various details that enrich our understanding of the whole. Some details are obviously motivic, perhaps part of a main theme; others are more subtle. For example, the "Lebewohl" motive, G–F–Eb, that opens Beethoven's *Les Adieux* sonata is a small-scale replication of the first movement's fundamental melodic line (hereafter *fundamental line*).[2] Less obvious perhaps, but no less significant, is the way in which the variation theme of the second movement of the *Appassionata,* which culminates in a descending fifth (Ab stepwise down to Db), punctuates its cadences with a melodic figure that also occurs as a diminution in the bass (ex. 2, see at "N.B.").[3]

Example 2. Beethoven, Sonata in F Minor, Op. 57, II, mm. 13–16

A similar relationship can be found in the second movement of Gershwin's *Concerto in F.* The first horn opens with the complete upper-neighbor-note figure Ab–Bb–Ab, followed by a return to Bb. The latter joins with the bottom voice of the clarinet trio entering after the double bar in m. 4 to make another, larger statement of the same figure at the same pitch level, as shown by the nested brackets in example 3. In the long trumpet melody that ensues, Ab, asserted in three distinct registers including that of the opening horn solo, emerges as the main melodic note. The entrance of the oboe at rehearsal number 1 (hereafter R1) shifts the melodic focus to Bb, returning to Ab four measures later. This reflects, over a span of more than twenty measures, the neighbor-note figure introduced by the solo horn. At the same time, the motive represented by the neighbor note (labeled *N;* other abbreviations are *P* for passing note and *Arp* for arpeggiation) continues to predominate at the surface level in both the main melody and the accompaniment, in both its pitch-specific form and in transposition. The trumpet solo begins with a transposition of the introductory horn solo (the nested neighbor-note figure

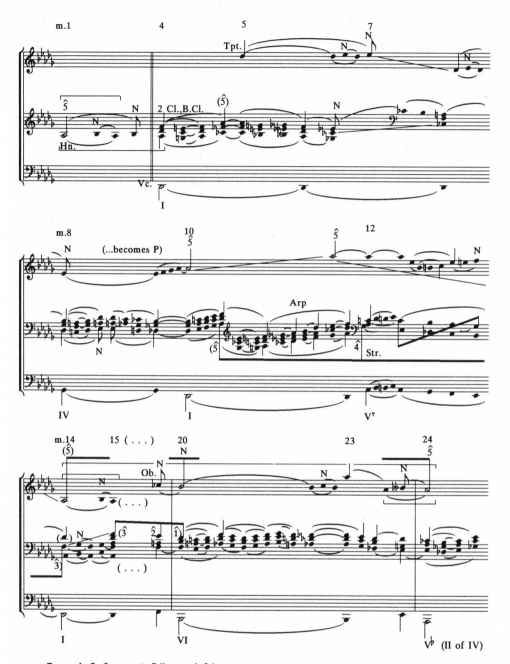

Example 3. *Concerto in F, II, mm. 1–24*

on Db–Eb) and comes to rest on Ab–Bb–Ab in the same register as the horn. And the oboe, which takes over the trumpet's role on the upbeat to m. 20, concludes with a flatted version of the same figure, an octave higher.

Example 3, which will be discussed further in chapter 7 (see ex. 75), also serves as an introduction to analytic pitch notation. The basic unit is the stemless, filled notehead. A stem on a filled note indicates the next higher (or deeper) level of structural importance, whereas the stemmed, open note is reserved for those tones most basic to the melody and bass. The Schenkerian terms for these three main structural levels are *foreground, middleground,* and *background,* respectively. Flags on individual notes are reserved for those with special function—most typically for middleground neighbor notes, sometimes for applied dominants in the bass. The barlines of the original music may or may not be retained, depending on the amount of detail included in the graph and the length of the piece or excerpt.

Continuity in an analytic graph is denoted by slurs (foreground and middleground) and/or beams (middleground and background); these may be nested, as, for example, is the smaller slur representing neighbor-note motion contained within the larger one at the beginning of (and throughout) example 3. The crosswise beam connecting stems that point in opposite directions (as in the inner voice, mm. 12–13) designates an *unfolding,* in which a harmonic interval occurs linearly (here C–Gb, belonging to V⁷).⁴ Background melody notes are normally labeled by numerals designating degrees of the tonic scale (here the fifth, Ab); appropriate arabic numerals are surmounted by carets (thus 5̂). Background and middleground bass notes are labeled in customary fashion by Roman numerals. Vertical intervals above the bass are also highlighted when they form significant patterns, such as the succession of parallel tenths between inner voice and bass in mm. 12–14, which in this instance belong to the foreground.

In terms of structural levels, the large-scale neighbor-note motion over the length of the passage belongs near, but not at, the background, whereas the nested neighbor-note motive announced by the horn is both at and near the foreground. The levels are best appreciated when seen in their relative positions; for the most part, discussions here concern the foreground and various sublevels of middleground.

The most important middleground event in most of Gershwin's music is the *linear progression* (which may or may not replicate the fundamental line); second to that is the *arpeggiation.* A linear progression may be either ascending or descending; what distinguishes it from a mere stepwise succession of notes is that its steps are each supported vertically. Schenker labeled linear progressions according to the interval spanned: that of a third would be a *third-progression;* that of a sixth a *sixth-progression;* and so on.[5] The steps of a linear progression may bridge some foreground discontinuities and frequently are themselves elaborated—or *prolonged*—in some way.[6] The latter is also true of the arpeggiation, which for analytic purposes is defined as a triad or seventh-chord broken in a single direction. The most basic type, the *first-order* arpeggiation, begins a piece and arpeggiates the tonic triad at the middleground level. (A close relative of the first-order arpeggiation is the *initial ascent,* an initial ascending line, which can be thought of as a first-order arpeggiation filled in by harmonically supported steps.)

A first-order arpeggiation followed by a descending linear progression—shown by the analytic graph in example 4—dominates the refrain of "Love

Example 4. "Love Is Here to Stay," refrain, mm. 1–16

Is Here to Stay," from the posthumously completed *Goldwyn Follies* of 1938. In registrally specific terms, the voice begins its three-note upbeat on c^1 (middle C),[7] then comes to rest at four-bar intervals on f^1, a^1, and c^2, at which point the linear progression begins its downward motion. Harmonically, overall, the arpeggiation proceeds from I to V, though local harmonization varies:

saliently, the chord G9 occurs on the downbeats of both mm. 1 and 5 (supporting f^1 and a^1, respectively), with different consequences in each case.[8]

The linear progression, meanwhile, begins in m. 9 with c^2 as the goal note of the arpeggiation and the *primary melodic tone* ("primary tone," for short) of the song. The successive descending steps of the progression, each prolonged by a neighbor note (a double neighbor, upper and lower, in the last instance), are readily apparent through f^1 (m. 13). The momentary reversal in m. 14 is interpreted as an upper neighbor to f^1 (itself prolonged by neighbor notes), whose return and implied resolution to e^1 (mm. 15–16) take place in an inner voice, below the ostensible melody note d^2. This shift in the vocal line is accomplished by *overlapping,* or the registral transfer of an inner voice to the top position. As the (now) inner voice F has an implied resolution to E, so the upper voice D resolves to an implied C on the downbeat of m. 16.

The matter of implied notes is open to question, more so in twentieth-century music than in the standard tonal repertoire of the eighteenth and nineteenth centuries. A note is implied because the rules of resolution demand it and because there is nothing present to contradict it. The question is twofold with music of this sort: First, do the rules still exist? Second, should the music be expected to obey them? While it is a truism that an analysis should represent what is actually heard, one can also argue that it should represent what the ear and the intellect together comprehend. In the case at hand, all that is physically present on the downbeat of m. 16 is the bass note C, which surely poses no conflict with the implied upper voices e^1 and c^2, especially since these notes are made explicit (albeit an octave lower) on the second quarter of the measure.

The linear progression in "Love Is Here to Stay" conforms to the Schenkerian model in that its interval (the descending sixth c^2–e^1) is a structural component of the underlying harmony (V), here present at both beginning and end. The intervening bass notes move through the circle of fifths, forming alternating sevenths and tenths with the structural upper voice. These constitute a variety of *linear intervallic pattern,* shown in the analysis by arabic numbers between the staffs (i.e., the repeating progression 7–10 in mm. 9–16).[9]

An ascending linear progression, also spanning a sixth, begins the refrain of another *Goldwyn Follies* song, "Love Walked In," shown in example 5. Arpeggiation is also a feature here, but at the foreground level—in contrast to the preceding example, where the arpeggiation belonged to the middleground. The ascent from g^1 to eb^2 (first eight measures) is supported by the

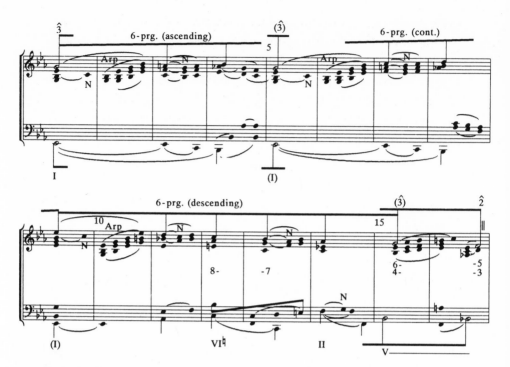

Example 5. "Love Walked In," refrain, mm. 1–16

tonic at both beginning and end, though movement toward the dominant occurs in between. A larger move toward the dominant takes place over the eight measures that follow, beneath a descending linear progression. The latter, like the ascent, begins with a foreground arpeggiation of the tonic triad, arriving back on g^1 in a reversal of the previous ascending linear progression and terminating on f^1 (end of m. 16). The caesura on scale degree $\hat{2}$ over V, after which the opening melody begins anew (this time completing its descent to $\hat{1}$ instead of stopping at $\hat{2}$), is a common occurrence in tonal music called *interruption,* indicated graphically by a double vertical line. In cases where the interruption and subsequent completion comprise the entire piece, the descent leading to the interruption, though partial, is accorded quasi-background status and graphed in open notes.

As mentioned earlier, the background is of secondary importance in most of the discussions that follow; however, there are times when it must be addressed. The background consists of both melody and bass, which together comprise the *fundamental structure* of a piece or movement; the melodic portion alone is called the *fundamental line.* The three basic models of fundamental structure depend on the fundamental line; a stepwise descent from the third, fifth, or octave of the tonic scale (i.e., scale degree $\hat{3}$, $\hat{5}$, or $\hat{8}$) to the prime (scale degree $\hat{1}$).[10] The head note of the fundamental line is called the *primary tone* (or *primary melodic tone* if further clarification is needed). As mentioned earlier, the primary melodic tone in example 4 is scale degree $\hat{5}$ in the key of F (in registrally specific terms, c²); as for example 5, a case could be made for either $\hat{8}$ (eb²) or $\hat{3}$ (g¹); the former is the more obvious choice, though the central role of the note G would, upon further consideration, point to the latter. The refrain of "Swanee" (ex. 6) is less ambiguous, owing to the com-

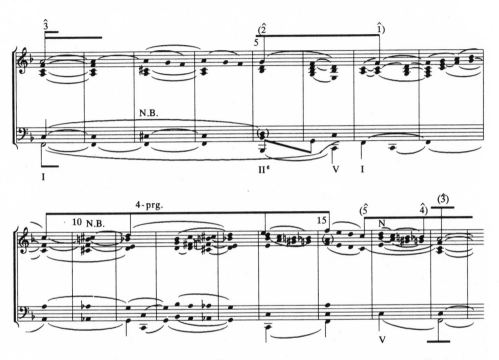

Example 6. "Swanee," refrain, mm. 1–17

plete descent from $\hat{3}$ to $\hat{1}$ within its first eight-measure period, which effectively places the subsequent excursion to and from $\hat{8}$ in the middleground. (An interesting motivic detail, marked "N.B." in ex. 6, shows the beginning of the inner voice, C–C#–D, replicated in the vocal melody at the start of the next eight-bar period.) In another early song, "Nobody But You," the $\hat{3}$–$\hat{2}$–$\hat{1}$ pattern achieves closure in only four measures (ex. 7). At its immediate repetition in the next four bars, the same melody is supported not by I but by V of V. The arrival on $\hat{2}$ over V, in m. 16, constitutes an interruption as defined above in connection with "Love Walked In," after which $\hat{3}$ is reasserted as the primary tone, as at the beginning. The final setting of the $\hat{3}$–$\hat{2}$–$\hat{1}$ motive (see ex. 7b) takes the V of V to its logical conclusion on a V–I cadence.

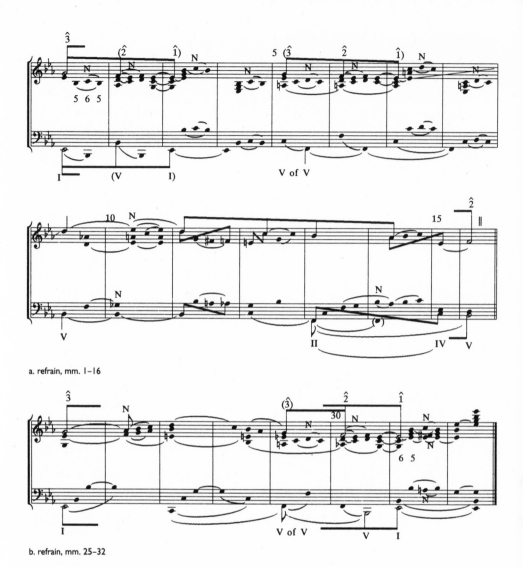

a. refrain, mm. 1–16

b. refrain, mm. 25–32

Example 7. "Nobody But You"

As the tonal literature abounds with instances of the interrupted $\hat{3}$–$\hat{2}$, it is no surprise that this should be the case with Gershwin as well. To cite every example would be both space-consuming and tedious; yet it would do well to mention two more in which the path from $\hat{3}$ to $\hat{2}$ is traced in an especially artful way. From *Porgy and Bess,* these are "Bess, You Is My Woman Now" (ex. 8) and "There's a Boat Dat's Leavin' Soon for New York" (ex. 9a). Each begins with an ascending third to $\hat{3}$; subsequently, each melody asserts the same scale degree in a lower register before progressing to $\hat{2}$.

The distinctive features of "Bess, You Is My Woman Now" are compound

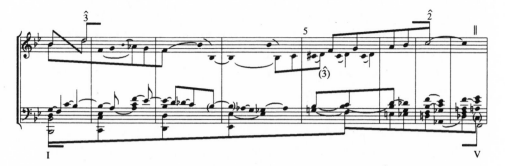

Example 8. *Porgy and Bess*, II.1: "Bess, You Is My Woman Now," mm. 1–8 (R95–R95 + 7)

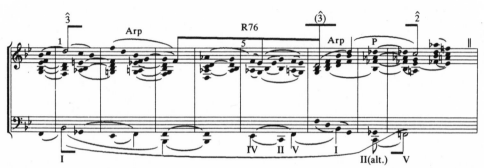

a. analysis of mm. 1–8 (R75 + 4–R76 + 4)

Moderato (Tempo di Blues) ♩ = 96

b. introduction (R75–R75 + 3)

(col 15b)

c. instrumental punctuation, m. 9

Example 9. *Porgy and Bess*, III.2: "There's a Boat Dat's Leavin' Soon for New York"

melody and linear progressions: the descending fourth bb^1–f^1, the ascending fifth f^1–c^2, and the intervening major third—replicating the fundamental line in reverse—bb–d^1. The first among the linear progressions is but one instance where one or more flatted scale steps—those much-vaunted Gershwinian blue notes—take the place of their diatonic counterparts. The latter involve as many as three strata, which the graph in example 8 attempts to show. The lowest, the ascent from b♭ beginning in m. 4, is clearly differentiated—even signaled—by the octave leap preceding it. The middle stratum comprises the descending fourth from b♭¹ (mm. 1–3) and ascending fifth to c² (mm. 5–7). The topmost stratum, initiated by the background note d², joins the middle when the ascending fifth reaches its goal.[11]

On the other hand, the surface of "There's a Boat Dat's Leavin' Soon for New York" is dominated by foreground arpeggiations. Just below this surface is a linear progression formed by successive low points in the vocal part: f¹ (m. 3)–e♭¹ (m. 5)–d¹ (m. 6).[12] This last note is then transferred by arpeggiation to d², thus joining it with the background 3̂, which proceeds to 2̂ (c²) via a chromatic passing note. The middleground F–E♭–D just described gives added significance to the events preceding, accompanying, and following the vocal passage, as illustrated by the remainder of example 9. In example 9b the introductory vamp, which continues below the first two bars of the vocal line, contains, in its upper voice or voices, both ascending and descending forms of this progression.[13] In example 9c, the close of the first period is punctuated instrumentally by a compound melody with F–E–E♭–D as its lower stratum.

Whether conscious on the composer's part or not, concealed repetitions such as these contribute greatly to the organic structure of a composition. The opening of *Rhapsody in Blue,* no doubt an intuitive creation, is nonetheless rich in concealed repetitions.[14] The graph in example 10 focuses on two main motives: *a,* the fourth, and *b,* the neighbor note. (An additional motive, the foreground arpeggiation, is labeled *c.*) The initial clarinet run spans a compound form of the ascending fourth and is labeled *a* in example 10. Two statements of the descending fourth, each filled in by step, follow (mm. 2–3 and m. 4); these are labeled *a'.* The same interval, ascending, then occurs sequentially as a melodic skip: f¹–b♭¹ (mm. 6–7) and b♭¹–e♭² (mm. 8–9). It is the descending form, the upper tetrachord of the scale with flatted seventh, which is most characteristic of Gershwin (we have already seen it in "Bess, You Is My Woman Now," ex. 8); it is emphasized here by its presentation in two registers. The repetition is "concealed" by virtue of the diminutions in the first presentation that are lacking in the second, and by the rhythmic differences that in themselves are interesting: the first statement is complete on the fifth quarter note, the second on the fifth eighth note.

Motive *b/b',* the neighbor note, first appears as a diminution within the first *a'* (mm. 2–3), then as a diminution of the lower note of the ascending fourths (*a* figures) in mm. 6–7 and 8–9. Finally, forms of both the *a* and the

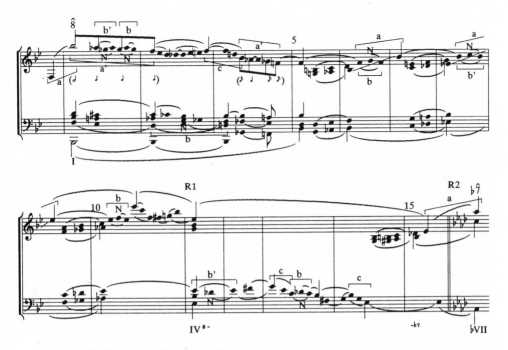

Example 10. *Rhapsody in Blue*, mm. 1–16

b motives combine to form the inner-voice melody of mm. 11–14, which will later become the principal closing theme of the piece.

In this sense, the concealed repetition can link two or more themes. In another, it can tie surface aspects of a piece to the deeper levels of middleground and background. The excerpt from the second movement of *Concerto in F* as analyzed in example 3 shows the neighbor-note figure both as a foreground element in the introduction and main theme and as the middleground relationship between sections of that theme. The latter—the background Ab and middleground upper neighbor Bb returning to Ab—comprises the concealed repetition. In the song "'S Wonderful," the skip of a third plays a similar role. As shown in example 11, descending foreground thirds, mostly minor, predominate in both the verse (where in sequence they form first an ascending, then a descending linear progression) and the refrain (the repeated, thematic Bb–G).[15] A harmonic type of concealed repetition exists between the A and B sections of the refrain: the middleground major third Eb–G. Another, melodic example closes the verse and leads into the refrain: the middleground linear progression Bb (verse, m. 19)—Ab (m. 23)–G (refrain, m. 1). This descending progression of a third, or third-progression, spans precisely those pitches so central motivically to the refrain. At the same time,

a. introduction and verse

Example 11. "'S Wonderful"

its context mirrors the opening of the verse in that, once again, foreground thirds occur in the service of a linear progression—only now their respective directions are reversed. The imitation between voice and accompaniment, where minor third answers major, is an added touch.[16]

It is a legitimate question whether the Schenkerian models of fundamental structure should apply—or be applied—to music which, tonal though it may be, falls outside the Classic-Romantic repertoire. It is one thing if a pattern fits; it is another if it must be made to fit. The end of "Love Walked In," whose beginning was cited in example 5, shows a complete stepwise descent to $\hat{1}$ (ex. 12), as does "Someone to Watch Over Me" (ex. 13). Both involve lines spanning an octave. In the first instance, a descending middleground line

b. refrain

Example 11. (continued)

from $\hat{8}$ joins with the background at scale degree $\hat{3}$; in the second, an octave line from d^2 to d^1 links two representations of the background note $\hat{2}$.

By way of contrast, the end of "'S Wonderful," graphed in example 11b, lacks scale degree $\hat{2}$. Missing as well from the vocal line is a structurally supported $\hat{3}$. One way to read the ending is to take scale degree $\hat{4}$ (mm. 29–30) via a change of register (ab^1–ab) to an inner-voice $\hat{3}$ (the g in m. 31), and thus obtain the background line—rather like a cantus firmus—$\hat{5}$–$\hat{4}$–$\hat{3}$. This is the same linear progression that (again, reaching into an inner voice) links the verse to the refrain (see the end of example 11a and the beginning of 11b), whose interval span, B♭–G, is replicated in the all-important "'S Wonder-

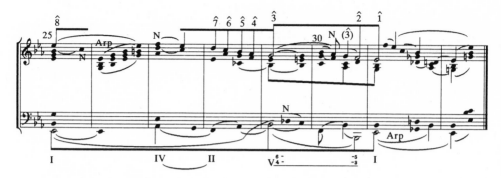

Example 12. "Love Walked In," refrain, mm. 25–32

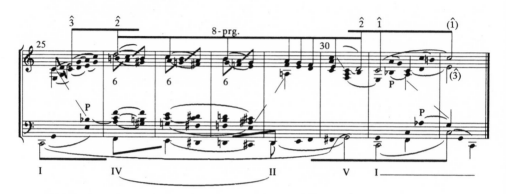

Example 13. "Someone to Watch Over Me," refrain, mm. 25–32

ful" motive. Closer to the surface, one can read scale degree $\hat{3}$ in the same voice's g¹ in the second half of m. 30. Interpolated between that note and the arrival of the tonic on the downbeat of m. 31 is an implied f¹ representing scale degree $\hat{2}$. But the chord supporting g¹, the so-called dominant thirteenth (in reality a ⁷⁄₆ substituting for—if not resolving to—⁷⁄₅), is so idiomatic to Gershwin and other contemporaneous songwriters in its unresolved state that one can rightly argue against changing it. Implied notes under these circumstances, in short, should be understood as logical (or intellectual) rather than aural phenomena.

A missing scale degree $\hat{2}$ likewise obscures the fundamental line in "I Loves You, Porgy" (*Porgy and Bess*, act 2, scene 3), a song in rondo form (ABACA) whose eight-bar refrain, or A section,[17] is graphed in example 14. The entire song abounds in interesting rhythmic features, one of which is the refrain's exclusive dependence on the rhythm of Porgy's entrance theme (see ex. 148), which resurfaces at the end of the refrain. This theme sneaks into the orchestral counterpoint in subsequent statements of the refrain, the last

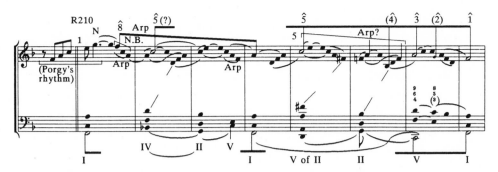

Example 14. *Porgy and Bess*, II.3: "I Loves You, Porgy," mm. 1–8 (rondo refrain)

Example 15. "How Long Has This Been Going On?" refrain, mm. 16–25

of which is a contrapuntal duet in which Porgy has joined Bess. The pitch structure of the refrain melody is a veritable nesting of arpeggiations at various levels (see, for example, the simultaneous foreground and middleground representations of f^2–c^2–a^1 in m. 1 and over mm. 1–4, marked "N.B."). At first glance it would seem that the descending arpeggiation from ff² also constitutes the background. But C (scale degree $\hat{5}$) is present in the first four bars, as is the high F ($\hat{8}$), and, through sheer repetition if nothing else, C receives greater emphasis. Moreover, a descending line from $\hat{5}$ may indeed be read in the next four bars: to $\hat{3}$ via a registrally displaced $\hat{4}$ (mm. 6–7); and to $\hat{1}$ via an implied $\hat{2}$. At the same time, there is no question that the scale degrees of the tonic triad are the prominent ones, even in places where they are not supported harmonically (as in the bracketed c^2–a^1–f^1 tagged with a question mark).

Implied notes and unresolved dissonances are further illustrated by "How Long Has This Been Going On?" from 1927, whose refrain has the standard form (AABA) of the thirty-two-bar chorus. A major-seventh-chord on C predominates during the first half of the B section (often called the bridge), as shown in example 15. The outer voices have the vertical C–b^1 alternating with

F–a[1] in a classic 7–10 pattern; however the phrase ends on the seventh and not the tenth. The next four bars continue the established melodic pattern a minor third higher, on the note d². Yet here the vertical support centers on the tenth (bass B) rather than the seventh—in other words, a stable interval as opposed to a presumably unstable one. What makes the bridge an organic part of the refrain is that its middleground melody notes, b¹ and d², join with the end of the second A section (g¹, m. 16) to form an arpeggiated tonic triad, whose goal happens also to be the primary melodic tone. The force of this arpeggiation tends to offset the effect of the vertically unstable middle note.

The final eight bars, meanwhile, stand as yet another illustration of the analytic uses of implied notes (ex. 16). The melody spans a descending fifth

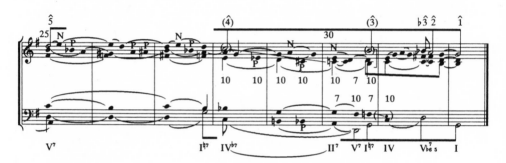

Example 16. "How Long Has This Been Going On?" refrain, mm. 25–32

from starting to ending point, yet without actually passing through steps $\hat{4}$ and $\hat{3}$. Their insertion as implied notes is justified by the following: First, c² and b¹ are both structural components of their respective supporting harmonies, so it is conceivable that, if expected, they can be interpolated by the listener. Second, in this instance they do actually appear, albeit an octave lower and in an inner voice. Further justification comes in m. 31, where the vocal part reaches scale degree $\hat{2}$ (a¹) by way of bb¹, thus returning to the register in which it began.[18] The note bb¹, on the surface an incomplete neighbor to a¹, becomes understood as a chromatic passing note once the implied steps in the fundamental line are inserted.

The examples in this chapter represent a sampling of Gershwin compositions from different stages in his career; they have been presented not in chronological order but as illustrations of concepts. The extent to which they conform to Schenkerian models demonstrates their connection to the larger body of Western tonal music. At the same time, their unique and endearing features have not been ignored.

Today you can see that the happiest men

All got rhythm!

"Slap That Bass" (*Shall We Dance,* 1937)

Where two hearts become one

Who could ask for anything more?

"Nice Work If You Can Get It"

(*A Damsel in Distress,* 1937)

3 Fascinating Rhythm

S urely the Gershwins were aware of the quality of déjà vu in these lines. This is especially clear in the first instance, where the textual reference to "I Got Rhythm" is joined with a musical one as well (i.e., the notes B♭, C, E♭, and F). But Gershwin's fascination with rhythm would be self-evident even without lyrics and titles. His early music showed his ready absorption of patterns idiomatic to ragtime and to the popular songs of the teens and twenties. The developing period (beginning with *Rhapsody in Blue*) saw the emergence of certain rhythms, singly and in combination, that one recognizes today as characteristic of the composer. In his mature and final periods (*Second Rhapsody* through *Porgy and Bess* and thereafter) Gershwin's rhythmic language, partly through the tutelage of Joseph Schillinger, reached new levels of complexity while retaining significant links with the earlier music.

It is neither unique nor surprising that Gershwin's early titles should reflect an interest in ragtime, nor that such titles should not guarantee the real thing. Imitations of ragtime were the rage in the early 1900s; predictably, such imitations tended to be superficial.[1] While this adjective is hardly appropriate to anything Gershwin wrote, it could be said that the more conscious the effort at imitation, the less likely it was to succeed. The 1918 song "The Real American Folk Song (Is a Rag)," noteworthy as the first George and Ira Gershwin collaboration, is one I find engaging, but it is not ragtime. As for the piano rag "Rialto Ripples,"[2] its opening assertion of I followed by IV, then V, evokes the blues harmonically, and (though this is not so with the syncopated second theme) its use of triplets (ex. 17a) is not typical of the rag-

a. "Rialto Ripples," theme 1, mm. 1–4

b. "Blue Monday Blues," mm. 1–8

c. Scott Joplin, "The Entertainer," refrain, mm. 1–4

Example 17.

time style as defined by the popular turn-of-the century rags of Scott Joplin. Rather, to this writer at least, the spirit of ragtime (bearing in mind Joplin's continued admonitions in his scores not to play ragtime too fast) is best captured by Gershwin in "Blue Monday Blues," the title song from the opera (ex. 17b). Its moderate tempo and syncopated rhythms most closely approach the classic Joplin model, the latter illustrated by an excerpt from "The Entertainer" (ex. 17c).

Rhythmic considerations were apparently the impetus behind the most successful of Gershwin's early songs. As Schwartz relates, "Swanee" was the result of Gershwin's and lyricist Irving Caesar's intention to write a one-step (quick foxtrot in cut time) in the manner of, though hardly resembling in more than the most cursory aspects, Harold Weeks's "Hindustan."[3] "Nobody But You" is a foxtrot. And "I'll Build a Stairway to Paradise," as befits its lyrics about dancing, is a shuffle in straight $\frac{4}{4}$-time.

Not surprisingly, 1924, the year of *Rhapsody in Blue* and of the song whose title was borrowed for this chapter, was a watershed in Gershwin's rhythmic development. What he had written before this time was sufficient to gain him a reputation as a songwriter of promise, but there is little that bears the stamp of uniqueness. A notable exception is "Do It Again!" (1922), with lyrics by B. G. DeSylva.[4] First there is the repeated title phrase, whose rhythm of four eighth notes, with the fourth tied over to a long note (and thereby accented), is at once an outgrowth from ragtime and a precursor of the superimposed threes-on-fours (i.e., notes simultaneously beamed in fours but accented in threes) that characterize *Rhapsody in Blue* and much that came thereafter. Then there is the ingenious redistribution of rhythms in the second group of eight measures, in which the "do it again" motive reappears, first a half-measure late ("waiting for you"), then two measures early ("know if you do"). The resulting impression of irregularity—in pop-music jargon, the song's hook—belies the constancy of the eight-measure periods (ex. 18). Also noteworthy

Example 18. "Do It Again!" refrain, mm. 1–16

are the juxtaposition of short and long note values with straight quarter notes and, finally, the elegant way in which the song's main verbal, rhythmic, and melodic motives are symbolically intertwined.

A song from 1924 worth noting for its rhythm is "Naughty Baby," for which Ira Gershwin shares the lyric credit with Desmond Carter, a young staff lyricist for Gershwin's publisher Harms.[5] (The line "Don't be a naughty baby," from "Embraceable You," may well be the first instance of Ira Gershwin's tendency to make occasional references to earlier songs in later ones.) The melody of the refrain, whose first four bars are shown in example 19, in effect imposes a $\frac{6}{8}$ metrical scheme on a $\frac{2}{2}$ framework.

In *Rhapsody in Blue* we find essentially the same rhythmic device that had been featured in "Do It Again!," now in a multitude of guises (ex. 20). The

Example 19. "Naughty Baby," refrain, mm. 1–4

a. mm. 3–4

rubato e legato

Andantino moderato

R28

b. transition and beginning of slow theme

Example 20. *Rhapsody in Blue*

first theme (mm 3–4) presents no fewer than four such rhythms in succession. The transition to the slow theme, four measures before R28,[6] begins with the same rhythm, as does the slow theme itself, which employs the rhythm in augmentation.[7] The dotted brackets below the inner voice (ex. 20c) highlight another instance of rhythmic superposition, in which repeated patterns of pitch (a three-note segment comprising two descending semitones) and rhythm (two eighths followed by three quarters) occur simultaneously, but not in phase. This happens to be one of the outstanding uses of counterpoint in *Rhapsody in Blue* and in Gershwin's early work generally, as it can be seen that the upper voice's sustained notes amount to a rhythmically augmented inversion of the inner-voice's three-note segment.

Another rhythmic pattern—the mainstay of the numerous transitional passages in the piece—imposes three on four by means of melodic contour and accent.[8] It consists of a series of equal durations beamed in fours, with articulations grouped in threes. In some instances the threes are given additional emphasis through the periodic use of triplets (ex. 21);[9] in others interest

a. R4 + 6

b. R5 + 16

c. R9

d. R24 + 4

Example 21. *Rhapsody in Blue*

a. R6 − 1

b. R18 + 5

Example 22. *Rhapsody in Blue*

is heightened by means of subdivision (ex. 22). The right-hand part in example 21d has, in addition, a repeating pitch pattern (see under the bracket) whose six notes enable it to be stated three times within the two-bar span, rather than merely twice. A consequence of the differing phases of the pitch and rhythmic patterns is that the triplet on the first downbeat captures notes 1–3, the second downbeat notes 4–6.

The technique of rhythmic superposition pervades not only much of *Rhapsody* but much of what Gershwin wrote thereafter. The triplet (now at the end of the pattern) is used similarly in a transitional theme in the first movement of *Concerto in F* (ex. 23a)—likewise subdivisions (now with two notes subdivided instead of one) in *An American in Paris,* at the *vigoroso* transition

a. *Concerto in F, I, R7*

b. *An American in Paris, R3*

c. *An American in Paris, R44+2*

d. *An American in Paris, R47+3*

e. *Second Rhapsody, mm. 3–7*

f. *Porgy and Bess, I.1, R59*

g. *Porgy and Bess, I.1, R71+5*

h. *Porgy and Bess, II.1, R95+4*

Example 23. Superimposed threes on fours

following the first theme (ex. 23b). Again in *An American in Paris,* the violin duet that retransitions into the slower tempo (at *più mosso e rubato,* R44+2) has straight eighth notes grouped in three against a pulse of four, as does a two-measure interlude for solo string quartet (*più mosso e meno,* R47+3) within the section that follows. These are shown in examples 23c and 23d; in both instances the articulation in threes is matched by a pitch sequence.

The remainder of example 23 draws from works written in the 1930s. In example 23e, from the introduction to *Second Rhapsody,* we find a sequence of pitch and rhythm in three-note groupings, initially superimposed as normal eighth notes on a $\frac{4}{4}$ framework, then finishing with triplets in $\frac{2}{4}$. In act 1, scene 1 of *Porgy and Bess,* in "A Woman Is a Sometime Thing," Sporting Life's echo of Jake's refrain is accompanied by an incidental passage in fourths for solo clarinet (ex. 23f) in groups of 3, 3, and 6, respectively, over a G-minor chord (not shown). Not long thereafter, in the same scene, Porgy's theme takes off with a consequent passage (ex. 23g); see also ex. 149), again in eighth notes, grouped mainly in threes, though not exclusively. Groups of three also predominate in the second line of "Bess, You Is My Woman Now" (example 23h).

Clearly, the superposition of one rhythmic grouping on another is a fertile idea and a salient feature in Gershwin's music. The technique takes on added dimension when the superimposed grouping is subdivided, as in the song "Fidgety Feet" (ex. 24a). The three-note motive spanning two chromatic

a. "Fidgety Feet," refrain, mm. 1–4

b. *Rhapsody in Blue,* R28+2 (top two voices)

Example 24.

steps is expressed first as two repeated eighths, then two quarters. The eighth notes, coming on the first beat of the superimposed pattern, are thereby positioned differently in the measure as the pattern is reiterated. The slow theme from *Rhapsody in Blue* (written some two years before "Fidgety Feet") comes to mind for the obvious reason that it uses the same pitch motive—in eighths and quarters in the inner voice and in rhythmic augmentation in the descant (ex. 24b). An important difference, however, is that here there is no superimposed three-beat rhythmic pattern; as a result, the paired eighth notes, which occur initially on the downbeat, remain there for each successive measure.

Though undoubtedly a favorite device of his, metric superposition was not exclusive to Gershwin. An example by Edward "Zez" Confrey, someone Gershwin both knew and admired,[10] is the 1922 song "Stumbling," in which, perhaps for the first time in the popular song literature,[11] a subdivided $\frac{3}{4}$ motive is set against a $\frac{4}{4}$ meter (ex. 25). "Stumbling," still recognized as a

Example 25. Edward ("Zez") Confrey, "Stumbling," refrain, mm. 1–8

minor standard from that period, could well have been a direct influence on this chapter's namesake, which was written for the show *Lady, Be Good* late in 1924, the same year as *Rhapsody*. The refrain of "Fascinating Rhythm" superimposes a pattern of seven eighths (six notes plus one rest) upon a meter that is one eighth note longer. There are three like statements that form a large antecedent; the fourth is the consequent. ("'You've got me on the go' indeed," writes Hans Keller: "every upbeat is an upbeat to an upbeat.")[12] As the annotations in example 26 show, the three $\frac{7}{8}$ phrases are followed—in effect

Example 26. "Fascinating Rhythm," refrain, mm. 1–4

answered—by one that is in $\frac{3}{8}$ plus $\frac{4}{4}$ (in other words, seven eighths with a written-out ritard), and whose pitches differ only in the octave placement of the final note.

In a more general sense, songs like "Fascinating Rhythm" and "Fidgety Feet" typify what would be a Gershwin staple throughout his career—a song in which the content of the lyrics would be reflected in a repeated rhythmic pattern. Predictably, the prime exemplar is "I Got Rhythm," whose refrain in AABA form keeps the same rhythm in both the A and the B sections. "I Got Rhythm" occupies a unique place within Gershwin's oeuvre. Its date, 1930, places it near the end of the developing period, but its role in the *"I Got*

Rhythm" Variations (written four years later while Gershwin was studying with Schillinger) gives it a foothold in the mature period as well.

The rhythm that pervades the refrain places four attacks within the space of two $\frac{2}{2}$ measures: a quarter rest, three dotted quarters, and an eighth tied to a half note (see ex. 121c)—or, in terms of the lowest common denominator, note durations of three, three, three, and five eighths following a two-eighths rest. At the same time, a steady bass pulse on each half-measure keeps the listener mindful of the meter. The latter is not a factor in the *Variations,* however; in fact, it is noticeably absent—with the result that our attention is drawn more to the durational aspects of the theme: first, that "I Got Rhythm" begins with three equidurational notes—a series that can easily be extended to four with the shortening of the fourth note; second, that these durations are initially triple. Correspondingly, the tendency to juxtapose duples and triples is characteristic throughout the *Variations.*

A case in point is the second variation (Allegretto: Valse triste)[13] in which the triple durations of the theme's first notes are each transformed into a $\frac{3}{4}$ measure. With the piano providing the pulse on beats 2 and 3, echoes of the downbeat on the second half of each second beat divide the measure in two (ex. 27a).[14] The third variation ("Chinese Variation" in the two-piano score), although reverting to the $\frac{2}{4}$ of the opening sections, is counterpointed by an ostinato in the xylophone that, in the form of subdivided triplet quarters, keeps the triple division alive for fourteen more bars, the last four of which reintroduce the original durational pattern of the theme in the winds and brass. (The piano makes its entrance following this, at R12+4, with the main four-note motive in quarters accompanied by sixteenths.) Before that, we find one manifestation of the new ways in which Gershwin was thinking about rhythm (and about melody also): a canonic, sequential treatment of the four-note "I Got Rhythm" motive in which the subject is palindromic in both rhythm and pitch (ex. 27b).[15] An additional element of interest in example 27b is that the repetition of the center pitch causes the pitch and rhythm palindromes to be one note out of phase in the second half.

A type of sequel to "I Got Rhythm," obviously less explicit than *Variations,* can be seen in "Shall We Dance," an exemplar from Gershwin's final period, sung by Fred Astaire in the 1937 film of the same name. Like "I Got Rhythm," "Shall We Dance" is characterized by a rhythmic head motive beginning with a quarter rest followed by equal durations of three eighth notes each; this time, however, the motive prevails in the verse as well. Two versions of this motive occur in the refrain: the first, labeled a_1 in example 28a, follows two dotted quarters with a whole note; the second, a_2, subdivides the whole note

a. two-piano score, R8 (variation 2)

b. orchestral score, condensed, R11+5 (variation 3, mm. 3–10)

Example 27. *"I Got Rhythm" Variations*

into three plus five eighths. The form used in the verse, a₃ (ex. 28b), divides the last five eighths into three plus two. It is in this guise, last to be listed here but first to be heard, that the two-bar pattern turns palindromic, yielding (2 + 3 + 3) + (3 + 3 + 2). This last pattern is also the mainstay of another song, "Wake Up, Brother and Dance," from the same film.

Rhythmic motives such as the above, even if their implications were not completely realized at the time, have plenty of precedent. Certainly the 3 + 3 + 2 division of the measure was a popular rhythm, both generally and with Gershwin in particular—in the syncopations of the teens and twenties (recall for instance the last line of "Fascinating Rhythm"), and as the basic rhythm of the rumba, which came into vogue in the thirties. *Rumba,* in fact, was the

a. refrain, mm. 1–16

b. verse, mm. 1–8

(2 + 3 + 3) + (3 + 3 + 2)

Example 28. "Shall We Dance"

title Gershwin first gave to *Cuban Overture* (1932), whose recurring two-bar vamp contains, in its first measure, both prime and retrograde versions of this rhythm: 3 + 3 + 2 in the bass, counterpointed by 2 + 3 + 3 in the upper voices (ex. 29).[16] In a similar vein is the song "Just Another Rhumba" (1937),

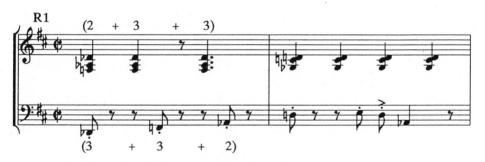

Example 29. *Cuban Overture*, mm. 6–7 (vamp only)

originally slated for *The Goldwyn Follies* (1938) but not used, and not published till 1959. While the 3 + 3 + 2 pattern persists in the bass, the vocal line of the refrain moves mainly in quarter notes, as illustrated in example 30.[17] This passage should be compared to the retransition from the trio section to the refrain reprise (cf. ex. 169), where the voice has an ascending scale set to the same durational pattern as the verse of "Shall We Dance," in rhythmic unison with the accompaniment. This is followed by a piano interlude of eighth notes articulated in threes and triplets—a pattern reminiscent of passages in *Rhapsody in Blue* and *Concerto in F* (see exx. 20 and 22a).

In short, many of the salient rhythmic events in Gershwin's later music have their foundation in patterns and preferences that first manifested them-

Example 30. "Just Another Rhumba" (unpublished 1937 version), refrain, mm. 1–4

selves relatively early in his career. In *Porgy and Bess,* the scene on Kittiwah Island (act 2, scene 2) is set by a pair of African drums playing triplet eighths (eventually triplet quarters) against an eighth and two sixteenths, within the context of a $\frac{2}{4}$ meter. The drums serve as prelude to the unison chorus "I Ain' Got No Shame" (both were cut from early productions), whose repeated opening line is punctuated by a $\frac{3}{4} + \frac{2}{4}$ pattern in the accompaniment, in which the drums are joined by piano, strings, and brass (ex. 31a). Together, the two bars represent the basic division of 3 + 2, while the $\frac{2}{4}$ measure is internally articulated as 2 + 3 + 3. Subsequently, beginning at R131, this pattern, expressed as a single, subdivided $\frac{5}{4}$ bar, becomes an ostinato accompaniment to a quasi-African chant with an ostinato of its own: a pitch group of five eighth notes (stated four times), which effectively divides the $\frac{5}{4}$ measure in two equal parts, while at the same time the added accent marks perpetuate the quarter-note pattern of 3 + 2 (ex. 31b).

Although these passages represent new levels of complexity for Gershwin, we can point to two specific ingredients that tie this music to the composer's earlier work: the use of pitch accents that differ from the prevailing meter on the one hand, and the division of the $\frac{2}{4}$ measure (or submeasure) into 3 + 3 + 2 on the other. Changing meters—and meters of other than two, three, or four beats per measure—are a rarity for Gershwin; indeed, the most remarkable rhythmic feature of Gershwin's music is the flexibility and, at times, complexity of rhythms that can coexist within metric frameworks that are basic and unchanging (there is a parallel with Schoenberg in this regard). Exceptions are few: portions of *Porgy and Bess* such as those described above; the rondo refrain from the finale of *Concerto in F,* with its shifts from $\frac{2}{4}$ to $\frac{3}{8}$ and back; and parts of *Second Rhapsody,* notably in the lyrical middle section. This section begins *sostenuto e con moto* at R21 with a theme in even quarters supported by half notes. Eight bars later, as if to contrast with the

a. R129: "I Ain' Got No Shame," mm. 1–4

b. R131+8

Example 31. *Porgy and Bess*, II.2

squareness of the initial slow theme, a new idea is introduced, featuring a metric change from $\frac{4}{4}$ to $\frac{8}{4}$ and back. As highlighted in example 32, the $\frac{8}{4}$ bar has its main points of attack on the first, second, and fourth half notes, which makes it a fourfold augmentation of the eighth-quarter-eighth pattern that immediately precedes it. That this is notated in one $\frac{8}{4}$ measure rather in two $\frac{4}{4}$ measures adds visual emphasis, and it thus encourages the smoothest possible articulation of the inner counterpoint.

We may now return to the distribution of rhythmic motives within phrases and periods. The song "Do It Again!" was previously cited as a demonstration of how changes in the placement of the main motive add an element of

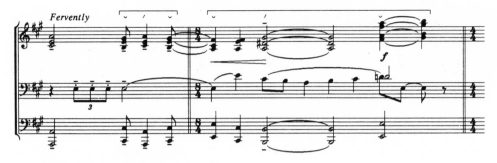

Example 32. *Second Rhapsody*, R21 + 8

surprise to an otherwise stable context (cf. ex. 18). That context, the structural medium in which virtually every songwriter worked, was the eight-measure period—and the ability to bring variety to this unchanging period structure was an important index of the composer's and lyricist's collective skill. In "Maybe," from *Oh, Kay!* (1926), with lyrics by Ira Gershwin, the thirty-two-bar refrain divides musically into 2 × 16, the halves into 2 × 8, although the lyrics add in effect an extra line to the first half of the song. The form, shown beside the lyrics in example 33 with each letter representing an eight-bar unit,

Section	Lyrics
A	Soon or late, maybe, If you wait, maybe,
B	Some kind fate, maybe, Will help you discover/Where to find your lover.
A	You will hear You-hoo, He'll be near you-hoo.
C (A'?)	Paradise will open its gate Maybe soon,/Maybe late.

Example 33. "Maybe," refrain: lyrics and musical form

can be expressed as ABAC; the A section, the only music that is literally re-peated, is a beautifully balanced pair of isorhythmic phrases (ex. 34a) (cf. exx. 58–59). The extra line of text in the B section is accommodated through rhyth-mic acceleration (ex. 34b). And the C section might alternatively be labeled A', for although the rhythm of mm. 25–26 is new, there is substantial pitch intersection with the opening material (ex. 34c, at "N.B.").

Although the eight-measure period remains the rule for most Gershwin songs, there are notable exceptions in the late years. In "(I've Got) Beginner's

a. mm. 1–8 (17–24)

b. mm. 9–16

N.B.

c. mm. 25–32

Example 34. "Maybe," refrain

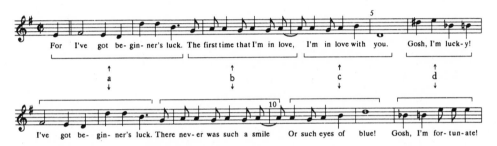

For I've got be- gin- ner's luck. The first time that I'm in love, I'm in love with you. Gosh, I'm luck-y!

a   b   c   d

I've got be- gin- ner's luck. There nev- er was such a smile Or such eyes of blue! Gosh, I'm for- tun-ate!

Example 35. "(I've Got) Beginner's Luck," refrain, mm. 1–12

Luck" (*Shall We Dance*, 1937) the first two sections of the refrain's standard AABA form have the nonstandard length of six measures each (ex. 35). In "Things Are Looking Up" (*A Damsel in Distress,* also 1937), the corresponding sections each comprise ten measures (ex. 36). Brackets and lowercase letters show the pacing of text lines: in "I've Got Beginner's Luck," line a occupies two measures; lines b and c are run together in the space of three measures; and line d, "Gosh, I'm lucky," takes but one measure. The last line in the next stanza, "Gosh, I'm fortunate," is verbally equivalent to its counterpart in the first; musically it uses three of the same pitches in a different order, with almost the same rhythm and with the same vertical support for each of the respective pitches (cf. ex. 164). In "Things Are Looking Up," the text lines take two measures each until line d, which takes four, and which contains five accented syllables instead of three.

This last line, the song's topic sentence, is the same for both stanzas. Its two settings, identical rhythmically and ending on the same tonic note and harmony, differ in melodic contour and harmonic detail (cf. ex. 167). There is, in addition (see ex. 36 at "N.B."), a permutational relationship between line a (G–A–F♯–D–E) and the first five notes of line d, first stanza (A–G–E–F♯–D).

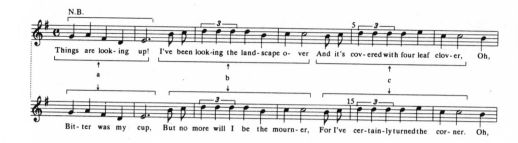

Example 36. "Things Are Looking Up," refrain, mm. 1–20

Obviously the subject of rhythm has not been exhausted in the remarks presented thus far. The various aspects of rhythm in Gershwin's music—meter, recurring patterns, characteristic subdivisions, phrase and period structure—will be continually revisited in the following chapters, as will the matters of pitch structure discussed in chapter 2.

4 The Early Period

We now turn to a closer examination of some of the more significant Gershwin compositions prior to *Rhapsody in Blue*—in other words, before February 1924. Several firsts are to be noted: There was Gershwin's first published song, "When You Want 'Em, You Can't Get 'Em, When You've Got 'Em, You Don't Want 'Em," in 1916.[1] The piano rag "Rialto Ripples" (see ex. 17a), written with Will Donaldson, a fellow song-plugger,[2] was the first Gershwin composition published by his erstwhile employer Remick. "The Real American Folk Song (Is a Rag)," one of his early collaborations with his brother Ira, was performed, along with the George Gershwin-Schuyler Greene song "Some Wonderful Sort of Someone," by the popular Nora Bayes in the 1918 revue *Ladies First;* it was here that Ira Gershwin first used the pseudonym Arthur Francis.[3] *Lullaby,* for string quartet (circa 1919), was Gershwin's first completed "classical" or concert work, while *Blue Monday,* produced as part of *George White's Scandals of 1922,* was his first essay in folk opera.

"The Real American Folk Song," which brought no financial gain from its initial exposure, remained unpublished until 1959.[4] It was included in a 1973 anthology[5] and, more recently, in the Broadway musical *Crazy for You* (1992).[6]

a. verse

Example 37. "The Real American Folk Song (Is a Rag)"

Its lyrics and music combine historical and contemporary commentary—from the perspective of 1918—on the state of popular music, the refrain extolling the rag as "a rhythmic tonic for the chronic blues." Though not in fact a rag, the music alludes—specifically in the transition to the refrain and in the bridge—to typical ragtime rhythm. An unusual feature of the verse, to my knowledge not encountered again until the composer's final period—in the quasi–English madrigal "The Jolly Tar and the Milk Maid" from *A Damsel in Distress*—is its ⁶⁄₈ meter. That and the siciliano rhythm suit the text, whose subject, the songs of the Old World (Italy included), is contrasted with the New World of the refrain. The verse has two stanzas, each consisting of two quatrains and a couplet; for the latter the meter shifts to a syncopated ⁴⁄₄ in preparation for the refrain. The song tonicizes III, then V, in the verse (ex. 37a) and flat VI, also followed by V, in the refrain (ex. 37b). Intentional or not, the symmetry of the major thirds above and below the tonic is inescapable.

The form of the refrain bears comment as well. Though it has its basis in the now-familiar AABA scheme (more common from the mid-twenties on-

b. refrain, mm. 1–16

c. refrain, mm. 17–20

Example 37. (*continued*)

ward than in the late teens), each of the A sections continues differently after
its identifying two-bar theme; the last is extended by five bars (for a total of
thirteen) and adds material recalling that of the B section. The result, expressible as AA′BA″, comes close to being through-composed. And, as if
to unite the seemingly disparate verse and refrain, the B section begins with
what is essentially a melodic recapitulation of the verse (ex. 37c). At the same

d. refrain, mm. 25–36

Example 37. (*continued*)

time, the chromaticism of the B section contrasts with the purely pentatonic melody of the refrain's opening bars.

The larger aspects of melodic structure, meanwhile, point to scale degrees $\hat{5}$ (g^1) and $\hat{8}$ (c^2) as focal points. As marked in example 37a, $\hat{5}$ is the first note in the verse; it also initiates an ascending linear progression at the end. In the refrain, $\hat{5}$ appears frequently in conjunction with both the natural and flatted forms of its upper neighbor (see the places marked $\hat{5}$–N in ex. 37b). $\hat{8}$, meanwhile, is represented in the verse by an octave line beginning rather tentatively with c^2 (mm. 1, 6) and continuing with the prolongation of b^1 (mm. 7–8) by a descending fifth-progression supported harmonically by III. The line gets stronger as it proceeds toward its close on $\hat{1}$ in m. 16. The final couplet of the verse follows, set to the ascending line from g^1 mentioned above, which skips to d^2 in the last bar. The two figures, ascending line and upper neighbor, point toward the reassertion of c^2 at the start of the refrain. There, as shown in the first bar of example 37b, this c^2 is coupled with its lower-octave replica c^1, which in turn begins a descending fourth-progression in the inner voice—a progression which, in passing through $b\flat$ and $a\flat$ on its way to g, hints at what would later become, from *Rhapsody in Blue* onward, a signal motive in Gershwin's music.

The concluding (A″) section of the refrain begins with the same inner-voice tetrachord, but with the natural instead of the flatted form of scale degree $\hat{6}$. The latter, m. 27, is transferred up an octave in the next measure, to the same register as the descent from $\hat{5}$ to $\hat{1}$ that occupies the song's final eight bars (ex. 37d).

Understandably, given the main locus of his activity at the time, Gershwin's early endeavors in the field of concert music were less sure than his songs. As noted in chapter 1, Gershwin used the main theme—to be more correct, the main motive—of the first of these, the *Lullaby for String Quartet* (1919 or 1920), in *Blue Monday* ("Has One of You Seen Joe?").[7] What is not so widely noted is that the actual material common to both is but a single motivic figure lasting two measures. In *Lullaby* this passage is immediately repeated and its main note sustained, resulting in a static treatment of scale degree $\hat{3}$ over a tonic harmony for a total of eight measures; the next eight are an analogous treatment of scale degree $\hat{2}$ over V. Following a brief excursion through IV and flat VI to V, a truncated recapitulation brings back the $\hat{3}$ over I of the opening and takes it to the close. The resulting measures, twenty-eight in all, shown here in condensed score with analytic overlay (ex. 38), comprise the refrain of a rondo form: they are repeated intact in a different setting (the final cadence spiced by flat II the second time) and followed by a first episode in VI, a second in IV. The episodes are separated by transpositions of the refrain's first two measures to IV, then flat VI, alternating with recitatives (in $\frac{3}{4}$-time) in the first violin and cello. The piece ends with a more forceful setting of the refrain, plus a two-part coda that first restates the two initial measures of the theme in harmonics, then pulls the notes B, B♭, and A out of an inner voice and takes them canonically through four ascending octaves in a rhythm—$\frac{3}{4}$ in a $\frac{4}{4}$ framework, with a resulting shifting of accents—that we can now recognize as a Gershwin trademark.

The new context given the *Lullaby* motive in *Blue Monday* is a distinct improvement (ex. 39).[8] Free from the repetitions and overall static profile of the earlier piece, the tune now "goes someplace" mm. 3–4 while the harmony, instead of sitting on the tonic, takes a decisive direction toward VI. The melodic background, still $\hat{3}$–$\hat{2}$–$\hat{1}$, is now enriched by middleground and foreground events.[9] Among these is the foreground ascent of the vocal line from g♯[1] to e[2], which is accompanied by an implied motion resolving the seventh of the secondary dominant of VI in an inner voice. This, being more basic to the underlying structure, is placed in the middleground as $\hat{2}$–$\hat{1}$, a descending third prolonging the background note $\hat{3}$. (Put another way, this expresses the simple truth that the interval of a minor sixth is an inversion of a

Example 38. *Lullaby for String Quartet,* mm. 9–36

major third.) In addition, the implied e¹ in m. 5 joins with one that is physically present as the head note of the inner-voice progression e¹–d¹–c♯¹.

This progression continues after a long hiatus in mm. 17–20, the last four bars of the aria, with b–a–g♯. Over this, an altered version of the opening motive replaces the expected c♯² with a chromatic passing note, rhythmically offsetting the arrival of c♯². Then, instead of continuing d♯²–e² as in mm. 4–

Example 39. *Blue Monday,* R18 ("Has One of You Seen Joe?")

5, the vocal line shifts downward to d#¹ at the point where the 4 of the cadential ⁶₄ resolves to 3, and where 6 resolves to 5. The latter, which physically takes place an octave lower, functions in the register above middle C as the implied $\hat{2}$ of the fundamental line.

Another selection from the opera, the title song "Blue Monday Blues," was cited in chapter 3 (ex. 17); a third, "I Want to See My Mother," "sung in true 'operatic tradition' by a dying man, is not distinguished,"[10] though its middle section bears quoting for its use, in an instrumental counterpoint, of what would become a familiar rhythmic pattern in Gershwin's later work (ex. 40 at "N.B.").[11] Apart from these three short arias, the vocal writing consists of recitative, some of it measured, with accompaniments and interludes that occasionally weave a song theme into a fabric of otherwise exclusively

Example 40. *Blue Monday*, R34 ("I Want to See My Mother," mm. 9–10)

Example 41. *Blue Monday*, prologue, mm. 21–33 (R7–R8 + 3)

instrumental material. The excerpt in example 41, the conclusion of the prologue sung by the tragic hero Joe, is a case in point. For eight bars Joe is accompanied by a sequence based on the motive borrowed from *Lullaby;* two bars later, at his exit, the orchestra echoes the overture's opening theme (see at "N.B.").

Also from the overture is the theme quoted in example 42, interesting be-

Example 42. *Blue Monday*, overture, mm. 30–32 (R4–R4 + 2)

cause of its resemblance to "I'll Build a Stairway to Paradise" (lyrics by B. G. DeSylva and Ira Gershwin),[12] whose success in *Scandals of 1922* contrasted with the ill fate of *Blue Monday*.[13] Though harmonically adventurous for its time, "Stairway to Paradise" may seem a bit dated today. If it does, it is largely because its piano style and rhythmic vocabulary are steeped in those of the twenties. The rolled open left-hand chords (in the verse), the straight $\frac{4}{4}$ time, the abundant dotted rhythms — features shared with the instrumental portions of *Blue Monday* — combine to mitigate against that quality of timelessness that one associates with the best of Gershwin's songs.

Nonetheless, "Stairway to Paradise" is remarkable, not only for its verve and sustained energy, but for the structural soundness of its pitch material, whose prime source — again (compare "The Real American Folk Song") — is the upper tetrachord of the major scale. The verse (ex. 43a) begins with the ascending form of the tetrachord, spanning the interval g^1–c^2 and filled in by chromatic steps (mm. 1–13). Vertical support comes from a sequential pattern that can be described contrapuntally as the alternation of the intervals 10 and 8 in the outer voices (in other words, the linear intervallic pattern 10–8), the harmonic consequence of which is a series of resolutions of applied dominant to tonic. The melodic component of the sequence next continues upward to db^2 (mm. 14–15), after which the vocal line returns to g^1 (mm. 15–17). The remainder of the verse embellishes g^1 with its upper neighbor before

a. verse

Example 43. "I'll Build a Stairway to Paradise"

taking the melodic line to b¹ and back; b¹ (also present in the verse's final piano chord) is leading tone to c², which enters with the second syllable of the refrain. (Here, too, is a parallel with "The Real American Folk Song.") To summarize, the path the voice takes over the entire twenty-four measures of the verse is as follows: g^1–c^2–g^1, then g^1–b^1–g^1 (b^1 resolving to c^2 in the first measure of the refrain). It remains, with the exception of the upper neighbor $d\flat^2$, exclusively within the compass of the upper tetrachord.

The same tetrachord is the most important motive, on multiple structural levels, in the refrain (ex. 43b). A relevant surface detail is the piano's recurring grace-note figure (see at "N.B." in ex. 43b), which presents the upper tetrachord in its ascending version. Its two main occurrences, in mm. 1 and 13,

b. refrain (to second ending)

Example 43. (*continued*)

embellish, respectively, the first and second notes of the title phrase, which are an octave apart. The figure also appears as a decorative comment on the fourth beat of m. 10, an octave higher still; and a chromatic variant spanning a minor third appears in the same register two measures later. In the course of presenting the main theme of the song, first over I, then transposed over IV going to V, Gershwin combines several foreground representations into a larger progression covering the same notes over a span of eight measures. With the exception of the implied a¹ in m. 5, all four notes of the large progression are attached to motivically relevant foreground events: c² ($\hat{8}$) heads both a skip and a stepwise descent to g¹ (mm. 1–2); b♭¹ (flat $\hat{7}$) is the upper component of an unfolding from the same g^1 (mm. 2–4); bb^1 and g^1 lead to the vertical f^1–a^1 (implied $\hat{6}$) on the downbeat of m. 5. The transposition of the theme (and hence of the descending fourth) in mm. 5–6 terminates on c^2 and joins with the ensuing descent to g^1 ($\hat{5}$) in m. 8.

Whether the larger progression just described is middleground or background rests on whether the primary tone is $\hat{5}$ or $\hat{8}$. This is a frequent ambiguity in pieces where the upper tetrachord is present; recall that in "The Real American Folk Song" we decided in favor of $\hat{8}$. What follows m. 8 is different here, however. There is an arpeggiation to e^2 in mm. 8–10 (whose first interval, g^1–c^2, essentially reverses the content of m. 1), raising the possibility (not present in the other song) of a background descent from this upper-octave version of $\hat{3}$ to the close on $\hat{1}$ via an implied $\hat{2}$. Endowing e^2 with such importance leads to a legitimate question about its preparation, however: did it just jump in at that point? On the other hand, if we took the descending line in mm. 1–8 as background, and continued it from the return of g^2 in m. 14, we would find ourselves at the end with an inner-voice E presumably taking precedence over the vocal line's more convincing close on C. Therefore, the first choice seems the more likely. As for the preparation of the primary tone e^2, it could be argued that d^2 in m. 6 of the refrain, ostensibly an upper neighbor to c^2 (as it is in m. 5), is instead the head note of a descending fifth and is an eventual passing note to e^2; the result, as suggested in example 43, is an initial ascent from c^2 in m. 1 (and in turn in the verse). Also graphed in example 43b is the piano coda, which, in recapitulating the descending upper tetrachord, introduces the flat form of scale degree $\hat{6}$ for the first time since the verse, thereby tying together the whole song with this single motive.

Gershwin's other big pre-*Rhapsody* hit, "Swanee" (lyrics by Irving Caesar), introduced in a revue for the opening of the Capitol Theatre in October 1919, attracted little notice until Al Jolson took it up the next year.[14] Thereafter it enjoyed a degree of success that some argue was disproportionate to its quality. Alec Wilder, for one, contends that "were it not known to be by Gershwin, I doubt if even the most observant authority could name the writer from the hundreds writing at that time."[15] Jablonski and Stewart, on the other hand, point out the "typical humorous Gershwin touch in the quotation from 'Old Folks at Home' in the last bar [of the trio]."[16] Another reference to the Stephen Foster original, less explicit and perhaps fortuitous, is that the first stanza of "Swanee" and the first line of "Old Folks at Home" coincide in pitch, or more precisely pitch-class, content: both make complete and exclusive use of the pentatonic scale (ex. 44a). Years later, as if to further the relationship between the two songs, Gershwin would see fit to conclude

a. refrain, mm. 1–8, compared with Stephen Foster, "Old Folks at Home," mm. 1–2

b. transcription in *George Gershwin's Song Book,* coda

c. analysis of verse

Example 44. "Swanee"

the piano solo version in *George Gershwin's Song Book,* with Foster answering Gershwin in imitative counterpoint (ex. 44b).

The refrain, as analyzed in chapter 2 (ex. 6), as an exemplar of the fundamental line $\hat{3}$–$\hat{2}$–$\hat{1}$. The verse, which differs in both mode and fundamental structure from the refrain, is distinguished by its minor key and its prominent inflection of D♭ to D♮ in the neighbor-note figure c^2–d^2–c^2. There was a logical programmatic reason for these exoticisms: the song was consciously patterned after one with an Eastern theme—and so perhaps there was a need to allude musically (and lyrically, inasmuch as the verse begins, "I've been away . . .") to another far-off place before bringing the locale closer to home. The resulting idiom, with its hint of eastern European Jewish folk music, was one that Gershwin came by rightfully.[17]

But aside from these considerations, the verse to "Swanee" (analyzed in ex. 44c) is forceful, direct, and well crafted. Its melodic profile, stated twice, is clear: an arpeggiation to scale degree $\hat{5}$, then the aforementioned neighbor note, and lastly a descending line. (The latter is incomplete in its first statement, ending on $\hat{2}$ over V, and represents a classic example of an interruption, as defined in chapter 2.) The opening arpeggiation made by the stemmed notes in mm. 1–3 is middleground in scope and fits the definition of a first-order arpeggiation (see chap. 2); moreover, in mm. 2–3, a foreground replica of the same arpeggiation (bracketed) joins to the primary tone as well. This motivic nesting is significant, as is the foreshadowing of the neighbor note (D♭, however, not D♮) in the left hand's upper voice (mm. 1–2). When the melody of mm. 1–4 is repeated in mm. 5–8, the accompaniment stresses the neighbor-note motive further, including the natural as well as the flat form. In addition, in mm. 15–16, the arpeggiation, transposed (and with each note preceded by an appoggiatura, or incomplete neighbor note), prolongs $\hat{2}$ while in the bass the flat form of the neighbor note prolongs V. In short, the two motives, arpeggiation and neighbor note, virtually saturate the verse. Following the vocal close on $\hat{1}$, a brief transition leading to the minor $\hat{3}$ prepares the major $\hat{3}$ of the refrain.

Of the works from Gershwin's early period analyzed in this chapter, only "Swanee" and "Stairway to Paradise" are still generally performed today. Yet there is insight to be gained from relationships between these better-known, later pieces and less familiar earlier ones. For example, "Stairway" has antecedents in both "The Real American Folk Song," composed four years earlier, and the contemporaneous *Blue Monday.* In "Some Wonderful Sort of Someone" (1918; lyrics by Schuyler Greene),[18] the melody in the bridge bears a distinct resemblance to the refrain of "Fascinating Rhythm."[19] Mention should also be made of such "exotic" numbers as "Limehouse Nights" (1919; lyrics by DeSylva and John Henry Mears) and "Mah-Jongg" (1923; lyrics by DeSylva).[20] In both, the accompaniment, rich in parallel fourths, takes on a life of its own to an extent not generally found until the 1930s.

Other instances exist as well. A cadenza for two clarinets in the Kilenyi notebook, dated September 15, 1921,[21] can be taken as a vague hint of the opening measures of *Rhapsody in Blue*. Another hint at *Rhapsody* can be seen in passages in the verse of "Stairway to Paradise" (mm. 7–8 and 15–16; cf. ex. 43), in which descending chromatic scale segments are supported vertically by parallel inverted dominant sevenths. Structures such as these are basic to those transitional passages, common in *Rhapsody* and subsequent works, that one comes to recognize as typically Gershwin. Finally, it is not hard to notice that *Blue Monday* was, at least in genre, a precursor of *Porgy and Bess*.

5 *Rhapsody in Blue*

Of the twenty-three numbers making up Paul Whiteman's famous "Experiment in Modern Music," *Rhapsody in Blue* was
the twenty-second. The first half of the program was a hodge-
podge of acts, ranging from a five-piece band performing
"The Livery Stable Blues" with barnyard sound effects, to a "melodious
jazz" treatment of "Mama Loves Papa" by the Palais Royal Orchestra, to a
quasi-anthropological analysis of "Yes, We Have No Bananas." Zez Confrey,
composer of "Stumbling" (ex. 25), played a medley of piano solos. The more
sedate second half included "semi-symphonic" arrangements of some Irving
Berlin songs and a new work, *Suite of Serenades,* by Victor Herbert.[1] "By this
time the listeners were beginning to lose interest in the experiment," write
Jablonski and Stewart. "The audience was becoming restless, bored. The
overfilled hall was hot. Standees began to slip through the exits."[2]

This was the context in which *Rhapsody in Blue,* as arranged by Ferde Grofé
for the Paul Whiteman Orchestra with Gershwin as soloist, was introduced
to the world at Aeolian Hall on March 7, 1924. History has left little doubt
that *Rhapsody* outclassed everything else on that famous program. And what
we have so far seen of Gershwin's work prior to that time should make it

equally plain that for all his promise as a songwriter, for all the earnestness of his early forays into "serious" composition, this new piece was unprecedented for him.

Apart from its novelty, *Rhapsody* had certain distinct qualities, the first being motivic interrelatedness. This was recognized as far back as 1931, as witness Isaac Goldberg's remark that "a surprising amount of the piece is embryonically suggested in the first three pages."[3] More specifically, as Charles Schwartz put it some forty years later, "the opening fourteen measures serve as the basis for much of the piece."[4] In these measures we now refer to the motives highlighted earlier (ex. 10): the fourth (*a* ascending, *a'* descending) and the neighbor note (*b* upper, *b'* lower). Not only do these motives pervade the famous clarinet solo of mm. 1–11; they are also the building blocks for the inner voice of mm. 11–14, whose eventual role as *Rhapsody*'s closing theme is significant both intrinsically and symbolically.

The first main theme of the work is introduced by the solo clarinet (mm. 1–5). Measures 6–9 present an important corollary wherein the neighbor note (*a*) and the fourth (*b*) are combined into a figure that is in turn treated sequentially at the fourth, thereby asserting motive *b* at the next higher level. An equally significant variant of this figure, in which the fourth is replaced by a minor third, follows subsequent statements of the first theme and is introduced with the entrance of the solo piano just before rehearsal number 3 (R3).

The thematic digest in example 45 shows just how motivically tight *Rhapsody* really is. Excerpts (a) through (c) comprise the first main theme, the first of two corollary themes, and the closing theme. These three themes are included within the first fourteen measures; moreover, the material that frames these fourteen measures frmes the first main part of the work. The latter concludes with the closing theme transposed to C, which in turn functions harmonically as an extended prefix to the dominant of G that comes just before R14 and the start of part 2. Analogously, the work as a whole ends with the closing theme in its initial key of E♭, whose harmonic function is as prefix to the dominant of B♭. The second corollary theme (ex. 45d) is the first new theme introduced after the initial fourteen bars; actually, it is a variant of corollary theme 1, with a minor third in place of the perfect fourth.

Part 2 begins with the G-major theme which Schwartz calls "a variant of the initial motif,"[5] and which will be referred to here as the transition theme (ex. 45e). In addition to the rhythmic aspects discussed in chapter 3, there are several connections based on pitch. The initial three pitches of the transition theme recall corollary theme 1, this time with an incomplete neighbor note.

a. main theme I, mm. I–5

b. corollary theme I, mm. 6–9

c. closing theme, mm. I I–I4 (RI–RI + 3)

d. corollary theme 2 (R3 − 2)

e. transition theme (R14)

N.B. (prime)

N.B. (inversion)

f. main theme 2 (R28)

g. "Funny Face," refrain, mm. I–4: for comparison

h. variant of closing theme with chromatic passing notes (R19)

Example 45. *Rhapsody in Blue:* summary of themes

i. corollary theme 3 (R33)   j. F#-minor variant of main theme 2 (R34)

Example 45. (*continued*)

The middleground descent from G echoes the descending upper tetrachord of main theme 1, though here only scale degree $\hat{7}$ is flatted, not $\hat{6}$.[6] Another element from main theme 1, the descending neighbor-note sequence, may be found in the counterpoint to the whole note in the fourth bar. Finally, the closing figure of this theme (see at "N.B.") quotes intact the germinal idea of corollary theme 2, first in its initial (prime) form, then—upon the theme's immediate repetition—in inversion.

The transition theme eventually leads to the second main theme, in E major. Its link with the earlier material, over and above the rhythmic correspondence noted in chapter 3, is the minor third spanned by its first three notes (ex. 45f). This is the operative interval in corollary theme 2, and in this regard main theme 2 also shares in the relationship between the transition and second corollary themes cited above. The interval in question here is, of course, the upper third of the E-major triad, whose lower third can be found as well—between the first and last notes of the theme's first two measures. The other noteworthy motivic element in this theme, the chromatic passing note, receives special treatment indeed: as the melody ascends in long note values, a descending form of the same motive counterpoints it as an inner-voice ostinato. The result is a significant instance of both the process of contrapuntal layering mentioned in chapter 1 and the technique of three-on-four superposition discussed in chapter 3. (As shown in ex. 45g, virtually the same figure forms the inner voice of the refrain of "Funny Face," composed three years later.) The conspicuous use of the chromatic passing note, like that of the minor third, has its precedent in earlier material, namely the variant of the closing theme in example 45h.

Ostensibly the last new material to be introduced, the F#-minor ostinato that begins the final portion of the work (part 3 or the conclusion of part 2, depending on one's point of view) once more features the minor third (ex. 45i). This links it with corollary theme 2—and, since this theme is also a corollary (i.e., to main theme 2), it is appropriately referred to here as corollary theme 3. (It should also be noted that corollary themes 2 and 3 both begin with neighbor-note figures, or forms of motive *b*, the former a major, the latter a minor second.) Below this ostinato, an F#-minor version of main theme 2 enters (ex. 45j). With the major and minor thirds of main theme 2 both recalled and reversed in position, the connection to that theme is complete and unequivocal.

Gershwin's penchant for counterpoint is in continual evidence throughout *Rhapsody*—indeed, from the very beginning. At its first appearance, main theme 1 is counterpointed by parallel descending chromatics in the inner voices (ex. 46a). The restatement in A♭, moments later, introduces the element of contrary motion—twice, in fact, within a single measure (ex. 46b). And not long thereafter, when the theme makes its first appearance in the piano alone, in A major (ex. 46c), contrary motion is pervasive: first, the de-

a. m. 3 (orchestra)　　　　　　　　　　　　b. R2 + 1 (orchestra)

c. R5 − 3 (piano solo)

Example 46. *Rhapsody in Blue*: successive settings of main theme 1

scending upper tetrachord a^2–e^2 is counterpointed by the ascending progression e^1–a^1 in the would-be tenor voice (see the superimposed beams); next, the filled-in skip e^2–c^2–e^2 is supported in like fashion by the bass $c\sharp^1$–e^1–$c\sharp^1$; finally, the lower-octave reprise of the tetrachordal descent from A, a^1–e^1, is set against the bass's ascending lower tetrachord A–d. The crisscrossed lines in example 46b–c highlight a special kind of contrary motion known as *voice exchange,* which typically involves notes a third apart within the same harmony (or two closely related harmonies, such as I–VI or II–IV), possibly with chromatic inflections, that exchange places in the opposing voices.

Inversional symmetry, in short, plays an important role in the treatment of the two main themes of *Rhapsody in Blue* as well as in the makeup of the transition theme that occupies considerable space between them. This space, or most of it, is generated by the sequential treatment of the theme through a recurring, recursive harmonic progression that proceeds by successive minor thirds, through G, B♭, D♭, E, and back to G.[7] In the course of one such sequence we find yet another manifestation of the inversional-symmetric trait, at R16 (ex. 47), where the trichord A♭–B♭–D♭ is counterpointed by its mir-

Example 47. *Rhapsody in Blue:* inversional symmetry, R16 (orchestra)

ror image D♭–C♭–A♭ in double augmentation. Also juxtaposed in this passage are two of the main rhythmic ideas in the piece: the two groups of four (eighths) joined by a tie in the descant, set against the superposition of three on four (quarters) in the bass.

Suffice it to say that *Rhapsody in Blue* abounds in ingenious passagework. Whether the product of Gershwin's conscious mind or the result of his natural pianistic gift, the music is there and its attributes are indubitable. The same is true of the numerous motivic connections that can be drawn between the various themes and subthemes. Yet questions remain as to whether one can find a coherent structure behind *Rhapsody* as a whole—and whether, given all the well-known, well-worn facts about the work, one even ought to try.

Answering the latter in the affirmative for the present, we begin with the analytic vocabulary and the depiction of main theme 1 from chapter 2. From example 10 alone it is possible to infer that either $\hat{8}$ or $\hat{5}$ could be the primary melodic tone. As we have already seen, the stepwise line between the two, through flat $\hat{7}$ and flat $\hat{6}$, is motivically paramount at the local level. At the same time, scale degree $\hat{8}$ (b♭²), initiates a larger, middleground progression whose second step, a♭², is already evident in example 10 at the start of the statement of main theme 1 in A♭ (R2). The next step, g♭², comes at R3, again as the head note of the next lower transposition of main theme 1. Vertical support for this sequence comes from a bass that moves through the circle of fifths: B♭, E♭ to A♭, D♭ to G♭. The bass pattern continues with B and E, but these are both successive dominants leading to A, the site of the next statement of main theme 1. The middleground melodic progression traced thus far—from bb² through gb²—continues into what turns out to be an inner voice, while the head note a² of the A-major statement of main theme 1 (solo piano at R5+2, orchestra at R6)[8] emerges as the second step in yet another descending line from the opening bb².

The schematic in example 48 presents a graphic summary of the fore-

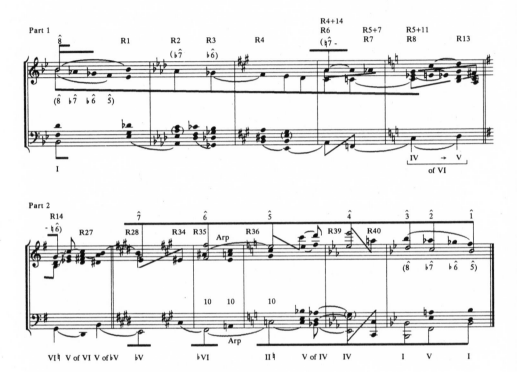

Example 48. *Rhapsody in Blue:* complete schematic

going discussion.[9] It attempts to show the essential voice leading, with upper registers adjusted downward (hence the beginning on bb¹ rather than bb²), and depicts the linear progressions in terms of their relative importance, or depth. The open note on the initial melody note bb¹ (supported by bass Bb, also an open note), indicates the deepest level, or background, which remains in force until the E-major Andantino and the introduction of main theme 2. (The hanging beam signifies that the background melodic line— likewise the bass—will continue.) The two descending lines described above, both middleground, are presented as filled, beamed notes; the first, descending through flat 7̂ and flat 6̂ (a larger reflection of the basic content of main theme 1 shown in stemless noteheads), eventually becomes an inner voice and therefore has downward stems; the second, which proceeds through natural $\hat{7}$ to natural $\hat{6}$ at the start of part 2 (R14), constitutes the descant at a deeper level (albeit still middleground) and has its stems pointing upward.

What we have, in short, is a nesting of descending lines at structural levels ranging from the foreground to two levels of middleground—and eventually to the background, shown in open notes over the entire span of example 48. The clue to the background structure, and to the identity of scale degree $\hat{8}$ as the primary melodic tone, is found in the Andantino, whose key, locally, is E major, and whose main melodic note is G♯ (or, to be registrally specific, g♯^{1}). This note, scale degree $\hat{3}$ in the key of E, can be interpreted enharmonically as flat $\hat{7}$ of B♭. It proceeds to the F♯ of the Misterioso, which likewise can be read as flat $\hat{6}$, then to E♮ (flat $\hat{5}$) at "Molto stentando" (R36). The conclusion, beginning with the Grandioso in E♭ (scale degree $\hat{4}$ over IV leading to V) and continuing with the final reprise of main theme 1, brings us firmly back within the orbit of B♭ and to the concluding descent of $\hat{3}$–$\hat{2}$–$\hat{1}$. This conclusion is overshadowed at the foreground level by the descant, which recapitulates the all-important descending upper tetrachord.

Thus it is possible, given a few compromises, to read a quasi-Schenkerian background structure in *Rhapsody*—a structure whose melodic component, the descent from scale degree $\hat{8}$, is reflected in the foreground and at various levels of the middleground. This is already shown to some extent in example 48, more so in the excerpts discussed below.

The first, graphed in example 49, follows the A-major version of main

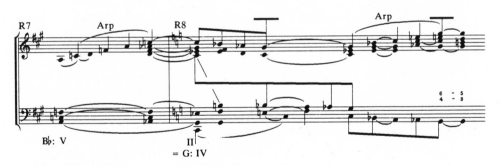

Example 49. *Rhapsody in Blue*: replications of motive *a'*

theme 1 introduced by the solo piano at R4+14 and taken up by the orchestra at R6. A new theme arpeggiates through an F-major triad to c^2, which then begins a partial quotation of main theme 1 in C minor, commencing with a transposition of motive a': c^2–bb^1–ab^1–g^1. This progression is foreground; at the same time, its terminus on g^1—step $\hat{6}$ of the tonic scale—coincides with (or at least anticipates) the tail note of the middleground progression $\hat{8}$–natural $\hat{7}$–natural $\hat{6}$, shown in example 48 (discussed above). A second occurrence of the C-minor version of motive a', an octave lower, can be seen in an inner voice. This progression is also at or very near the foreground, though it is less readily apparent. At precisely the point where it concludes, the bass enters with yet another stepwise descent from C to G, one more octave lower (i.e., c–Bb–Ab–G). These four notes now support a harmonic progression from I to V in the local key of C, leading to an episode in the major mode of that key, beginning at R9. Dovetailed with the conclusion of this episode, at R11, is a second bass progression covering the same ground—that is, from c to G with emphasis on the flatted scale steps in between (ex. 50). This pro-

Example 50. *Rhapsody in Blue*: motive *a'* with complementary fifth (at "N.B.")

gression supports a sequence based on the closing-theme derivative depicted in example 45h, and leads to a full-blown statement of the closing theme in its entirety, with corollaries. The central foreground idea in the episode, the descending fifth from G to C (marked "N.B."), is the complement of the descending fourth, and it is thus significant that this idea returns in the pickup to the closing theme at R12.

Another instance worthy of mention in which the expansion of motive a' is registral as well as temporal, occurs within the lengthy opening section of part 2 (ex. 51). A six-note figure drawn from the third measure of main theme 1, linking the arpeggiated triad and descending upper tetrachord (and thus related to a portion of the closing theme, as in ex. 10), is first treated sequentially (beginning one measure before R24). Then, upon its arrival at G major, it is repeated against a rhythmic ostinato in three successively higher registers. The passage culminates on a doubled F♮ (f^{3-4}), which can be under-

Example 51. *Rhapsody in Blue:* expansion of motive *a'*

stood as proceeding from g³, continuing to an arpeggio that takes E♭ down
four octaves (from e♭⁴ to e♭¹), and concluding on d¹ over V of G major.

The centerpiece of part 2—some would say of the entire *Rhapsody*—is the
celebrated Andantino, which is graphed in its entirety in example 52. Melodically, its theme (main theme 2) emphasizes the third of the local tonic E major
(interpreted at the background level as flat VI of B♭ major), with subsidiary
motion occurring both above and below the central pitch of G♯. This note
has background status, not only with respect to this section, where it is locally
interpreted as 3̂ of E, but with respect to the entire work, where (as in ex. 48)
it is equated enharmonically with flat 6̂ of B♭. The Andantino contains three

Example 52. *Rhapsody in Blue,* Andantino: analysis

complete statements of main theme 2, their lengths varying slightly depending on their endings. Statements 1 and 2, by the orchestra alone and by piano with orchestra, respectively, each end on the dominant of E; statement 3, by the piano alone, ends on a somewhat veiled local tonic.

A striking contrapuntal feature of main theme 2 is the juxtaposition of the ascending chromatic passing note in the descant with the descending chromatic passing note, repeated in rhythmic diminution, in the inner voice directly below. More basic and no less elegant is the inversional balance exhibited in the very first measure, where descant and bass exchange the notes G♯ and E. These two elements—the chromatic passing note (labeled CP in example 52) and the exchanged third—account for much of what happens in the rest of the section. Notice, for example, the descending line in the inner voice beginning $c\sharp^1$–c^1–b shortly before R29. The same melodic segment, an octave lower, occurs at the cadence at R29, where it joins with the bass on B. At the close of the second statement of the theme (R31) the same notes reappear, now as the bass line itself. The chromatic passing note then continues in its rhythmically diminished ostinato form as accompaniment to the piano's parallel tenths that begin at R32. This passage (shown only in a telescoped form in ex. 52) serves as a retransition to the third statement of main theme 2. This, the last such statement in the Andantino, and the first by the solo piano, essentially duplicates its predecessor in the orchestra. It, too, ends with a whole-tone variant of the initial gesture, which serves, the second time around, as a transition to the F♯ minor of the Misterioso.

The unfolding symbol—the diagonal beam connecting two notes with opposing stems—has some fairly clear-cut uses in the foregoing analysis. Foremost among these is main theme 2 itself, whose first two bars articulate the major third G♯–E over an E-major harmony. This is the first requirement: that the unfolded interval be a structural component of the locally prolonged harmony. The second, which applies to unfoldings in the upper voices, is that the unfolded interval have voice-leading consequences, i.e., that it proceed to or from another interval, which may be either unfolded or simply stated as a vertical. Instances of both possibilities may be found in the present example.

Unfoldings can also embrace linear intervallic patterns, as demonstrated by the retransition in the solo piano beginning at R32. At that point the descant has G♯ (specifically, $g\sharp^1$), the bass E. At the end of the fourth measure (R32+3) the outer voices are, respectively, D♮ (d^2) and B. The unfoldings $g\sharp^1$–d^2 and E–B combine to make a recognizable harmonic entity, one that makes sense in light of the implied A major that ensues (R32+4), although ideally the descant d^2 should resolve to $c\sharp^2$ (the latter shown in parentheses, indicating an implied note). The outer voices e^2 and c♯ on that downbeat continue upward to c♯^{3} over a, resulting in the unfoldings e^2–c♯^{3} and, in the bass, c♯–a. The role of this resultant A-major harmony as subdominant of E is made evident at the end of the passage, where the inner voices d♯^{2} and f♯^{2}, added to the outer voices a–c♯^{3}, impart a dominant function.

The Misterioso begins with a four-bar introduction ("leggiero") leading to a segment labeled "Agitato e misterioso" in the published score.[10] Its only new material, the ostinato in example 45i, is the underpinning—more precisely the overpinning—for a sequence based on a variant of main theme 2, whose harmonic center ascends by minor thirds: from F♯ minor, to A major, then to C major (Molto stentando, R36), recalling the minor-third sequence that dominates part 2 prior to main theme 2. C major is then the starting point for a recapitulation of the agitato transition first heard at R5+14, where it makes a circuitous return to the local key of A major. Now, however, the dominant of A reached at R38+10 (Molto marcato) is taken, via chromatic contrary motion, to the dominant of E♭.

The E♭ reached at R39 (Grandioso) is a crucial part of the fundamental structure as shown in example 48. Melodically it is scale degree $\hat{4}$ of the fundamental line; harmonically it is IV (going to V) of the home key of B♭. E♭ is also a minor third above C—and thus the harmonic sequence of minor thirds commenced with the Misterioso is taken one step further. Moreover, the choice of E♭ for the final statement of the closing theme returns the piece full circle to the close of its expository first fourteen measures.

In short, *Rhapsody in Blue* is not nearly as rhapsodic as it may first seem. Its themes are joined by a multiplicity of motivic relationships. It has a coherent fundamental structure. Where it does appear to meander somewhat, it does so in a controlled way. The processes whereby this control is achieved are central to Gershwin's compositional technique. One is the recursive harmonic progression, which gives the illusion of motion to passages that begin and end in the same place (such as the succession of minor thirds from G to G that is the harmonic basis for the opening of part 2). The other is the transitional passage, a device for which Gershwin, for better or worse, has become well known.

Two such passages make their initial appearance early in part 1. The first, transition 1, begins at R4+6 (ex. 53a) and leads to the A-major entrance of main theme 1 at R4+14, or three bars before R5. Though harmonically static, its upper voices provide considerable interest from the standpoint of both the small and larger dimensions. The initial three measures comprise an ascending sequence supporting the top voice e^2–f^2–g^2, whose vertical cross-

A: V

(to c♯², R5-3)

a. transition I (R4+6)

Arp

N

N

N

(etc.)

10 10 10 10

b. transition 2 (R5+14)

Example 53. *Rhapsody in Blue*

sections are each based on the corresponding dominant seventh. The descending portion also begins on an E7 chord with e² in the top voice, whose notes alternate with their upper neighbors (diatonic in the first three bars, chromatic in the fourth), creating a whole-tone scale of semitonal dyads. In the fourth measure (whose immediate repetition is not shown), the emphasis shifts from the first to the second note of each dyad, then shifts back at the measure's end.

The larger significance of the upper voices is identical with the underpinning of the entire passage—namely, the dominant of A. The resolution of this dominant provides the clue to the larger melodic progression beamed in example 53a: from e² (the starting pitch) to d¹ (the registrally displaced passing seventh, unfolding to g♯) to c♯². The latter, the resolution of the passing seventh, is absorbed into an inner voice by virtue of the overlapped entrance of main theme 1.

The second transitional passage (ex. 53b) first appears following the C-minor statement of main theme 1, at R5+14 (Poco agitato). Its antecedent portion, based on corollary theme 2 (the theme of the piano's initial entrance), features a broad arpeggiation of a diminished-seventh chord, while its consequent portion, like the passage cited in example 53a, descends in whole tones. The featured vertical is once again the dominant seventh—though it must be emphasized that "dominant sevenths" in parallel motion are not dominants at all. As with functional dominant sevenths, the operative interval is the tritone—which now, instead of resolving to a third or a sixth, moves by step to another tritone. In the first transitional passage the parallel tritones are straightforward; their voice leading in the second transitional passage, on the other hand, includes overlapping between measures in the ascending phase of the passage (e.g., d♯–a to g–db¹, first and second measures), plus one functional resolution (e♯–b to f♯–a♯, third and fourth measures).

The two passages in example 53 are intertwined. The first ends with the bass progression F♯–F♮–E (supporting E7); the second has F♯–F♮ in preparation for E (and E7) on the next downbeat. The first statement of the second passage leads, in fact, to a restatement of the first (at R5+24);[11] the second (at R37), enhanced by orchestral accompaniment, joins with the Molto marcato (ex. 54), in which functional dominant sevenths—now the dominants of A

Example 54. *Rhapsody in Blue:* transition to closing theme

and E♭, respectively—are bridged by nonfunctional ones in stepwise—now chromatic—succession. In this instance the unidirectional motion of the lower voices is relieved, on the downbeats of the second and third measures, by an upward skip of a fifth. It is noteworthy that in these two places the descant is in an octave relationship with the bass—in other words, with the "root" of the so-called dominant seventh. It is also possible, as shown by the diagonal lines in example 54, to interpret the skips as the products of overlapping. By this reasoning the bass c♯ at the end of the first measure continues its chromatic descent not in the bass but in the inner voice, commencing with c^1. Similarly, one measure later, the chromatic steps transfer from bass f to the inner voice e^1.

Rhapsody in Blue is at once Gershwin's most famous and possibly his least understood composition. Easily dismissed as a piece of popular music, or at the very least as a youthful work by one not exactly steeped in formal musical training, it turns out to be a better-written piece than anyone could first imagine it to be. *Rhapsody* already displays Gershwin's technical gifts—of counterpoint, of rhythmic invention, and of a large-scale structure of melody and harmony which succeeds with against-all-odds bravado—which would only get better as time went on. In short, *Rhapsody in Blue* is a work of achievement and promise.

6 The Road to "I Got Rhythm"

After *Rhapsody in Blue,* from 1924 through 1930, Gershwin's technique as a songwriter developed considerably. This development was largely chronological in that the songs from the middle of the 1920s and before tend to have a distinctly "period" quality that had substantially disappeared by the decade's end.

"Oh, Lady Be Good!" (1924), from the show of the same name, reflects the earlier style: simple, direct, with clearly definable hooks. The latter—the vernacular for those quirks or details which give a popular song its particular appeal—are two in this case: the minor-mode opening of the verse, and the subdominant ninth with flatted seventh in the refrain. Though each has its precedent in an earlier Gershwin song ("Swanee" in the one instance, "Stairway to Paradise" in the other), there are differences as well. The verse, for one, opens in the relative (not parallel) minor and, unlike "Swanee," does not remain there, but goes first to G major, then to E major, and back to G for the refrain. The use of the altered subdominant is different here as well: in "Stairway" it occurs in the context of a transposition of the theme (and a lyric that declares "I've got the blues"), while its function in "Lady" is admittedly local and coloristic—as a substitute for an expected tonic within the theme itself.

Unlike these earlier tunes, "Oh, Lady Be Good!" is unremarkable melodically. Repeated notes abound in both verse and refrain; in the latter the primary tone and its upper neighbor (d^2 and e^2) are emphasized to the point of obviousness. But "Oh, Lady Be Good!" is a rarity among Gershwin's songs from the twenties in that there is an extant manuscript comparable to those which exist for the late songs. This manuscript is the closest thing to a composer's fair copy that we have; as with the other songs (as opposed to the concert works), the copy is in pencil, in what Wayne Shirley calls the composer's informal hand.[1] It has blank measures for the four-bar introduction; otherwise the accompaniment is completely written out, with dynamic markings that are at times even more detailed than those in the published score. The main differences are in the piano's right hand, where parallel octaves and reaches larger than an octave are routinely modified in the published version by deleting or transposing the lowest voice. The verse illustrates the first situation, the refrain the second (exx. 55a–b). The manuscripts make it clear that Gershwin viewed his songs as compositions and gave the accompaniment as much attention as the vocal part. It is thus not unreasonable to assume, in cases where manuscripts are not available, that the published piano parts likely reflect, for the most part, what Gershwin actually wrote.

Insight into the composer's thought processes in general, and during the post-*Rhapsody* twenties in particular, can be gleaned from what Ira Gershwin describes as "a hasty lead-sheet" for "I've Got a Crush on You," which was featured first in the 1928 show *Treasure Girl* and subsequently in the revised (1930) production of *Strike Up the Band* (ex. 56).[2] Although the manuscript specifies no chordal structures in either musical or letter notation, it does show an inner voice at the start of the refrain. Characteristically, this inner voice is both stepwise and chromatic (recalling Kilenyi's watchword *Stufenreichtum*), suggesting that counterpoint, rather than harmony, is the prevailing factor in Gershwin's song accompaniments.

There are two songs from the twenties whose accompaniments bear notice. "Fascinating Rhythm" has a piano part which, in just those sections that are so distinctive rhythmically, forsakes all root-position chords for patterns of parallel sixths underpinned by leading tones (see ex. 57a). The accompaniment acquires a more conventional texture in the middle and closing portions of the refrain, just when the rhythm of the song falls into line with the $\frac{4}{4}$ meter. The tonic triad, too, is delayed until these sections (ex. 57b).

Another piano part that goes beyond the routine belongs to "Maybe," from *Oh, Kay!* (1926) (cf. exx. 33–34). As in "Fascinating Rhythm," the vocal line gets its harmonic support chiefly from the middle register. Freed much

Example 55. "Oh, Lady Be Good!" manuscript and published score

Example 55. (*continued*)

Oh, Lady Be Good!

Words by
IRA GERSHWIN

Music by
GEORGE GERSHWIN

7271_3

a. verse (beginning)

Example 55. *(continued)*

4

b. refrain (beginning)

Example 55. *(continued)*

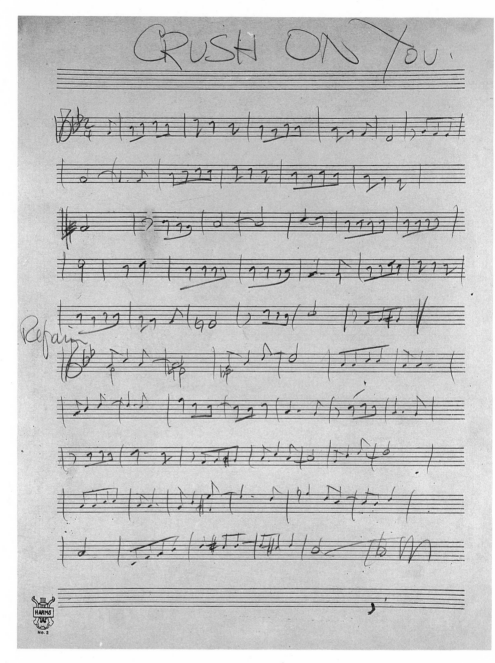

Example 56. "[I've Got a] Crush on You," leadsheet, manuscript

a. refrain, mm. 1–5

b. refrain, mm. 9–12

Example 57. "Fascinating Rhythm"

of the time from providing a bass line, the left hand alternately doubles the vocal line an octave lower and takes over the right-hand part while the latter echoes the voice an octave higher (ex. 58a). The song is further integrated by an introduction that uses the material of the refrain (ex. 58b) and a coda that refers back to the main motive of the verse (ex. 58c).

The refrain melody, meanwhile, is a notable example of the pentatonic, plagal Gershwin[3] — a dual trait that extends back to "Swanee" and foreshadows "I Got Rhythm." The same can be said of "Clap Yo' Hands," also from *Oh, Kay!*, whose refrain opens with a melody that is almost a duplicate of the opening of "Maybe" (ex. 59a).[4] But what is outstanding about "Maybe" is the symmetry of its antecedent and consequent phrases (ex. 59b). Measures 5–8, descending from d^2, are a near-perfect mirror image of mm. 1–4; the sole difference, for which there is ample and deep-rooted precedent, is that the ascending fourth is answered by a descending fifth. There are interesting parallels here: to "I Got Rhythm" in the former respect; to "Fascinating Rhythm" in the latter (cf. ex. 26). (Shades of "Fascinating Rhythm" also occur in "Clap Yo' Hands"—in the way the melody, rhythmically foreshortened and offset, is retraced.)

a. refrain, mm. 1–4

b. introduction

c. refrain, first and second endings

Example 58. "Maybe"

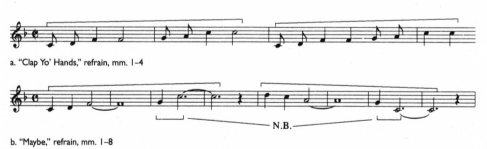

a. "Clap Yo' Hands," refrain, mm. 1–4

b. "Maybe," refrain, mm. 1–8

Example 59.

An intriguing step on the road to "I Got Rhythm" is "Liza," a number written for Florenz Ziegfeld's *Show Girl* (1929)[5] and, like "Swanee" some ten years earlier, popularized by Al Jolson. Boldly, the refrain begins with repeated half notes that sound out B♭, C, E♭, F (ex. 60). Transposed, these are the same four pitches that earlier opened the refrain of "Maybe" and "Clap

Example 60. "Liza," refrain, mm. 1–4

Yo' Hands" and which would, a year later, declaim the title phrase of that most famous of Gershwin's songs. In "Liza," however, this motive occupies the upper portion of the melodic range; unlike the others, its melodic framework is authentic rather than plagal. And the harmonic progression supporting it moves toward IV rather than V.

But it is the contrapuntal aspect of this support that distinguishes the song still further: the left hand's stepwise succession of arpeggiated parallel tenths. The right hand, whose top voice doubles the song melody, can be read as the result of overlapping descending steps, as shown by the voice-leading lines in example 60. The composer himself has, in effect, corroborated this reading in *George Gershwin's Song Book,* where "Liza" is the last, the longest, and pianistically the most difficult of the eighteen song arrangements. There, with evident relish, Gershwin draws attention to the overlappings with a sequence of afterbeat flourishes that double the pattern two octaves lower, where it joins with the left hand's parallel tenths (ex. 61).[6]

"Liza" is also an interesting study in relationships between verse and refrain. From the analytic graph of the entire song (ex. 62) we see that both the verse and the middle section (or bridge) of the refrain are dominated by the upper tetrachord of the scale. Descending fourth-progressions from eb^2 occur four times in the verse: at mm. 1 and 5, and, embellished by foreground replications, at mm. 10 and 14. The bridge begins with yet another such progression (refrain, mm. 17–20), which turns out to be in the service of a larger progression—beamed, with scale-degree numbers in ex. 62b—leading to the resumption of the main theme at m. 25. This progression also spans the upper tetrachord. The bass at m. 17, meanwhile, prolongs VI by means of a descending fourth from c.

These motivic links between verse and bridge, in the form of various representations of the descent from $\hat{8}$ to $\hat{5}$, are complemented by the descent from $\hat{5}$ to $\hat{1}$ that dominates the outer portions of the refrain. These, the A sections in the standard AABA chorus form, also contain activity in the

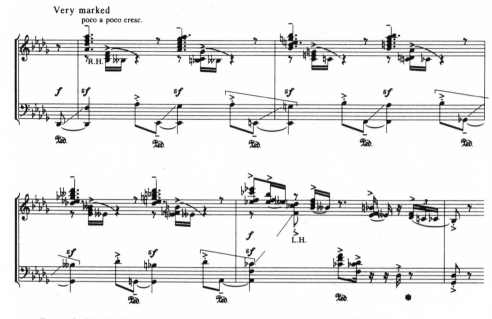

Example 61. "Liza," transcription in *George Gershwin's Song Book,* mm. 33–37

a. analysis of verse

Example 62. "Liza"

b. analysis of refrain (repeat notation mine)

Example 62. (*continued*)

upper tetrachord—including the all-important motive that would eventually be identified with "I Got Rhythm"—as the result of the successive overlappings detailed in example 60. And although the descent from $\hat{5}$ is judged to be the background line (and is thus represented in open notes at its final appearance), it is paralleled above by successions of what in Schenkerian terminology would be called *cover tones:* stepwise from eb^2 in m. 3, then, a third above, stepwise from f^2 in m. 4. (Both lines drop out in m. 8, where their respective resolutions to bb^1 and g^1—shown as implied notes in the graph—are physically present an octave lower.)

Overlappings, cover tones, and motivic connections between verse and

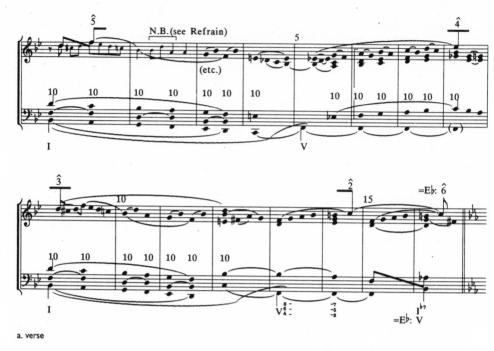

a. verse

Example 63. "Soon"

refrain are also integral to an exceptionally elegant ballad from the same year, "Soon," written for the second version of *Strike Up the Band* that opened in January 1930. The verse, in the dominant, traces the melodic line f^2–eb^2–d^2–c^2: in other words, $\hat{5}$–$\hat{4}$–$\hat{3}$–$\hat{2}$ in the key of Bb (ex. 63). This progression leads by step directly into the initial bb^1 of the refrain, which is scale degree $\hat{5}$ of the tonic Eb and the primary melodic tone. The underlying melodic profiles of verse and refrain taken together thus form a continuum; taken separately, one is reflected in the other. Not only does each descend from the fifth of the scale, but in each there is a stop on scale degree $\hat{2}$—the phenomenon that Schenker called interruption (cf. ex. 5).

An interesting foreground connection between verse and refrain is the motive marked "N.B." in example 63, comprising an ascending third followed by a descending fourth. Having been featured prominently in the verse, its recurrence in the refrain—in the same rhythm—seems more than a coincidence. And in what Ira Gershwin referred to as the "vest"[7]—that portion of the verse which leads into the refrain with a distinct thematic idea—the two ascending lines, each spanning a fifth, can be seen as a foreground reflection (indeed, a mirror image) of the descending fifth-progressions that dominate the song's middleground and background.

b. refrain (to second ending)

Example 63. (*continued*)

  An equivalent balance is achieved in "Embraceable You" from *Girl Crazy* (1930), where a verse dominated by descending lines (ex. 64a) leads into a refrain in which ascending figures predominate (ex. 64b). The form of the refrain, typically described as ABAC,[8] is in a larger sense two parts rather than four, with the consequent portion different for each. Though different, both consequents revert to descending motion as the prevailing melodic ingredient—in part, to descending spans of a third. The interval of a third, filled in by step, is an important motive throughout the refrain. The ascending form, labeled *a* in example 64b, governs the antecedent periods; the descending form, labeled *a′*, pervades the consequents. This is evident in the way each section begins—and, at deeper levels, in the way each section continues.

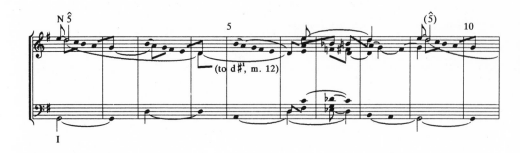

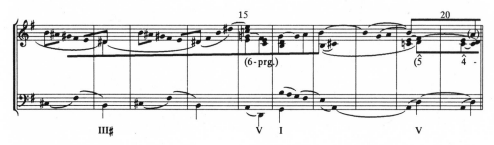

a. verse

Example 64. "Embraceable You"

Taken in its entirety, the refrain's A section is a classic instance of an *initial ascent,* a middleground linear progression leading to the primary tone. The first note of the progression, beamed in example 64b, is g^1 (mm. 1–2), the goal note of the first statement of motive *a;* the next is a^1 beginning m. 3. How it continues is open to interpretation, however. At first reading it seems almost second nature to follow the scale upward from a^1 at m. 5 to d^2 on the downbeat of m. 7. The result, an ascent of a fifth, shown by the upward stems and beam, fits in admirably with the descending fifth that opens the verse; the primary tone in this reading is, of course, scale degree $\hat{5}$, or the note d^2.

At the same time, a purist could conceivably see weaknesses in this read-ing, namely the unsupported b^1 and the upward-resolving c^2. The alterna-tive, notated with downward stems, would treat the first b^1 as a passing note to a flagged c^2 (thereby making clear the replication of motive *a* as stated in m. 1) resolving downward to an implied b^1 in m. 7.

If the first reading had two weaknesses, then the second would have one big one, namely the suggestion that the main note of the song—the culmina-tion of the initial ascent—is there only by implication. But this is not entirely the case. The note B appears two measures later, in the same register as the one implied (i.e., b^1), at the start of the second eight-bar period. It is found a measure sooner, in m. 8, in an inner voice an octave lower, as the goal of

b. refrain (to second ending)

Example 64. (*continued*)

the descending progression d¹–c¹–b — the same inner-voice progression that connects the verse to the refrain. Looking at the pattern of the inner voice as related to the descant, one can see, through the octave doublings and couplings, an underlying structure that gives primacy to scale degree $\hat{3}$. Yet the fifth remains stronger, from a sheer melodic standpoint; purism aside, it is probably the more honest reading.

The ambiguity as to whether $\hat{5}$ or $\hat{3}$ is the primary melodic tone is not unique to "Embraceable You"; indeed, there are numerous examples in the classical tonal literature.[9] From the Gershwin songs of the period between *Rhapsody in Blue* and "I Got Rhythm" come two further instances of such ambiguity.

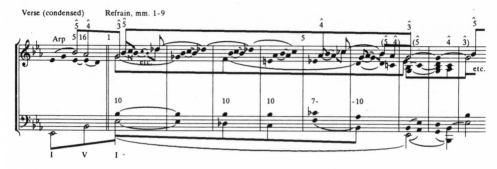

Example 65. "The Man I Love"

One of these is "The Man I Love," composed in 1924.[10] As shown in example 65, the nuclear neighbor-note motive of the refrain initiates a descending sequence spanning the line $\hat{5}$–$\hat{4}$–$\hat{3}$. Competing with this is a strong inner voice, later doubled in octaves, which descends from $\hat{3}$. The result is a central role for scale degree $\hat{3}$ as head note of one progression and tail note of another. As in "Embraceable You," the inner voice $\hat{3}$ is also the tail note of a large $\hat{5}$–$\hat{4}$–$\hat{3}$ progression initiated in the verse.

The other instance of ambiguity is the evergreen "I Got Rhythm," which would eventually be the basis of the *"I Got Rhythm" Variations* composed in 1934. Surely a major reason for the song's fertility is the elegance of its material. The initial four-note motive, already seen as operative in several other Gershwin songs, is symmetrical; it is also an essential ingredient in the pentatonic scale, which Gershwin favored. The symmetry of the motive is reinforced by that of the first two lines of the refrain, which present this motive in both prime and retrograde forms—and here, moreover, the retrograde is also the inversion.

Here, as in the preceding examples, a case can be made for either $\hat{5}$ or $\hat{3}$ as the primary melodic tone. Both possibilities are shown relative to the key of F in example 66.[11] In the first interpretation (detached stems, numbers in parentheses) the melody is neatly framed by the two representations of $\hat{5}$: c^1 and c^2. But whereas the melody's lowest note, c^1, is continually present from the beginning, the role of its high point, c^2, is ambiguous. Its one occurrence is not within the basic thirty-two-measure form but in a four-measure coda (appropriately on the word "more"), where its harmonic support, V^7 of II, demands resolution. And it should be noted, as a matter of performance practice, that intrumental jazz improvisations on "I Got Rhythm," including pieces that use what are colloquially called "'Rhythm' changes," characteristically do not use the coda and hence do not reach the high C.

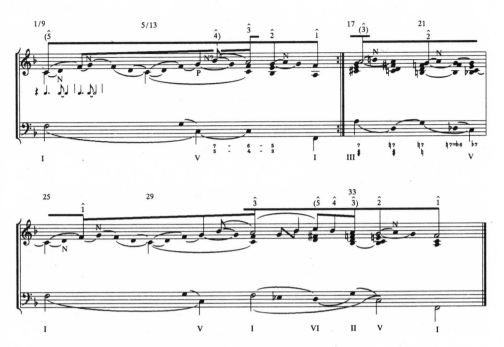

Example 66. "I Got Rhythm": analysis of refrain (repeat notation mine)

One may therefore prefer to give greater value to a¹, or scale degree $\hat{3}$, which is the structural high point during most of the body of the refrain (and, incidentally, in the verse as well). C nonetheless remains an important inner voice which fulfills its potential as a cover tone in the *"I Got Rhythm" Variations* (cf. ex. 127).

But it would be remiss, amid this discussion of pitch, not to mention the obvious element that ties the refrain together and directly binds it to its subject matter: the isorhythmic pattern that persists from beginning to end. It starts on the second quarter and superimposes a series of three eighth-durations concluded by a duration of five eighths (seven including the first quarter of the next measure). The implications of this rhythm and its inter-action with the prevailing meter, along with those pertaining to pitch, were later exploited in the *Variations*. One can also find a sequel in the title song from the 1937 film *Shall We Dance,* in which a similar rhythmic pattern dominates both verse and refrain.

7 *Concerto in F* and *An American in Paris*

Gershwin's credibility as a composer of concert music was greatly enhanced by his next two major works. *Concerto in F,* written in 1925 and premiered in December of that year, was a logical sequel to *Rhapsody in Blue.* Not only was it longer and more elaborate, but it was cast in a form that made clear its intention to be taken seriously—and which in actuality did not fall far from the Classic-Romantic model to which Gershwin aspired. On a different front, the model for *An American in Paris,* whose first performance was three years later almost to the day, would come to have a similar purpose.[1] After all, a tone poem suitable for a ballet (and posthumously realized as such, albeit abridged, in the 1951 film of the same name) would place Gershwin in the company of the most au courant of French composers (or in his own contradictory pairing, "Debussy and the Six"),[2] not to mention the adoptive Parisian Stravinsky. Perhaps most significantly of all in the eyes of some, Gershwin orchestrated both works himself.

Concerto in F and *An American in Paris* both excel in the area of melodic development. So, also, did *Rhapsody in Blue;* there, however, the development was mainly confined to one idea at a time, or to ideas in sequence.

What we now find, in contrast, are a number of instances where more than one melodic idea is used and developed simultaneously. This process, which I call contrapuntal layering, becomes increasingly important in Gershwin's later work.

A case in point is the expressive theme introduced by the piano in *Concerto in F* as the second subject of a modified sonata form. Its initial presentation, prefaced by bass C and arguably supported harmonically by that note as an implied pedal point, is accompanied by parallel $^{10}_{6}$ verticals beginning with db–b–e^1 on the first downbeat (ex. 67). The topmost stratum of this accompaniment then becomes the basis for a countermelody in the violas and English horn (ex. 68),[3] which joins the piano at the next statement of the theme twenty measures later, at R5.[4] This countermelody subsequently comes to the fore in the solo part, when the full orchestra takes up the theme at the close of the exposition. When the theme last appears in its grandioso version, identical in both the first-movement recapitulation and its reprise as the last episode of the rondo finale, the aforementioned counterpoint is in all four horns in unison while the piano has a repeated-note triplet version of what was originally a pair of inner voices in the left hand (ex. 69).

The fit between the first movement of *Concerto in F* and the Classic-Romantic notion of sonata form is best in the exposition. The concept of the lyrical second theme harks back to the eighteenth century. That this theme would also be initially reserved for the solo entrance is but one step removed from the classical practice of introducing the soloist through a distinct theme within the first subject area. And the latter, again in keeping with tradition, is a series of ideas rather than a single theme — ideas which, in a well-composed piece, will join to reinforce a common structural background.

The ideas in this case are, in the main, three: (a) a wind-and-percussion fanfare; (b) a widely-cited Charleston motive; and (c) an arpeggiated figure in a dotted rhythm. The material of these ostensibly discrete events (ex. 70) is joined in more than one way.[5] The percussion component of the fanfare is continued through the Charleston figure, whose close echoes the fanfare's high point both harmonically and rhythmically. The semitonal neighbor-note figure C–Db, introduced by the bass clarinet trill, reappears transposed as the only moving voice in the Charleston chords (see at "N.B."). The bassoon arpeggiation that follows prolongs D♮ over the sustained fifth F–C, with the combination of C and D representing, in the same register, the whole-step counterpart of C–Db. These neighbor-note embellishments of C set the stage for the emergence of that note — scale degree $\hat{5}$ in the key of F — as the primary melodic tone of the piece.

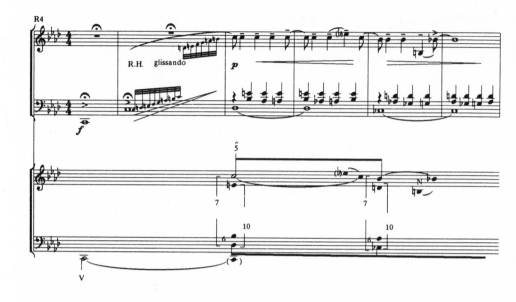

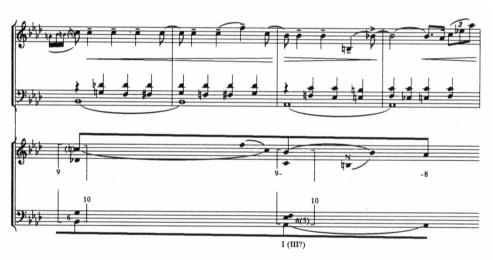

Example 67. *Concerto in F, I*

Example 68. *Concerto in F, I, countermelody at R5*

Example 69. *Concerto in F,* I

Expansion of these three ideas begins almost immediately. A six-bar transition beginning at R1+9 combines the dotted rhythm of the arpeggiation with a juxtaposition of parallel verticals in the upper voices in chromatic contrary motion with the bass. Then the arpeggiation itself is the basis of a sequence rooted in ascending minor thirds (not unlike the beginning of part 2 of *Rhapsody*) whose support component grows steadily more complex (R2–R3+9). This sequence is interrupted and then followed by single reprises of the fanfare (at R2+9 and R3+9 respectively), the second of which omits the bass clarinet trill accompanying the snare drum roll—perhaps in preparation for the recasting of the pitches C and D♭ as the opening vertical of the ensuing second main theme and solo entrance. The same two pitches (more precisely pitch classes) feature prominently in the transitions bridging the successive statements of theme 2 in the second part of the exposition; they also form the bass at the close of the cadenza linking the exposition with the development section.

The development proper begins at R14 with a return to F major and the Charleston motif, out of which grows a new, lyrical melody which eventually becomes the subject of its own mini-section (Moderato cantabile, from R20). The latter in turn gives way to a procession of like-length episodes based on the Charleston and arpeggiation figures.

The recapitulation, greatly foreshortened, opens with a reprise of theme 2 a fourth higher (the Grandioso at R29) and closes with a quodlibet formed

Example 70. *Concerto in F,* I, mm. 1–12

from the three elements that comprise theme 1 (Allegro con brio, from R34). These are connected by a relatively lengthy and elaborate transition that likewise presents previously heard material in simultaneous fashion. As per the dictates of conventional sonata form, the two main themes are now stated in the tonic, inasmuch as the transposition of theme 2 places it harmonically on IV of IV—in other words, I.

In an evaluation of the movement as a whole, the weakest portion would

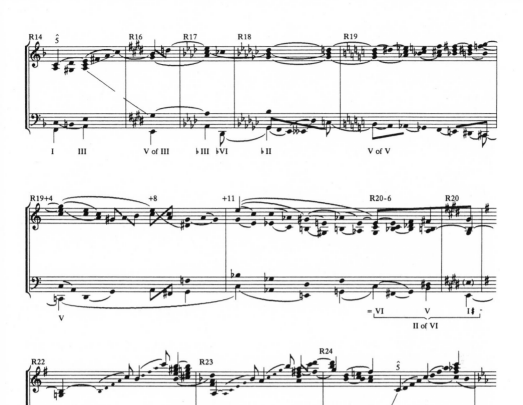

Example 71. *Concerto in F,* I: analysis of development

have to be the development section, whose content, save for its inspired beginning, amounts to a linear succession of variations on the same theme, lending at least a germ of truth to descriptions such as that attributed to Prokofiev, whom Gershwin had met in Paris, as "thirty-two-bar choruses ineptly bridged together."[6] Yet the local changes of key and the ways in which they are connected are both inventive and structurally meaningful.

The development is shown schematically in example 71. The first harmonic change is from F to E, with A minor as intermediary. In the course of moving from I to III in F, Gershwin sets the melody c^1–d^1–e^1 in contrary motion with the would-be tenor c–B–A. (This, depicted as the essential content for the span from R14 to R16, actually takes place at the third and fourth measures after R15.) The last note of the tenor then becomes the bass,

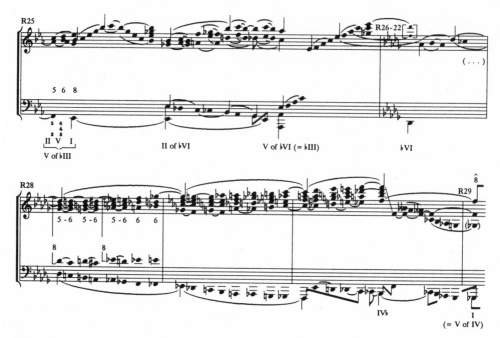

Example 71. (*continued*)

whereas the first note of the descant is retained as an inner voice. The latter, transposed up an octave to c² by arpeggiation, leads to b¹ as the bass proceeds to E.

The key of E returns with the Moderato cantabile (R20), where an outgrowth of the Charleston motif emerges from beneath a countermelody of descending thirds. Its harmonic predecessor this time is C; and the connecting chords, which begin six measures before R20, accompany the melodic progression d¹–f#¹–g#¹ (highlighted by the beam in ex. 71). As with the passage described just previously, there is a play of registers: e¹ is the tail of a descending coupling from e², and g#¹ is actually a normalized representation of the piano's unexpectedly high g#³ on the downbeat of R20.

The question remains whether there is any logic in Gershwin's choice of keys. There is some resemblance here to portions of *Rhapsody*—for example, in the widespread use of E major in a seemingly remote context. In *Rhapsody,* the E major of the Andantino was interpreted enharmonically as flat V of B-flat, its main melodic note G# as flat $\hat{7}$. Here, where the tonic is F, E makes the most sense as a secondary function: at its first appearance (R16) it is an intermediary between III and flat III; subsequently, where a segment in E major (the aforementioned Moderato cantabile at R20) is followed by a sequence beginning with E minor (Allegro molto, R22), the two modes of E act collectively as II (leading to V) of VI.

From there, beginning at R23, the harmonic direction is stronger and more straightforward. With raised third, VI becomes V of II, and at R24 there is a II–V–I cadence on F. The same pattern a step lower (at R25) leads us to E♭ (flat VII, or V of flat III), then to D♭ (flat VI). The latter, at twenty-two measures before R26, begins the last portion of the development, whose climactic moment is the retransition beginning at R28.

The retransition, also graphed in example 71 (see at R28), is interesting in several respects. With the progression d♭–E♭–F₁ the cellos and bassoons effectively retrace the F–E♭–D♭ sequence cited above—in reverse order and in registrally expanded form, with the seconds transformed into descending sevenths filled in by step. At the same time, the string basses, timpani, and percussion reintroduce the lower component of the opening fanfare (not shown in the two-piano score or in the analytic graph), with the timpani reiterating the original pitches f–c–F while the basses alter the motive to fit the local harmony. Meanwhile, the top three voices move upward in parallel superimposed thirds, with voices 1 and 3 proceeding either in alternating fifths and sixths (the linear intervallic pattern 5–6) or in parallel sixths. The piano doubles the upper orchestral strands in every voice but its lowest, which moves up the chromatic scale in a succession of descending, rather than ascending, semitonal dyads.

In short, while the above passage is made up of sequential patterns, it is apparent that Gershwin had no compunction about altering these patterns for the sake of the passage's overall direction. The result gives credence to the contention that Gershwin's transitions are not as aimless as some critics would have us believe. The same, moreover, can be said of the other transitional passages in the movement. Each characteristically makes its point: in the way certain notes are emphasized or, to use the Schenkerian term, prolonged; and in the relationship of these notes to the larger structure of the work.

This is true even where the stage is not quite fully set—as at the end of the second statement of theme 2 (see ex. 68). There, at R6, in the solo piano, an ascending sequence based on the closing figure of the theme gives way after four measures to a descending passage in sixteenth notes, whose sudden appearance is underscored by the direction "Molto meno mosso" and by its very anatomy: a compressed statement of the total chromatic built on representatives of all three diminished-seventh chords. Yet a broader view of

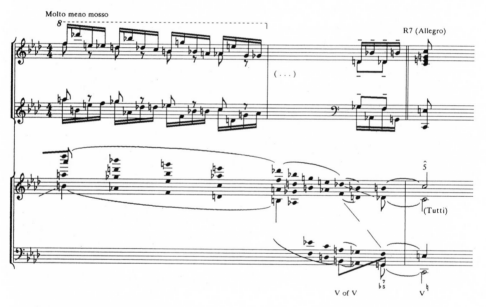

Example 72. *Concerto in F, I*

this antecedent-consequent pair (ex. 72) reflects a solid foundation both harmonically and melodically. The ascending sequence takes place over a pedal
B♮; the latter, a major third above the previous bass note G, joins with the
descant beginning on D♮ to form an extension of the preceding harmony—
II with raised fifth and third, or V of V. Conversely, the sixteenth-note passage begins with B♮ as its lowest voice and ends with bass G in the same har-

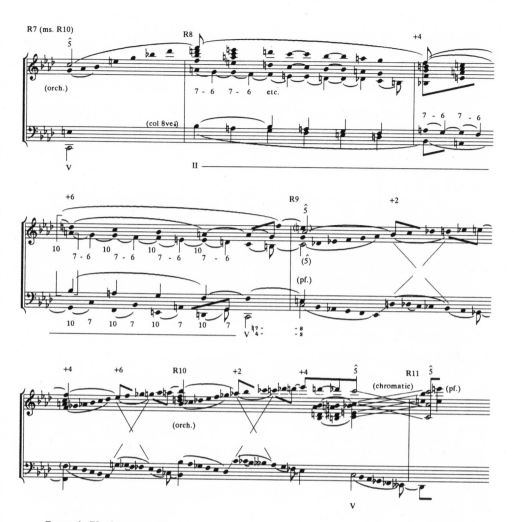

Example 73. *Concerto in F, I*

monic context as before. Melodically, the antecedent portion concludes with the interval C♯–E—whose lower note is the enharmonic equivalent of the D♭, asserted in no fewer than four registers, that dominates the consequent.

 This D♭ resolves to C, the primary melodic tone, on the downbeat of R7;[7] the music that ensues (graphed in ex. 73) remains rooted in a dominant prolongation, which is manifested in three distinct phases. In the first ten measures, a sequential use of the motive previously cited in example 23a results in an arpeggiation of the three upper degrees of the dominant seventh over a root pedal, whose foreground realization is also an arpeggiation. Next, at R8, a vertical forming II⁶₅ is transferred down an octave through a series of 7–6 progressions between the bass and an inner voice; then (R8+4) the descant starts a descending line spanning the seventh f^2–g^1, which is here represented as an unfolding—as is the bass B♭–G. (Both intervals are components of the prefix II, which will move back to V shortly.) The linear intervallic pattern changes in the last two measures (R8+6): the 7–6 is now between two inner voices; at the same time, the lower of these voices forms alternating tenths and sevenths with the bass while proceeding in parallel tenths with the descant. Third and last is another sequence, in a contrasting contrary motion, whose beginning coincides with the reentrance of the piano on the dominant at R9. As shown in the concluding portion of example 73, this partially chromatic wedge may be interpreted as a series of overlappings through the circle of fifths, with each arrival point preceded by leading tones above (bass) and below (descant). The pattern continues when the orchestra takes over at R10, only to be short-circuited back to V four measures later.

The thirty-two measures summarized above comprise, more or less, the transition theme proper of the first-movement sonata form—a role that is confirmed by the recurrence of key elements later on. In the recapitulation, following the Grandioso reprise of theme 2, the combination of first-theme reprise and coda is heralded (at R31) by a simultaneous return of the first and third segments, with the first continuing thereafter as a lower counterpoint. The third segment—the contrary-motion sequence—makes an appearance in the finale, four measures before the penultimate statement of the rondo refrain at R20.

Gershwin's concern for formal unity is evident in the way themes from the first two movements return as episodes in the third; likewise in the reappearance of the one transitional passage. Other connections exist at deeper levels. One is in the choice of D♭, a prominent secondary key area in the development section of the first movement, as the tonal center of the second. Like the first movement, the second has scale degree $\hat{5}$, now A♭, as its primary melodic tone. This new primary tone is asserted unequivocally at both start and finish of the second movement and connects convincingly with the finale.

The second movement is a song form turned rondo; its formal scheme, ABACA, is detailed in example 74, and the salient motives of the rondo refrain are identified in example 75 (see also the analysis in ex. 3). Opening the work, in the solo first horn, is a lower-register representation of the primary melodic tone A♭ ($\hat{5}$), in a nesting of upper neighbor notes in which a complete formation (a') is overridden by a larger one that is incomplete (a). This entire figure materializes transposed as the incipit of the lengthy trumpet solo which follows. At the same time, the original pitch (which also com-

Section	Key(s)	Location; Remarks
introduction	(D♭)	mm. 1–3; unaccompanied horn
A (refrain)	D♭	mm. 4–47 (R2+14)
B (episode 1)	D♭, D, F♯	upbeat to R3 through R6+11
transition 1	V of D♭	R7 through R7+8
A (refrain)	D♭	R8 through R9+3
transition 2	V of E (bass progression A♭[G♯]–B)	R9+4 through R10 (piano cadenza); features preview of episode 2 counterpointed by minor third ostinato
B (episode 2)	E	upbeat to R10+1 through R16+10; miniature ternary form with middle section based on variant of episode 1
A (refrain)	D♭	R17 through end; flute has former trumpet line, piano has accompaniment originally in clarinet trio and cello; concluding melodic figure (motive b) echoed by oboe and then piano to end the movement

Example 74. *Concerto in F, II: summary of form*

pletes the incomplete neighbor note of the horn solo), now embellished by its lower neighbor (here labeled a''), is the point of departure for the lowest voice of the accompanying clarinet trio.

Both components are thematic. The parallel $^6_4$ triads in the clarinets enter first. Over these, one measure later, the first trumpet commences with one of Gershwin's longest and grandest melodies. It begins with the nested neighbor note (motives a and a') in two successive registers, comprising the pitches db^2–eb^2 and db^1–eb^1. Added to these is the stepwise ascending fourth to ab^1 (motive b), which rounds out the first phrase and connects via an octave skip to the beginning of the second. The latter begins on the upbeat to m. 12 with a repeated note in a distinctive rhythmic pattern (motive c) and proceeds to another form of the nested neighbor note: two incomplete upper neighbors (motive a), each with a chromatic passing note, a perfect fourth apart. A dramatic leap of a thirteenth (m. 13) takes the melody down to its lowest pitch ab —the same lower-octave replication of the primary tone played by the opening solo horn—and to the punctuation of the phrase (m. 14) with the same neighbor note, bb. The trumpet continues for four more measures with what is essentially a repetition of the second phrase with added melodic diminu-

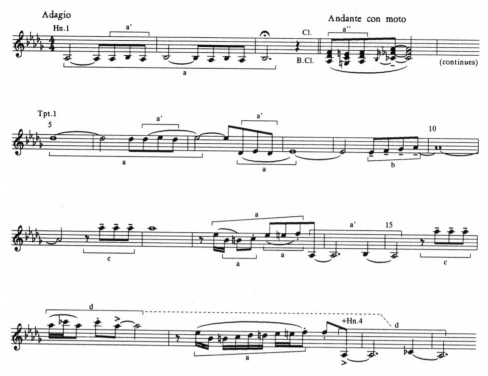

Example 75. *Concerto in F, II: main motives identified, mm. 1–19*

tions. Most noteworthy among these is the minor third that embellishes the high point ab² (m. 16); identified as motive *d*, the same interval returns two octaves lower, two measures later, as a revised closing gesture. There, on the pitches ab–cb¹–ab, the trumpet is joined by one of the horns in a clear reference back to the opening in both specific pitch and timbre, albeit with the fourth horn instead of the first.[8]

With this opening refrain Gershwin lays the groundwork for a second movement that is very different from the first. It is, instead, reminiscent of *Rhapsody,* with its long, initial melody in a featured solo instrument: a melody whose motivic potential is realized both in the foreground of subsequent themes and at the deeper levels of linear structure. An instance of the latter sort occurs immediately after the trumpet finishes, where (at R1, shown in analytic notation in ex. 3) the oboe takes over with a lengthy bb¹ followed by an equally long ab¹, thus forming a complete neighbor with the multiregistered Ab of the trumpet tune.

Unity at the foreground level, meanwhile, is most notably manifested in the way each new theme begins with the rhythm of motive *c*. In the case

a. refrain, trumpet melody, mm. 12–15

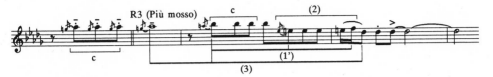

b. episode 1, theme (piano in octaves)

Example 76. *Concerto in F,* II

of episode 1, which begins with the upbeat to R3 (ex. 76), the correspondence includes the repeated note, which occurs first on a♭² as in the refrain. There are also certain coincidences of interval and contour, as suggested in example 76, between this new melody and that of the refrain. One, a faint parallel between the bracketed segments labeled (1) and (1′), is admittedly approximate. Another, the punctuation of both these segments by the chromatic passing note—bracketed and labeled (2)—is exact. A third exists in the beamed three-note cells, or trichords, marked (3), which each consist of an ascending major second followed by an ascending minor third (or descending sixth, or thirteenth).[9] These connections, while somewhat evanescent and probably subconscious on the composer's part, serve to reinforce the more tangible associations that come by way of motive *c* and the repeated notes.

The rhythm of motive *c* minus the repeated note serves as the springboard for episode 2, which continues with what amounts to the same rhythm shifted back an eighth note. This pattern, marked *c′* in example 77a, also occurs in augmentation at the close: four quarters, with the last tied over the barline. A retroactive connection can be drawn to the beginning of the movement: to the introductory pronouncement of the solo horn (the rhythm of *c* itself); and to the clarinet trio (the rhythmically shifted version, or motive *c′*). Another link with the opening section of the movement is the prominence of motive *d,* the reversed skip of a minor third, in the transition to this episode: the cadenza identified as transition 2 in example 74 (shown in part in ex. 77b). There, after twenty-one bars of rest, the piano enters with an ostinato on motive *d* in a high register, on the same two pitch classes as in the refrain. The same ostinato, transposed, subsequently accompanies a preview of the episode's theme.

R10+1

c (rhythm)   c'

c   c'

c

c' (augmented)

a. episode 2, theme

R9+4

Tpt.

d
p rubato

rit.

Moderato

R9+12

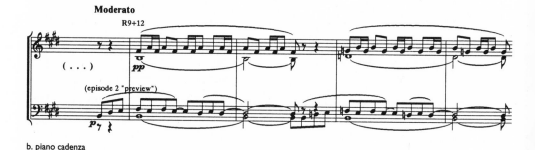

(. . .)   *pp*

(episode 2 "preview")

p

b. piano cadenza

Example 77. *Concerto in F,* II

Taken in its entirety, episode 2 is a miniature ternary form whose middle section, which extends from the upbeat to R12 to the upbeat to R13 and includes a four-bar retransition, is based on an altered reprise of the theme from episode 1 (ex. 78), the latter bringing with it a reminder of the initial, repeated-note form of motive *c*. As it turns out, an interesting converse of this relationship is found within episode 1, where amidst the strummed strings of the accompaniment the opening phrase of episode 2 is twice stated by paired woodwinds in octaves—at R3+8 by the first flute and first clarinet and at R3+10 by the first oboe and English horn (ex. 79). In each of these passages the triple upbeat, ostensibly missing, is in effect supplied by the repeated eighth notes in the theme of episode 1, played by the solo piano.

Example 78. *Concerto in F, II*

"Again and again one comes back to the wonderful second movement, on which Gershwin expended more care than on any other comparable piece of music." So goes an account in a mass-market paperback published more than thirty years ago.[10] Others whose credentials are better known corroborate this: "The second movement, which took George the longest to compose, is one of his loveliest creations and is probably one of the finest pieces of writing by an American composer."[11] Even in the context of faint praise, as in the New York *Times* review of the first performance, Olin Downes managed to cite the refrain theme, "a stopped trumpet playing a 'blue' melody against a sensuous harmonic background," as being "perhaps the best part of the concerto."[12] Thus it is no surprise that even a routine scratch of the surface will reveal an organic coherence between the movement's various parts. And

Example 79. *Concerto in F, II*

there is more than a passing significance to the first writer's feeling that in this movement "there is a quality of humanity, which we will not hear again until . . . *Porgy and Bess*." [13] For it is here that we find, for the first time in Gershwin's writing, the use of thematic preview as a compositional device — a technique that he uses to great advantage in that other work.

Relationships of like quality can be found even in the transitional material. One such theme, an outgrowth of episode 1, makes its initial appearance in the first violins at R4+2. Eight bars later, a second statement pitched a major seventh lower, divided between first violins and violas, is counterpointed by the solo piano. The piano counterpoint is complementary in both contour and rhythm; yet, remarkably, it uses the same pitch classes — more specifically, the same semitonal dyads in reverse order. This relationship is highlighted in example 80a, where other interesting aspects of this transitional theme are also illustrated. Example 80b shows its return in the context of episode 2, at the climactic moment. In example 80c we see (at "N.B.") a very close variant of this theme reborn as the consequent portion of one of the recurring themes of — once again — *Porgy and Bess.*

Commensurate with the stature of the second movement as a distinct composition is its integration into the scheme of the concerto as a whole. Its main key of D♭ is prepared by its introduction in the development section of the first movement; this is also true of the secondary area of E major. Melodically, the trumpet's long initial d♭[1] can be interpreted as an upper neighbor to the primary melodic tone of the preceding movement.

The connection between the second movement and the finale is stronger

a. *Concerto in F,* II, transition theme: contrapuntal setting (R4 + 10)

b. *Concerto in F,* II, transition theme: climactic setting at R16

c. *Porgy and Bess,* humoresque theme (first appearance over vocal)

Example 80.

still. The former concludes with the closing figure of what was initially the trumpet tune, now played by a solo flute: the ascending fourth to ab^1 (labeled *b* in ex. 75). Echoes of this motive in the oboe, then the piano, expand the A♭ to three successively higher registers, to an upper limit of ab^3. This reinforces the semitone relationship between the slow movement's last descant note and the heavily doubled G (including g^3) that begins the finale. The linear progression continues with the piano's entrance on F, initiating the second statement of the rondo refrain, now in its home key. From a melodic standpoint, the finale's initial G thus turns out to be a large-scale passing note between A♭ and F, whereas harmonically the anomalous G minor of the opening may be seen as a prolonged dominant preparation—that is, II of F (ex. 81).[14] That

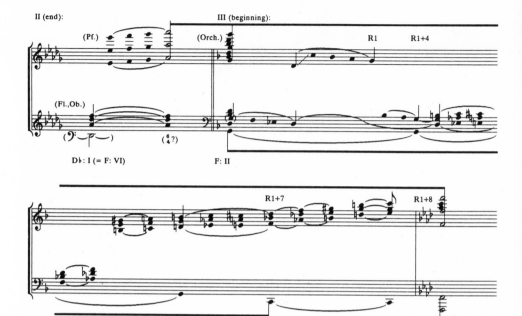

Example 81. *Concerto in F,* end of II and beginning of III: analysis

Gershwin may have heard it this way as well is evidenced in part by the key signature of one flat (i.e., F major) in both the manuscript and published versions of the orchestral score—although the piano score, which preceded the orchestration chronologically, does show two flats. A more substantive indication is the movement of the bass to C just before the arrival on the tonic (see at R1+7), with the upper voices completing the dominant triad on the last sixteenth note.

The refrain itself, as graphed in example 82, is a closed form both melodically and harmonically, with tonic beginnings and endings in both dimensions. Despite the local persistence of scale degree $\hat{5}$, the large picture of refrain plus episodes makes scale degree $\hat{8}$ the most likely choice for primary melodic tone; the result is an octave line complicated by register transfers in both directions. Rhythmically there are two aspects that are particularly noteworthy: the repeated sixteenth notes, useful in transitions and as accompaniment to other themes; and the temporary shift to triple meter, which links the refrain to the second episode.

Although the finale may be closer in spirit to the traditional rondo than the second movement, its form (tabulated in ex. 83) is less easily delineated. Elements of the refrain appear within as well as between the episodes, and the episodes themselves are not treated equally. All but one are based on themes

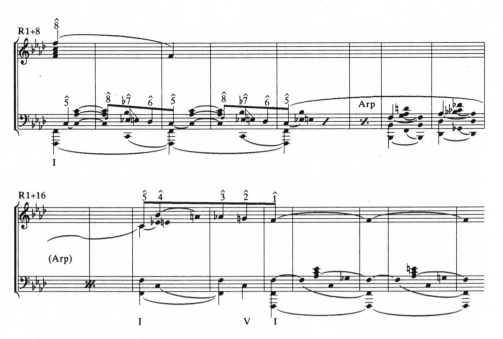

Example 82. *Concerto in F,* III: analysis of rondo refrain

from the earlier movements. The second theme from the first movement is the source for both the first and the final episodes (1*a* and 1*b* in ex. 83). Episodes 3 and 4 recapitulate, in reverse order, the two episodes from the second movement. But it is the one exception, episode 2, that predominates. After its initial appearance (episode 2*a*) it makes at least four returns that can be considered sections in their own right (episodes 2*b* through 2*e*). Other than the refrain, it is the only theme to undergo musical development.

The refrain and this main (albeit second) episode share a rhythmic trait in the form of a temporary shift to triple meter. This is accompanied by a certain melodic affinity: the refrain has an upper neighbor note; the episode, a nested neighbor-note formation which becomes a passing note at the middleground level. The analysis in example 84 reveals a larger melodic similarity when compared with the profile of the refrain in example 83. Both themes feature a descent from scale degree $\hat{8}$ by way of flat $\hat{7}$—this despite one theme's being nominally minor, the other major (ex. 84). A motivic link can thus be seen not only between two themes of a single movement but between the concerto and the two major works that came respectively before and after.

The opening theme of *An American in Paris,* like those of *Rhapsody in Blue* and the slow movement of *Concerto in F,* is multiregistral. It begins with

Section	Key(s)	Location; Remarks
A (refrain)	G minor (orchestra) to F minor	orchestral opening is a prolonged II leading to V of F; piano enters at R1+8 with refrain in tonic; some development, R2+2–R3+15; repeated F used as transition to episode 1
B₁ (episode 1*a*)	F (V of IV)	R4–R4+31; up-tempo version of I, theme 2 (same key as recap, but with key signature of four flats instead of five); sixteenths reintroduced in piano beginning R4+16
A (refrain)	F	R5–R6+7; includes eight-bar transition (repeated open fifths)
C₁ (episode 2*a*)	F	R7–R8+11; episode theme followed by quasi-variation ending on V
C₂ (episode 2*b*)	C, G, D	R9–R10+15; development of episode theme counterpointed by elements from refrain; $\frac{3}{8}$ passage used as transition
C₃ (episode 2*c*)	F	R10+16–R12+9; episode theme in solo piano minus $\frac{3}{4}$ measures; orchestral recap of episode 2*a* prefaced by mm. 1–4 of refrain in F major
D (episode 3)	B♭	R12+10–R13+16; recaps II, episode 2, prefaced by refrain mm. 1–3; sixteenths continue in piano
C₄ (episode 2*d*)	B♭	R14–R17+2; reprise with quasi-variation, followed by fugato on same theme
A (refrain)	B♭ to E♭ (II–V of A♭)	R17+3–R19+1; repeated E♭ as transition to triple upbeat of episode 4
E (episode 4)	A♭ to C	R19+1–R17; sixteenths continue in piano (cf. episode 3 and subsequent portion of episode 1)
C₅ (episode 2*e*)	C (V of F)	R19+18–R39; reprise with quasi-variation, followed by four-bar transition identical to I, R9–R9+3
A (refrain)	F	R20–R21+8; full orchestra plus piano; last complete statement of refrain

Example 83. *Concerto in F,* III: summary of form

Section	Key(s)	Location; Remarks
B₂ (episode 1b)	F (V of IV)	R22–R22+15; grandioso reprise of I, theme 2, identical with first movement until the last two bars
A (refrain/coda)	F minor to F major	R23 through end; refrain theme extended by sequences based on successive perfect fourths, then minor thirds; final segment in F major (beginning R23+24) recalls arpeggiation motive from I, theme I

Example 83. (*continued*)

Example 84. *Concerto in F,* III: analysis of theme, episode 2

the notes c²–d¹–e¹, whose collective role as a registrally transposed third—motive *a* in example 85—is confirmed by the subsequent entrance of c¹. The note d² is also introduced at virtually the same time, initially as an upper neighbor to c², then as a passing note to e². The latter, which completes an upper-octave replication of motive *a,* is also leading tone to f², whose direct approach is from the opposite direction as terminus of the descending third from a². The arrival of this f² (at R1), the end of the theme proper, initiates the descending fourth f²–e♭²–d♭²–c², which is subsequently echoed at the next lower octave. Marked as motive *b* in example 85, this descending upper tetrachord is partitioned exactly as in the first main theme of *Rhapsody* and almost as in the rondo refrain of *Concerto in F.* Underscoring its importance as a closing figure is the way in which the lower-octave imitation is followed by the complementary descending fifth (motive *b′*), which reaches down into the bass ostinato with which the passage started.

This matter aside, *An American in Paris* is unique within Gershwin's output. Virtually absent are those "generic" transitions that abound not only in *Rhapsody* and *Concerto* but in *Second Rhapsody* and even *Porgy and Bess.* Where transitions do occur, they are either clearly based on portions of the main

Example 85. *An American in Paris,* main theme 1: initial setting

themes or they introduce transitional themes of a more distinct character. The piece is far more advanced than its predecessor, not only harmonically and contrapuntally but also rhythmically.

Unprecedented as well is the rapid shifting of themes and tempos that occurs throughout the piece, in part owing to programmatic considerations.[15] Beneath this cluttered surface one can discern three main sections (in Jablonski's term, "minimovements") followed by a combined recapitulation and coda.[16] Each large section is distinguished by the introduction of one or more new themes. In the first two sections these themes, once introduced, become parts of the general vocabulary, and so the second section freely uses material from the first. Only the third section, which is based entirely on its two contrasting themes, is distinct in this regard. The sections themselves are as follows: section 1, from the beginning through R28+9; section 2, from R29 through R45+3; and section 3, from R45+4 through R67+7. The recapitulation-coda, which begins at R68, draws on all three sections.

A thematic digest parallel to that of *Rhapsody in Blue* (cf. ex. 45), is presented in example 86. Shown first is main theme 1 with its constituent motives *a* (the ascending major third) and *b* (the descending upper tetrachord, appended as a closing figure) plus the descending major third (motive *a'*) and the repeated-note rhythmic figure of four sixteenths and an eighth (motive *x*). Accompanying main theme 1 at its first appearance is a counterpoint an-

a. main theme 1; counterpoints 1 and 2

b. transition themes 1, 2, 1a, 1b

c. transition theme 3

d. main theme 2

Example 86. *An American in Paris:* summary of themes

e. transition theme 4

f. main theme 3a and 3b

g. transition theme 5

Example 86. (*continued*)

chored on a sustained C (counterpoint 1); subsequently (beginning at R1+4), a second counterpoint of rising chromatic steps is added—the latter eventually inverted, as at R9.

As in *Rhapsody,* there are several transitional themes; what is different in the present work is their often close relationship with the main material and to each other. At R3 a "vigoroso" passage leads to a "giocoso" whole-tone

R45+8 (Andante ma con ritmo deciso)

Tpt.1   R46

analysis: R46+2

h. main theme 4

Allegro (R57)
Tpt.

Tb.

analysis: a   or   a

i. main theme 5

Example 86. (*continued*)

figure four bars later; both may be considered transitional themes (ex. 86b).
The first builds upon the repeated-note motive *x,* extending it into a melodic
figure (motive *z*) that is on the one hand pentatonic, on the other a product
of neighbor notes. Rhythmically, it is typical of Gershwin in its superposition of triple on duple meter; it does so, moreover, at the levels of both
the eighth note and of the quarter note. Transition theme 2 juxtaposes the
neighbor note with the repeated note, the latter now comprising three accented eighths (motive *y*), which will later be associated with the infamous
taxi horn (see at R14+5). These follow in direct succession, as does an important variant of transition theme 1 that begins at R4. Identified as transition
theme 1a, this corollary theme retains the rhythm of transition theme 1 in the

descant while presenting its pitches, transposed, in diminution. This descant of flutes and xylophone counterpoints itself in augmentation three octaves lower (bassoons and lower strings). One could say that transition theme 1a combines the pitch motive z with the rhythm of motive x; the latter, differentiated by not being applied to a repeated note, is labeled x'. Meanwhile, motive x proper returns again at R8+9 in canonic imitation, in a passage here labeled transition theme 1b that serves as a retransition to the third statement of main theme 1 at R9.

Transition theme 3 (ex. 86c) is more an episode than a transition theme; along with the taxi horn, this quotation from "My Mom Gave Me a Nickel," if not the most memorable part of the piece, is the part most likely to be remembered by the lay listener. Its profile resembles main theme 1 in its use of the upper tetrachord in ascending followed by descending motion; the difference, of course, is that in main theme 1 the descent involves flatted seventh and sixth degrees.

The second main theme of section 1 (main theme 2) enters "con umore" at R13. Like transition theme 1 and its variants, main theme 2 draws on the rhythmic figure x, which first appears almost in its original form, but offset by half a beat; then, as a closing gesture, figure x occurs on the beat, but with a repeated dyad instead of a repeated note. Tonally, main theme 2, a closed structure both harmonically and melodically, is—along with the finale (main theme 5)—the simplest in the piece. Its main role as the work progresses is as a source for developmental material, where its identity tends to merge with the related portion of main theme 1. It is the first element from section 1 to return after section 3 (at R68), and thus may be considered the beginning of the recapitulation-coda.

Of the five transitional themes identified in example 86, only two are not materially related to the main themes of the work. The first of these, transition theme 4 (ex. 86e), occurs twice: between sections 1 and 2, in two flutes (at R28, the version shown here); and between sections 2 and 3, in two violins (beginning at R44+2).[17] (The latter, a half step lower, concludes on the vertical sixth a–f^1 over an F-major triad, the dominant of the opening key of section 3—and of the key of the second theme of section 1.) In addition to being uniquely transitional, transition theme 4 comprises a pattern that reproduces at the interval of a minor third. In both respects, transition theme 4 is reminiscent of some of the transitional material in *Rhapsody* and the *Concerto* (compare, respectively, the theme cited in ex. 45e and the "molto meno mosso" passage in ex. 72).

The second of these transitional themes, labeled transition theme 5 and cited at its initial pitch level in example 86g, occurs between sections 2 and 3 (and briefly in the coda, at R69+7). Essentially an arpeggiation, it is more a motive or figure than a full-fledged theme. Its final statement in the transition to section 3, on a Db-major triad (beginning at R44), appends yet another arpeggiation that takes its expected concluding note, ab^2, to an A♮ an octave higher. The latter, sustained, joins with the remaining notes of the F-major triad that underpins the reprise of transition theme 4.

The remainder of example 86 cites the main themes of sections 2 and 3. In example 86f is the theme of section 2, whose two parts, main theme 3a and main theme 3b, are subsequently treated separately. Together, their melodic profiles trace an ascending major third, $e^1–f\#^1–g\#^1$, which is followed immediately by a descent along the same path; these are, respectively, middleground representations of motives a and a'. Another such representation, of a only, can be traced over the span of the last new theme of the work, the "hot" second theme of section 3, shown as main theme 5 (ex. 86i). For the latter we show two analytic interpretations. The first verticalizes the arpeggiations and minimizes the register transfer; the second, although omitting some interior detail, shows the register transfer more clearly—virtually a middleground reflection of the displaced major third that begins main theme 1.

But the most eloquent profile belongs to the theme that resembles the others least, namely the first theme of section 3 (main theme 4, ex. 86h), whose outline forms a descending fifth. Initially stated by the first trumpet through a felt crown, it recalls the second-movement theme of *Concerto in F* both timbrally and in its perfection of design. Though not a blues in the structural sense,[18] it has often been referred to as such—by Gershwin himself, among others[19]—no doubt because of its prominent use of flatted scale degrees within its overall major context. As the unfoldings in the analysis show, these flatted scale degrees occur on two distinct contrapuntal planes.

The discussion now turns to how these themes are developed over the course of the composition. The relationship between the first main theme and those that follow is one aspect of the process; another is the way in which this theme, at its successive reappearances, is layered with a continually changing series of counter-melodies. Most persuasive, though, are those places where motivic elements, such as those identified in example 86, are extracted and built into true developmental passages.

Such is the case with the stretto leading to the climactic moment of section 1. It begins at R20 with a pattern of stepwise parallel triads grouped in threes, which moves sequentially upward beginning four measures later. Entering at this point, where the condensed score in example 87 begins, is a

Example 87. *An American in Paris*, section 1, stretto

dialogue based on main theme 2, whose anchoring pitches form a sequence of minor thirds iterated at successive perfect fifths (F♯–A, D♭–E, A♭–B). The bass, which begins on C♯, also follows in perfect fifths with the pitches A♭ and E♭. Next, at R21, we see a return of the key element of main theme 1, namely motive *a* in its registrally displaced form, in rhythmic augmentation. This augmented version of motive *a* is followed by a second statement of the same motive a fifth lower; together they span a minor tenth (b♭^{2}–g^1)—or, in registrally reduced terms, a major sixth (B♭–C–D, E♭–F–G). At the same time, an upper counterpoint brings back an extended version of transition theme 1a (featuring motive z), which is immediately linked with the initial gesture of main theme 2. Meanwhile the bass, which has held a sustained B♭ for the first two measures, launches an abbreviated statement of main theme 1 (with a flatted third in its second measure).

The sequence based on main theme 2 returns at R21+5 for four measures and leads to the climax at R22 ("con fuoco"), which puts a cap not only on the stretto but on section 1 as a whole. This passage, whose beginning concludes example 87, incorporates virtually all the thematic source material of the section. The bass has a descending sequence built on main theme 1 while the topmost stratum (flutes and piccolo) features the main motive of main theme 2. There are also two inner strands that operate essentially within the same register. One, a unison line in the clarinets, recalls the clarinet parts introduced at m. 5 and at R9 as inner-voice counterpoints to main theme 1. The other, aurally the strongest element in the passage, presents the stepwise major third, both ascending (motive a) and descending (a'), as an ostinato in parallel diatonic triads. The latter can also be seen as an outgrowth of the parallel-triad pattern shown at the start of example 87, whose continuing presence ties the entire stretto together.

The juxtaposition of the registrally displaced and non-displaced forms of motive a, which occurs in one way in main theme 1 and in another in this climactic stretto, can hardly be ascribed to mere chance. Moreover, section 2 concludes in parallel fashion, with another stretto featuring the same motives in a similar but varied treatment. It begins "deciso," at R41 and comprises three four-bar segments. In the first, the triplet motive from example 87 (in parallel thirds rather than triads, with the accompanying trill below rather than above) is counterpointed by sequences based respectively on main theme 2 and main theme 1, the latter in the bass. The next four measures are dominated by an ascending pattern of sixteenth notes that—once again—emphasizes the third in stepwise progression. This is done most clearly in the upper string parts, shown in the first half of example 88, where at once we see motive a in a threefold presentation, each time on the same pitches: in its most basic form (violas), with registral displacement (second violins), and in rhythmic augmentation (first violins). The ensuing ascending sequence leads to a reprise of the opening bars of main theme 1 accompanied by descending parallel triads in the lower parts. A detail worthy of note is the voice exchange between descant and bass on the last of the major thirds, highlighted here by crisscrossed lines. Also present, though not shown in the

Example 88. *An American in Paris:* sequential treatment of motive *a*

example, are dialogues in the woodwinds recalling main theme 3b and the opening clarinet counterpoint.

To summarize, *An American in Paris* is distinguished by two significant traits: an economy of theme and motive whose roots can already be seen in *Rhapsody in Blue,* and a thoroughgoing use of the contrapuntal layering process found in *Concerto in F.* In both respects, Gershwin goes far beyond his previous achievement. But there is more: for one, the subtle formal aspects revealed by the seemingly capricious tempo changes. For example, each of the strettos discussed above is followed by a "calmato" segment featuring the first main theme of the large section that precedes it. Thus, beginning at R23, a solo by the English horn dreamily recalls main theme 1 (ex. 89), whereas at R43 parallel chords sound out the first six notes of main theme 3a (ex. 90). Harmonically, these two excerpts contain some of the most inspired writing in the entire work, and they readily reveal the source of the inspiration. In the first instance the verticals, all diatonic, move in contrary planes of parallel traids and fifths; they begin with the same pair of chords that began the piece, transposed. With its wash of diatonic dissonance, this recasting of main theme 1 is the most French-sounding portion of the piece; at the same time, the not-incompatible influence of Stravinsky can be seen in the rather un-Gershwinesque pattern of changing meters. In the second excerpt, the

Example 89. *An American in Paris*

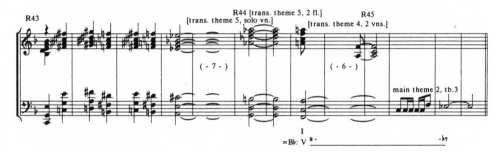

Example 90. *An American in Paris:* transition to section 3 (condensed)

verticals are in parallel motion in all voices; though the melody is diatonic, the verticals are not. Their structure, consistent from chord to chord, may be interpreted as two major triads a tritone apart—the same harmony that Stravinsky made famous as the so-called "Petroushka chord," and to which Gershwin would eventually return in *Porgy and Bess.*[20]

Matters of influence aside, there remains the question of the larger role played by these often-brilliant details. In the case of the "parallel Petroushka chords," for example, the bass, which begins on C, comes to rest on A at the end of the thematic quotation. It proceeds to G eight measures later (at R44), supporting a vertical of the same type (with "roots" on G and Db); it then moves to F two measures after that, where it supports a plain triad. The flatted seventh subsequently added to this chord (by a variant of main theme 2 in the bass trombone) underscores its harmonic function as the dominant of Bb, the local key that begins section 3. The underpinnings, in other words, are still tonal; moreover, they recapitulate the harmonic relationship between the two main themes of section 1.

The prominence of Bb as a secondary key area, in association with the second themes from the beginning and from the end, in sections 1 and 3 respectively, is just one way in which the work achieves a sense of balance and coherence. Another can be found in the relationship between the opening

Example 91. *An American in Paris:* complete schematic

theme and its return in the coda: the latter, beginning on III and ending on I, adds a harmonic dimension to the theme's all-important major third. Third-relationships play a role in section 2 as well: in the profile of its bipartite main theme (ascending in main theme 3a, descending in main theme 3b), and in the harmonic succession E–C–A♭–F reflected in the section's four key signatures.

These and other attributes are depicted graphically in example 91. This overview of the entire work combines a comprehensive background-middle-ground sketch with annotations that refer to the themes listed in example 86. It begins with main theme 1 and the background notes c² and F.[21] Of these two basic components, descant and bass, the latter is considerably easier to trace, largely because of the abundance of pedal harmonies. In the upper

Example 91. *(continued)*

voice (or voices), the guiding principles are twofold: first, the basic rule of melodic voice leading that places a premium on progression by step or common tone; and, second, the need to take into account the local primary tone of each theme or segment of the work. As examples, the melodic background B♮s, each labeled as scale degree $\hat{4}$ and representing main theme 2 and main theme 4 in sections 1 and 3 respectively, are relatively unproblematic: in the first instance B♮ is the main melodic note of main theme 2, and in the second it is the terminus of the descending line from what is locally $\hat{5}$ in main theme 4 (see ex. 86h). On the other hand, the G♯ joining main themes 3a and 3b in section 2 requires an enharmonic reading as A♭, which makes it equivalent to flat $\hat{3}$ of the tonic scale. The same scale step is also reached in the bass via descending major thirds from E, which proceed first to C (R38) and then to A♭ (R39). From R38 to R39 one can also read the melodic progression C–B♭–A♭ in the flutes and upper strings; this is represented as the inner-voice progression $\hat{5}$–$\hat{4}$–flat $\hat{3}$. Following on the heels of this progression is another descending line from C leading to A♮. The accompanying harmonic progression to F completes section 2 and leads into section 3.

That there should be a network of relationships based on major and minor thirds is not unusual. What gives it significance is the multifaceted treatment of the major third that occurs very early in the piece, within the confines of the opening theme. The resulting added dimension is illustrated by the return of this theme (main theme 1) in the coda, in the local key of A (III♯ in relation to the tonic F), where the foreground melodic third e^2–$f\sharp^1$–$g\sharp^1$ establishes a pitch-specific link to the middleground ascent that opens section 2. The interplay of major and minor has motivic value as well. We see it in the descending lines from C cited above and in the connection between the exposition of main theme 5 and the reprise of main theme 4 that begins at R65, where D–E–F♯ (see ex. 86j) is changed to D–E–F♮, thereby joining it to the dominant of the ensuing local key of C.

While the focus of example 91 remains on the work as a whole, it also seeks to show how certain noteworthy middleground passages fit into the larger scheme of things. First among these is the stretto chronicled in example 87, which serves to connect the unfolded third (a^1–$f\sharp^1$) initiated at R19 with the tenth ($b\flat^2$–g^1) spanned by the extension of motive a at R21. Another, not yet discussed, occurs in section 3, beginning at R52. A developmental offshoot of main theme 4, this passage (including the temporary resting place at R53) reduces to a succession of ascending parallel sixths a minor third apart and ends an octave higher than where it began. The result is a recursive progression prolonging the dominant of II, whose resolution (R54+3) slides into the tonic three measures later, with only a scant reference to anything resembling a dominant.

It is there, at R54+6, that we have the final assertion of the background note $\hat{5}$ over I, in the form of a compressed version of main theme 4 in the tonic key. The last new theme to appear, main theme 5, does so in the context of a prolongation of the dominant of II, or sharp VI—the same as in the above passage of parallel sixths. A return of main theme 4 in the dominant key leads to scale degree $\hat{4}$, whereas an implied $\hat{3}$ can be read in the A-major return of main theme 1 that starts the coda. The background moves to $\hat{2}$ over V at R70, and to $\hat{1}$ over I at R74, at which point the work is structurally complete. The thematic reprises that follow remain on the tonic and thus do not alter the background.

If Gershwin had the work of certain other composers in mind when he wrote *An American in Paris,* then it must be said that he chose his models well and that he executed the design with uncommon skill. Scarcely a note is wasted. To close with one more example, we go back to a countermelody added to main theme 1 beginning at R9, in the bassoon and celli. As shown in example 92a, its nucleus is a chromatically filled descending minor third

a. R9 (bassoon, voice)

b. R56 + 3 (violin solo)

Example 92. *An American in Paris:* countermelody to main theme I

—a variant of motive *a'*—which forms a voice exchange with the stepwise major third comprising motive *a.* This descending figure is then balanced by motion in the opposite direction, also in stepwise thirds. Variants of this melody reappear subsequently, but none is more exposed than that shown in example 92b. Predictably labeled *calmato,* this violin solo follows the climactic passage (cited in connection with ex. 91) that reinstates $\hat{5}$ over I, where the same material has just served as the basis for the parallel inner voices. Its content clearly relates to that of example 92a, except that now the thirds are all major and centered on one in particular—the third from C♯ to A. This interval can be found not only in the foreground of the melody but in the middleground that coincides with its successive downbeats, where motive *a'* (C♯–B–A) is followed by motive *a* (A–B–C♯).

If this were an operetta
We'd sing of him for days.

"Dancing in the Streets" (*Pardon My English,* 1932)

8 New Musicals

The 1930s brought a change in Gershwin's output that was both unmistakable and multifaceted. This change was first evident in the musical comedies at the start of the decade, where the pastiche of earlier times gave way to well-written scripts, to which the Gershwins responded with music and lyrics of increasing sophistication. This was true not only of the songs themselves but of the way the songs would fit into each show as a whole. The first steps had already been taken with *Strike Up the Band,* whose revised version of 1930, with book by Morrie Ryskind based on George S. Kaufman's original script from three years earlier, brought together the two writers who would subsequently collaborate on *Of Thee I Sing* (1931) and *Let 'Em Eat Cake* (1933). In between came *Pardon My English* (1932), whose score was first-rate in spite of any reservations one may have about the show. Together these three plays make an eloquent statement about where Gershwin was heading during this period, in which the distinction between the "popular" and the "serious" Gershwin would become ever more difficult to draw.[1]

The most apparent consequence of these "new musicals" was a reduction in the number of potential standards—that is, songs capable of surviving on their own, out of context. Five songs from the original *Strike Up the Band* were published, of which the best known by far are the title song and "The Man I Love." The latter, withdrawn from *Lady, Be Good* three years earlier, was not successful here either, leaving "Strike Up the Band" as the show's only real hit tune and the only clear musical link to the 1930 revival.[2] As if recognizing the source of his bread and butter, to say nothing of the personal satisfaction derived from having his tunes remembered, Gershwin added to the later show the love songs "Soon" (new) and "I've Got a Crush on You" (from the "tuneful but ill-fated" *Treasure Girl* of 1928).[3] In *Of Thee I Sing*, the title song, "Love Is Sweeping the Country," and "Who Cares?" are all tied to the book, yet each can be performed alone; all three are widely known. By way of contrast, *Let 'Em Eat Cake* had only one such song, "Mine."[4] Seven songs from *Pardon My English* were published, of which three—"Isn't It a Pity," "Lorelei," and "My Cousin in Milwaukee"—are in print as of this writing.[5] All three are of considerable interest, not to mention charm; yet none has received the kind of universal recognition that the term "standard" would imply.

Of Thee I Sing was Gershwin's first—and, as it would turn out, his only— unqualified success in this new genre. The theatergoing public was evidently ready for a satirical musical in 1931—in the midst of the Great Depression— in a way that it was not in 1927, and the show had a healthy run of 441 performances. It won the Pulitzer Prize in 1932—the first musical comedy to be so honored—but since the award was in drama rather than music, it officially went only to the authors of the book and lyrics.[6] As if to indicate the new direction it represented, its published vocal score declared it to be an operetta—"The Pulitzer Prize Operetta" at that. Its orchestration, though publicly not by Gershwin, had more of his involvement than would be expected for a typical Broadway show,[7] and its overture had sufficient stature in the composer's mind for him to use it (in an abridged arrangement for the house orchestra) to inaugurate his radio program "Music By Gershwin."[8] The "operatic" quality of the score is evident in the widespread use of recitative within the musical numbers, and in one obvious use of thematic recall: the quote from *An American in Paris* representing the French ambassador and his entourage.

Symbolic of the show as a whole, the overture to *Of Thee I Sing* is marked by economy throughout, both thematically and tonally. It opens with "Wintergreen for President" in C minor and ends with the title song in Eb, with "Who Cares" in G—then C—in between. The overall span of the minor third is characteristic of the composer; Eb is also the key of the choral reprises of "Of Thee I Sing" that conclude both acts of the operetta. Preceding "Of Thee I Sing" in both the overture and the choral reprises is a fanfare consisting of a repeated minor third (B♭–D♭) in the upper stratum counterpointed by chromatically descending ⁶₃s in the lower. This passage is used only in these contexts, and not when the song appears in scene 5 of act 1.

Tying the overture together is a simple motive found there and nowhere else: the repeated descending whole step—an incomplete upper neighbor note—in dotted rhythm. This figure, introduced over a C-major chord at m. 16,[9] can be seen in part as an outgrowth—more properly a mirror image—of the repeated semitonal neighbor-note figure that punctuates the opening line of "Wintergreen." Its pitches, meanwhile, echo the D and C of the minor third appended to the "Wintergreen" motive in the bass in mm. 13 and 15. These details, highlighted along with other salient features of the overture's first seventeen measures (first-order arpeggiation, linear progressions, and the temporally expanded reprise of the filled-in fourth G–C), are shown in example 93.

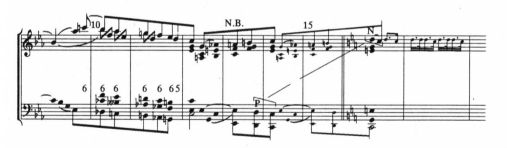

Example 93. *Of Thee I Sing,* overture, mm. 1–17

The motive of the repeated dyad, once established, persists through the remainder of the overture in ways that reflect both motivic fluidity and contrapuntal acumen. At m. 34 (ex. 94a), a downward chromatic extension of the figure is overlaid by the first line of the title song, whose ascending chromatic

a. mm. 34–39 (brackets show mirror relationships)

b. mm. 55–58

Example 94. *Of Thee I Sing,* overture

steps can be seen as a reassertion of the mirror-image process cited above, as can be the counterpoint formed by the semitonal neighbor notes in mm. 36–37 and 38–39. Another extension of the repeating-dyad figure accompanies the prefatory first chorus of "Who Cares?" beginning at m. 55 (ex. 94b).

The first passage, particularly, is rich in implications. On the one hand it harks back to the Andantino of *Rhapsody in Blue* (ex. 45f), where the chromatically filled whole step, ascending in sustained notes, is set against an ostinato based on its inversion. On the other, it looks ahead to the process of thematic foreshadowing used in *Porgy and Bess.*

No less significant is the way the "Of Thee I Sing" refrain (the verse, of less-than-usual quality and importance, was omitted in the New York production) uses this very simple, elemental motive.[10] Identical with the vocal line at the start, it continues as an inner voice when the song melody skips to a higher pitch. The first time it does this, at m. 5, the path is altered slightly, from G–G♯–A (motive *a*) to G–B♭–A (motive *a'*); the second time, sixteen measures later, it retains its original form. This feature is isolated in example 95. In the remaining portions of the refrain melody, shown in example 96, the ascending chromatic steps of motive *a* are balanced by the two diatonic steps in the opposite direction comprising motive *b*. The latter motive, the descending third, is derived from the five-note figure that occurs three times in sequence in the original melody, as shown by the brackets on the top staff. The analysis on the lower staff places motive *b* in some

a. mm. 1–8

b. mm. 17–24

Example 95. "Of Thee I Sing": motives *a* and *a'*

a. mm. 9–16

b. mm. 25–32

Example 96. "Of Thee I Sing": motive *b* and variants

larger contexts: the ascending third spanned by the first half of the melody (motive *b'*); the stepwise descent of a sixth in the second (motive *b''*); and the voice leading, complicated by register transfer, which connects the two. The latter is highlighted by the unfolding symbols, which reflect voice leading by maintaining a consistent direction of stem for each structural voice: for example, e^1 in the first interval leading to d^2 in the second (downward stems), and similarly g^1 to f^1 (upward stems).

The concluding portion of "Of Thee I Sing" (from m. 25 onward) continues to link melodic thirds at and below the surface level. The large motive b closes the melody, with the voice's penultimate note d^2 leading from the inner voice e^1. The smaller descending thirds, labeled b''', represent a variant form of the motive in which the skip of a fourth replaces the passing note. As in mm. 9–16, a larger voice-leading pattern can be discerned; in this case the unfolded third a^1–f^1 leads into the vertical g^1–e^1. This pattern, with a^1–g^1 in its upper voice, is more straightforward than its predecessor; it also brings to the fore a pitch-specific association with the whole step g^1–a^1 that begins the refrain (see at the first "N.B."; compare motive a in ex. 95). In two other places (also marked "N.B.") the chromatic note is brought in as well: with $g\#^1$–a^1 in m. 25, and with ab^2–g^2 in the instrumental close.

Suffice it to say that the "Of Thee I Sing" refrain is extremely tightly written and that its motivic content has ample precedent in Gershwin's earlier work. The same applies to its form, which combines the standard length of thirty-two bars with the non-standard thematic scheme ABAC (as opposed to the more common AABA). The same form can be found in "Embraceable You" (ex. 64); there as here, the concluding C section contains elements common to sections A and B.

Inviting comparison with *Of Thee I Sing* is its sequel, *Let 'Em Eat Cake,* which covers the dissolution of the Wintergreen presidency even more irreverently than the first play chronicled its establishment. Yet despite every expectation to the contrary, *Let 'Em Eat Cake* did not achieve the popularity of its predecessor. It closed after only ninety performances, and neither a piano nor an orchestral score has been published.[11] The trend set by *Of Thee I Sing* was taken a step further in this new operetta, whose score consists not of songs bridged together by incidental music but of complete musical scenes, nine in all, from which an occasional song may be extracted.

The integrated scene provided, for Gershwin, the perfect medium in which to explore his interest in counterpoint. Gershwin's writing was already heavily contrapuntal in his concert works (as witness *Concerto in F* and *An American in Paris*); in *Let 'Em Eat Cake,* fueled by his concurrent studies with Schillinger, he allowed this tendency to expand into his songwriting as well. A perfect opportunity existed in the opening of act 1. It begins like that of *Of Thee I Sing,* with "Wintergreen for President." This is followed by a reprise of the conclusion of the "Of Thee I Sing" refrain. Then come the supporters of Wintergreen's opponent Tweedledee with a song of their own—whose lyrics mimic, in places, those of "Wintergreen."[12] Even-

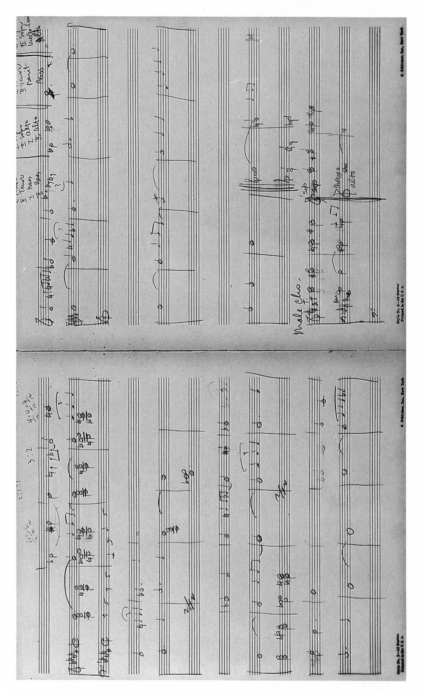

Example 97. Sketch for "Mine," *Schillinger A*, pp. 44–45

tually the Wintergreen and Tweedledee tunes are juxtaposed contrapuntally in "Wintergreen's" original key of G minor, the arpeggiation motive of the former meshing with the repeated notes of the latter.[13]

The other instance of song-countersong in *Let 'Em Eat Cake* is "Mine," whose off-key rendition by Robert Alda (as Gershwin) and Oscar Levant (as himself) was the comic high point of the biographical film *Rhapsody in Blue* (1945). In its original context, "Mine," in the key of C, comes at the end of a continuum (act 1, scene 4a, "The Store") that begins in E♭, resulting in an overall harmonic span that echoes both the overture to the present operetta and, in retrograde, that of *Of Thee I Sing* discussed above.[14] The start of the song refrain coincides with the arrival of C as the goal harmony of the scene, an arrival made all the more dramatic by the extended G7 of the preceding recitative.

The key of C is used in the manuscript score as well as the published song. Earlier manuscripts indicate, however, that Gershwin first conceived the refrain of "Mine" in D♭. On page 5 of the *Tune Book (1933–37),* colloquially known as the "Black Note Book" (Gershwin Collection, box 1, item 1), are seven bars of untexted voice and six of piano accompaniment bearing the working title "Love is O.K.," with "'Mine' I. G." added by Ira Gershwin in parentheses. Save for a couple of slight rhythmic differences, the tune is indeed "Mine." The other source is the exercise in the first Schillinger notebook.[15] Untitled, it begins with a complete statement of the refrain melody, also in D♭, over an incomplete accompaniment. This setting, shown in example 97, differs from the *Tune Book* version in that it is more a short score and less clearly for voice and piano, with the bottom two staffs accommodating both the tune and its accompaniment. A third staff adds an upper counterpoint.

The latter, with its odd chromaticism, is quite unlike the countermelody to "Mine" that eventually saw publication. Yet both are founded on the progression of three-part chords that forms the nucleus of the accompaniment.[16] In the published song, the countermelody follows the top voice of this progression without exception. The counterpoint in the sketch draws instead on the more chromatic middle voice, with a crossover into the upper voice that adds an augmented second to its vocabulary. This it does simultaneously with the accompaniment, though elsewhere it attempts to imitate the song melody a major sixth below and one measure later.

This initial experiment with a countermelody combined derivatives from the accompanying chordal pattern with imitations of the main song. What Gershwin settled on was simpler and from a practical standpoint wiser: a

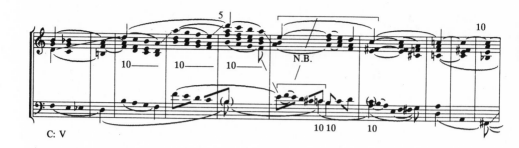

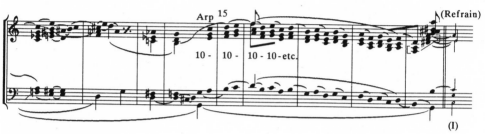

a. analysis of verse (recitative)

Example 98. "Mine"

companion song that followed, exactly, the top voice of the accompaniment chords and whose rhythm was complementary to the main song melody. The song is sung by the male romantic lead, John, to his female counterpart Mary. Although the score assigns the song to John alone, it is possible for Mary to join in, perhaps in the repetition of the refrain. The countermelody, however, is clearly intended not for Mary but for a chorus of two or more voices.[17]

The score of "Mine" is available in anthologies and need not be reproduced here. In its stead is a representation of the song in analytic notation. Example 98a shows the introductory verse-turned-recitative. The vocal part, though not explicitly delineated in the analysis, mostly follows the top voice of the accompaniment. The one real exception is that the voice asserts d^2 as a main melodic note within the first bar and, in mm. 3–5, remains on that note during the sequence of register transfers described below. (It should also be noted that the recitative and main song, intended as they are for a male tenor voice, are pitched an octave lower than written—though it could be argued that psychologically the male voice "sounds higher" when in the tenor range. To avoid confusion, all references to specific pitches will be to what is written.)

Harmonically the recitative functions as a prolonged dominant to the refrain's key of C. This dominant is asserted in several ways. First and not least

b. analysis of refrain

Example 98. (*continued*)

are the surface representations, such as the V$\frac{4}{2}$ that begins the recitative. The altered root-position V that concludes the recitative and, at the same time, connects it to the refrain is also a surface representation, but with larger implications. Its raised fifth, D#, is a passing note from the D that precedes it to the third, E, of the tonic triad (the open note following the double bar in ex. 98a). This progression, d^1–d#^{1}–e^1 in registrally specific terms, foreshadows the prominent use of the same pitches in the topmost inner voice of the refrain and, in turn, the companion song.

The bass note G does not stand alone: it is a recurrence of the first assertion of that note five measures earlier; moreover, nothing in the span from

m. 14 to m. 19 in that register contradicts the presence of that G. This larger presence, or prolongation, of the bass G is reflected by the dotted tie in the analysis. That this note is preceded in the same register by its leading tone (see the dotted slur from m. 10) is significant as well. Again, this connection is based on a broader way of looking at things: in this case, notice how F# occurs within the context of an embellishing secondary dominant, as can be seen by a perusal of mm. 7–13. Melodically, the featured note in these measures is C: c^2 in mm. 7–11, moving upward to d^2 in m. 12, then transferring down to c^1 in m. 13. This c^1 resolves to b on the downbeat of the next measure, whereas the bass G enters shortly thereafter within the same measure.

Bridging the two occurrences of bass G, in mm. 14 and 19, is a complex of upper-voice activity that confirms the presence of the dominant throughout this time span. From the downbeat of m. 14 to that of m. 16 we can trace an arpeggiation of the upper notes of the dominant seventh (see the slurs and the label "Arp") compounded by a register transfer back to the upper octave—that is, $b–d^2–f^2$. The goal note of this arpeggiation initiates a stepwise series of descending thirds, from $f^2–d^2$ down an octave to $f^1–d^1$. The resultant interval from f^2 to d^1, an expansion of the initial minor third, is highlighted in the analysis by a large unfolding symbol. In registrally reduced form, this interval converges on e^1, shown in example 98a as an open note following the double bar.

Other features of the recitative merit discussion as well. One is the abundance of vertical structures in parallel motion, with outer voices in tenths. Such structures accompany the upper voice in the passage outlined above. They also occur near the beginning of the recitative, in mm. 2–4, where a descending passage is transferred upward in each successive measure, resulting in a middleground octave transfer from d^1 to d^2 in the topmost voice. The d^1, in turn, was reached via an overlapping from the inner voice d in m. 1.

The overall prominence of the melody note D throughout the recitative strengthens the D–D#–E progression that leads into the refrain. Another motivic link to the refrain can be found in the melodic progression E–D–C in mm. 6–7. The parenthetical nature of this progression is underscored by the way it is set in the score—as a rhythmically contrasting passage in $\frac{6}{8}$-time. Another representation of the same third occurs in the lower staff, where it is depicted as an unfolding (ex. 98a, at "N.B."). This compressed version of E–C, or $e^1–c^1$, voice-leads to the unfolded ascending third $b–d^1$; the latter, in turn, proceeds to the vertical $a–(c^1)$. The resultant lower voice, shown with downward stems in example 98, forms a succession of parallel tenths with the stemmed $e^2–d^2–c^2$ in the upper staff. Parallel tenths, marked by arabic numbers (i.e., 10–10–10) in the analysis, are a prevalent feature of the recitative as a whole.

We now move on to the refrain. Although in the score the main song is sung once through before being joined by the countermelody vocally, both melodies coexist from the beginning thanks to the direct relationship between the companion song and the topmost inner voice. Hence the analysis in example 98b presents both melodies simultaneously and draws from them a common background structure.

The melodic component of this structure begins with the countermelody's e^1—scale degree $\hat{3}$ over bass I. This note and its harmonic support remain active during the first eight-bar period, while the main song hovers about the sixth a^1. The two parts switch roles beginning at m. 9, when the countermelody shifts to a position above the main song rather than below. The respective axes of the two tunes remain the same relative to the bass (i.e., the third for the countermelody, the sixth for the main song), but now it is the sixth that is important—this by virtue of IV progressing to V at the close of the second period. The note in question, d^1, thus eventually becomes the fifth of the dominant—that is, degree $\hat{2}$ of the tonic scale supported by V.

The result, as depicted by the open notes in example 98b, is a background structure of $\hat{3}$–$\hat{2}$ over I–V for the first sixteen measures of the refrain. In the second sixteen measures this path is retraced and closed, melodically and harmonically, with $\hat{1}$ over I. This is a good example of interruption, as introduced in chapter 2 in connection with "Love Walked In" (ex. 5), which differs from "Mine" in that its melodic background descends from $\hat{3}$ rather than $\hat{5}$. In both instances there is a preliminary descent to $\hat{2}$ over a harmonic progression to V, which is then repeated and completed. It is the logical pause, denoted graphically by the double vertical line (ex. 98a, m. 16), which may be said to constitute the interruption per se.

The conclusion of the refrain of "Mine" not only closes the background line; it also takes it up an octave. While this is happening, the countermelody dissolves in favor of a divisi harmonization of the main song, whose last line ("To know that love like yours is mine") underscores the feeling of completion and reconciliation. This last line begins with an arpeggiation bounded by scale degree $\hat{3}$ (e^1–a^1–c^2–e^2), which then proceeds to $\hat{2}$ (d^2) and to $\hat{1}$ (c^2). Though only the final $\hat{1}$ is background, one cannot ignore the way in which it is prefaced by $\hat{3}$ and $\hat{2}$ in a progression that constitutes a foreground reminder of the fundamental line in the climactic higher register.

Preceding *Let 'Em Eat Cake* was *Pardon My English,* which began its brief run on Broadway in January of 1933 after uneven tryouts in Philadelphia,

Boston, and Brooklyn. The show's failure led to its score being indefinitely shelved, or in this case put away in a trunk until fairly recently.[18] Of the published songs, "Isn't It a Pity" is probably the best known. Although it can readily be performed out of context—and indeed has been, notably by Mabel Mercer—it is more of a book song than it appears to be at first. It is a love duet between Michael Bramleigh, a career diplomat, and Ilse Bauer, a German student and the daughter of the town commissioner. The particulars emerge in the bridge, sung first by Michael ("You, reading Heine, / I, somewhere in China"), then by Ilse ("My nights were sour / Spent with Schopenhauer"). Thus, although one might see these lines as a whimsical reflection by Ira Gershwin on his college days, they fit their respective characters in quite specific terms.

Musically, too, there is more than meets the eye (or ear). The refrain has more of a "white-note" quality than is typical for a borderline late Gershwin song: the outer sections are in C, the bridge is in E minor, and both outer sections and bridge feature the melodic note E. The verse, on the other hand, is more chromatic, as can be seen in its opening lines, which use the pitches C–B–A and C–B♭–A♭, respectively—that is, a descending minor third followed by its alteration into a major one (ex. 99a).

a. verse, mm. 1–2　　　　b. verse, m. 7 (cf. refrain, m. 5)

c. refrain, mm. 16–24

d. verse, mm. 13–14 (inversion)　　e. refrain, mm. 2–4 (cf. introduction, mm. 1–2)

Example 99. "Isn't It a Pity," vocal line: melodic and rhythmic recurrences

But there is more carryover than contrast between verse and refrain. Though one cold make the broad observation that both share the vocal range e¹–e², the correspondences of detail are more striking. One such correspondence can be seen in the anticipatory occurrence of the line "Isn't it a pity?" in the verse, with the same rhythm and almost the same melody as its setting in the refrain (ex. 99b). Another is the way in which the first two measures of the verse (already shown in ex. 99a) recur, minus the chromatic alteration, as the motivic mainstay of the bridge (ex. 99c). Within the confines of the verse the unaltered version of this two-measure theme is inverted in mm. 13–14, resulting in ascending rather than descending thirds stated in exactly the same rhythm (ex. 99d). Another important motive, also spanning a third, is the triplet figure used sequentially in both the introduction and the refrain (ex. 99e).

The two other songs mentioned above, "Lorelei" and "My Cousin in Milwaukee," also strike a balance between their relationship to the show and their out-of-context appeal—or potential appeal, as they both deserve to be better known. Both songs feature a certain amount of the dialect humor that runs throughout the show: the "ja ja" in the bridge of "Lorelei," and the Polish accent of "My Cousin in Milwaukee."[19] Each is distinguished by certain details of a purely musical nature that help to take it beyond the realm of the ordinary.

In "Lorelei" it is the way the melody repeats the same arpeggiation to land on the same note, f^1, in the second and fourth measures of the refrain. The first time it is supported by the tonic, as expected; but on the second occurrence the harmony makes an engaging shift to IV so that the F in question is now a ninth above the bass rather than a fifth.[20] In "My Cousin in Milwaukee," the unusual feature is the accompaniment in parallel triads, whose stepwise progression contrasts with the fourths and fifths of the vocal line. This is what is immediately heard, although these triads are actually inner voices that move over an implied pedal point (or more than implied, as witness the grace notes in the score): B♭ for the first four measures moving to E♭ for the next two. In the key of B♭, this would be the chord change of I to IV (with flatted sevenths) that characterizes the blues—and which is as close to the blues as Gershwin ever came. But the home key of the refrain is E♭, not B♭, and what is first felt as a shift from I to IV is in fact V to I.

Still, the truly intriguing portions of the score are among those recently unearthed and as yet unpublished. In keeping with the play's German setting, a large percentage of the songs are waltzes.[21] One example is the first number in act 1, aptly titled "In Three Quarter Time." Another is "Tonight," sung by the same duo as "Isn't It a Pity," with Michael transformed into his romantic alter ego Golo. It comes at the opening of act 2, where Michael (now Golo) and Ilse, amidst effusive proclamations of love, check into the bridal suite of an inn. Two waltz tunes ensue, first sung separately, then together. These waltzes were the basis for the posthumous piano piece *Two Waltzes in C* (1971), the vehicle by which this number is chiefly known today.[22]

a. analysis, waltzes I (Golo) and 2 (Ilse)

Example 100. *Two Waltzes in C:* "Tonight"

"Tonight," in its original format, begins with an introduction in C, followed by a transition to E major leading to the innkeeper's verse in A (and with it a momentary metrical shift to $\frac{4}{4}$). The latter is omitted from the piano version, as are the dialogue and dance sequences, whose principal keys are E♭, B♭, and—finally—E. The vocal presentations are nonetheless uniformly in C. The waltzes, each thirty-two measures long, are in binary form, each section of the form consisting of an antecedent and consequent portion corresponding to the scheme ABAC. This is a form that Gershwin had used before ("Embraceable You," for example) and that he used again—in "Mine."

As a contrapuntal tour de force, "Tonight" goes beyond "Mine," whose

b. vocal score, mm. 220–27

Example 100. (*continued*)

writing it predates by the better part of a year. Whereas the countermelody in "Mine" is essentially the upper voice of a vamp, and as such distinctly "counter" in nature, the second song in "Tonight" is fully the equal of the first. Though each sounds complete by itself, their performance together reveals the subtle interplay of melody and rhythm between the two.

Example 100a presents an analytical view of the section headed "Waltzes I and II" in *Two Waltzes in C,* which corresponds to mm. 212–43 of "Tonight."[23] In the latter, the vocal parts are completely contained in the piano accompaniment, save for some obvious differences in register (compare ex. 100b). To aid in identification, the characters' names are appended to the two melodies.

Although pitch is the main focus of this analysis, two rhythmic figures bear notice: the dotted quarter, eighth, and two eighths; and the dotted quarter, eighth, and quarter. These, identified in example 100 as motives *a* and *b* respectively, always occur in conjunction with melodic segments in stepwise motion (be it diatonic, chromatic, or a mixture) in a uniform direction. Each is represented several times in each of the two waltzes. In the simultaneous presentation graphed in example 100, we first see motive *a* in waltz I (Golo) directly followed by motive *b* in waltz II (Ilse). These appear again in tandem four measures later, as a result of repetition; after that, at the beginning of the second eight-measure period (m. 220), we see motive *b* in a quasi-sequence, alternately in one waltz, then the other, for five consecutive measures.

The third eight-measure period (beginning at m. 228) repeats the essential contents of the first, with some changes. Those affecting the accompaniment only are the exchange of the positions of the two waltzes, with Golo's now on top, and the general amplification of each. In Golo's waltz this takes the form of the doublings in parallel augmented triads; in Ilse's, it is the prolongation of C#—and then D#—by a descending arpeggiated diminished-seventh chord. (This expanded accompaniment is identical with the ten-measure introduction except that the latter has an extra measure of punctuation at the end of each four-measure phrase.) More to the point, however, is the melodic change in the second half of Ilse's waltz—from the contents of mm. 212–13 (upper staff) to those of mm. 228–29 (lower staff). This change, which also occurs when the waltz is presented alone, conveniently produces a mirror image of what Golo is singing at the same time. As shown in the analysis, this mirror image results in the inversion of motive *a*.

Harmonically, the two waltzes are painted with broad strokes, with a basic framework of four measures of V followed by four measures of I holding for each of the first three eight-measure periods. Melodically, however, these portions are not quite so easy to read. Both songs include periodic emphases on the pitches D, E, F, and G, often in the form of paired thirds or sixths, as shown by the unfolding symbols in the analysis. Another manifestation of this emphasis begins in Golo's part with a descending linear progression from d^2 (m. 221) to e^1 (m. 228), which can be read as a registrally transposed step proceeding to f^2 (m. 229). The larger progression thus becomes D–E–F, which is then recapitulated in reverse order by the unfolding that coincides with Golo's motive *a* (same measure).

It is not until the final eight bars—the C section of the ABAC form—that we find a clear statement of the background structure of $\hat{3}$–$\hat{2}$–$\hat{1}$. This again invites comparison with "Mine" (cf. ex. 98b, mm. 25–32), but in the latter the two tunes come together for the entire section—or, to put it another way, the countermelody simply disappears. Here the two tunes remain distinct through the end, not coming into phase until the final $\hat{2}$–$\hat{1}$ of the cadence. The setting of scale degree $\hat{2}$ is noteworthy for the voice exchange between the two parts (D–C–B in Golo's part versus B–C–D in Ilse's) and for rhythmic identification of each component of the exchange with motive *b*.

As the original incarnation of *Two Waltzes in C*, "Tonight" is an impressive find. Yet there is another song from *Pardon My English*, also from the so-called Secaucus Trunk, that is at least its equal—and is still largely unknown to the musical public. It is a group number from act 1 titled "Dancing in the Streets." The scene is the streets of Dresden, the occasion, the birthday of Commissioner Bauer (Ilse's father). The lyrics are delightfully tongue-in-cheek, as in the verses quoted in the epigraph of this chapter and in the lines "Play the piccolo, sound the cello— / You must pardon us while we bellow. / He's a jolly good German fellow!" (The latter hints at one likely reason for the show's failure, as jolly good German fellows were not exactly bankable material in New York in the 1930s.)

"Dancing in the Streets" opens (*Andantino festivo*) to music strikingly reminiscent of the festival music in Stravinsky's *Petroushka*, initially in C major but moving quickly to the home key of Eb, which subsequently shifts to G and back again. This harmonic plan, Eb–G–Eb, is reflected in the three main sections of the song and within the first section alone. The compound ternary form, sixty-six measures in length (minus the eight-bar introduction), can be summarized as follows:

$$\begin{array}{ccccc} \text{A} & & \text{B} & & \text{A} \\ a_1 \quad a_2 & b_1 & b_2 & b_{1+2} & a_3 \end{array}$$

The score of "Dancing in the Streets" is shown in example 101 from the introduction through the start of section a_2 (m. 23). This span of music is sufficient to show, among other things, the ways in which the opening white-note ostinato—that uncanny evocation of *Petroushka*—is adapted to fit the ensuing keys of Eb and G while remaining no less identifiable with the indication "accordion effect" in m. 1. The latter, though perhaps redundant, is a noteworthy sidelight in support of the *Petroushka* connection, as is, in the version in Eb, the registrally displaced whole step in the bass straddling the inner-voice pedal—a rather Stravinskian detail.

Also apparent in this excerpt is the ease with which Gershwin handles the harmonic progressions cited above. The first of these is accomplished within the space of one measure, from the downbeat of m. 6 to that of m. 7, by a

Example 101. "Dancing in the Streets," vocal score, mm. 1–23

sequential treatment of the opening pair of chords that descends by successive minor thirds until it reaches E♭.[24] From that point the bass continues its
stepwise descent, to B♭, the confirming dominant, which is enriched by the
superposition above it of the same thirds that figured in reaching E♭ — that
is, the vertical F♯–A–C in the inner voices, plus the third C–D–E♭ in the instrumental line just prior to the vocal entrance.

The shifts between E♭ and G are done with even more dispatch. These,

Example 101. *(continued)*

too, rely on the strength of stepwise motion, which here is in the upper voice or voices: the instrumental descant (top voice) e^1–$f\sharp^1$–g^1 leading from $e\flat^1$ in mm. 18–19; and the ascending parallel $\frac{6}{3}$s with descant moving from g^1 through e^2 in the G-major scale, followed directly by f^2 through $e\flat^3$ in the E♭ scale in mm. 21–23.

"Dancing in the Streets" is also remarkable for its use of counterpoint, in which it is easily the equal of "Mine" and "Tonight." The first inkling comes

at m. 13 (and at corresponding points in sections a₂ and a₃), where a countermelody to the vocal part emerges from the top voice of the ostinato. An
interesting detail in the setting of this new tune occurs in m. 14, where the
notes eb^1–f^1–g^1 form an exchange with their mirror image, g–f–eb, in what
is effectively an inner voice—in other words, a voice exchange. This detail,
highlighted at "N.B." in example 101, returns in the subsequent a sections
with each recurrence of the countermelody.

The counterpoint in the opening portion of "Dancing in the Streets" foreshadows greater developments in the song's midsection. This large B section
comprises two themes, sung first in succession and then together—in short,
a miniature version of what takes place in "Tonight." And, like the songs in
"Tonight," the tunes shown together in example 102 are waltzes. The first,

Example 102. "Dancing in the Streets," mm. 52–59 (vocal parts only)

on the upper staff, is for divided female voices; the second, on the lower
staff, has the males in unison in a tenor range. The harmony, of necessity
the same for both, alternates between tonic and dominant on each downbeat, and the difference in range eliminates any chance of melodic conflict.
Though not shown here, the initial setting of the second tune as a bass, supporting a quasi-Mozartean accompaniment, adds to the graciousness of the
entire number. The heading for the B section, *Tempo di Ländler,* complements
the *festivo* of the outer portions. Meanwhile, the lyrics to this section contain

two of the best lines in the show. This is indeed an operetta, even if the song does not go on for days.

Let 'Em Eat Cake—which succeeds *Pardon My English* chronologically, despite the reverse order in which the two plays have been considered—offers an example that, from a technical standpoint, stands alone. Its source is "Blue Blue Blue," a number whose subject matter, a proposal by the Wintergreen administration to paint the White House blue, gave it limited prospects for being remembered outside the confines of the show. The song is complete on three pages,[25] with a refrain lasting twenty-four measures (alternating periods of eight and four) instead of the more customary thirty-two. The verse is shorter still: thirteen bars, including a two-measure introduction. The refrain, although chromatic in the vocal line, remains procedurally tonal. The verse is the opposite: a vocal part containing only the pitches F♯ and A, each repeated for four measures straight, pitted against an accompaniment that is as close as Gershwin ever came to atonality.

The introduction and verse to "Blue Blue Blue" are depicted in analytic notation in example 103. Though the reconciliation with tonality is clear in the transition to the refrain and in the single measure between the two four-bar periods that constitute the verse proper, the bulk of the excerpt is, from a tonal standpoint, ambiguous at best. Rather, the logic of what takes place seems to rest on sequential groups of pitches that, at junctures which match the phrase and period divisions in the music, form complete cycles (albeit with internal repetitions) of the twelve notes of the chromatic scale. These cycles are identified in example 103 (see the bracketed segments marked "all 12") by the numerical equivalents of the pitches represented in the musical notation, with the numbers 0 through 11 corresponding to the chromatic scale (regardless of spelling), starting with C.[26] Those which have already appeared at least once within a given cycle are shown in parentheses.

The two-measure introduction constitutes a cycle in that its four chords, of which three are distinct, collectively contain all twelve notes. The first two chords, in m. 1, are the same except for the transfer of G from the lowest (g) to the highest (g^2) position; their pitch content, expressed within a single register on the added staff below, consists of the pentatonic scale C–D–F–G–A, whose equivalent in number notation is 0,2,5,7,9.[27] The two chords in m. 2 are also pentatonic but at different transpositions: A♭–B♭–D♭–E♭–F for the first chord, B–C♯–E–F♯–G♯ for the second. These three pentatonic scales contain all twelve notes, with three repetitions. The first two scales contain F (whose number equivalent is 5) as a common tone in the same register,

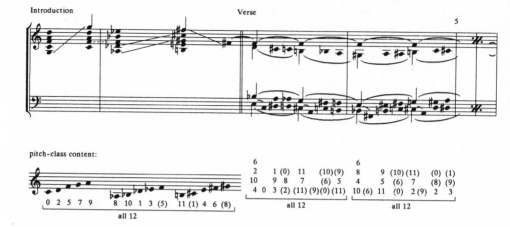

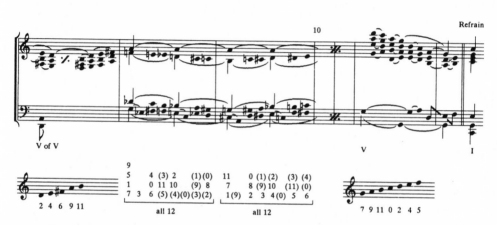

Example 103. "Blue Blue Blue": analysis of introduction and verse

whereas the second two share A♭/G♯ (number 8) and D♭/C♯ (number 1). The perfect fourth formed by these two notes remains intact in the last chord but is transposed up an octave. As if to compensate for this upward transfer (as well as for the upward transfer of the Gs at the beginning of the passage), the top note of the last chord, f♯², is taken down an octave to begin the vocal portion of the verse.

Pentatonicism played an important role in Gershwin's music almost from the beginning; thus one can see a natural extension of this tendency in his use of pentatonic figures to build chromatic entities.[28] Within the same brief verse he also uses the pentatonic scale in a tonal context, as in m. 7 of example 103, where the notes D–E–F♯–A–B (2,4,6,9,11) are rooted in D major or V of V. A further reconciliation with the upcoming refrain in C is represented by the two-measure transition beginning in m. 12. The verticals are rich in fourths, like those of the introduction, and the horizontal lines are still pentatonic—or at least pentatonic subsets (for example, reading from the top for the first four notes: D–C–A–G; A–G–E–D; G–A–D–E). The context, however, has changed to a single diatonic scale founded on a dominant seventh.

The chromatic cycles displayed within the verse itself—that is, in mm. 3–6 and 8–11—are quite different from that of the introduction: not only is the result chromatic, but so are the building blocks—three layers of parallel six-note chromatic scale segments beneath an upper-voice pedal (ex. 103). Each measure completes one cycle on its last attack point; the second measure in each two-measure group is a retrograde of the first; and the last two of every four measures are a repetition of the first. Finally, the second four-measure period (mm. 8–11) is an exact transposition of the first, a minor third higher.

Alec Wilder writes, of the song as a whole, that "it puzzles while it pleases." Concerning the verse, he observes that "the piano part looks as if Gershwin were making a sketch for a new concerto."[29] One clue to the puzzle can be seen in Gershwin's persistent use of the minor third, both within each four-bar segment and as an interval of transposition between them. This interval has been, and will continue to be, important to Gershwin's music throughout his career. In addition, the vertical structures within these passages, moving chromatically in parallel diminished fifths and major thirds, are familiar ingredients in Gershwin's piano writing from *Rhapsody* onward.

In short, Gershwin was, by the early 1930s, a mature composer in full command of his craft, using tools that he had developed through the years in new and exciting ways. This is true of the new musicals, or operettas; it is also true of the instrumental works that are the subject of the next chapter. The secure position he had built himself in the previous decade allowed Gershwin the luxury of being less prolific, giving him the time to pursue matters of technique on a more sophisticated level. On the negative side, the music from this period—the songs surveyed in this chapter and the concert works to be discussed in the next—has garnered the reputation of lacking, somehow, in that plangent, soulful quality that is supposed to be the hallmark of a great Gershwin tune. Such matters are, of course, highly subjective. The fact remains that the chief influences on Gershwin's music from the late twenties through the early thirties were nonindigenous: Stravinsky; Satie, "Les Six," and things French in general; and, in the political operettas, more than a hint of Gilbert and Sullivan. Wearing one's heart on one's sleeve was scarcely in vogue in this milieu; thus it can be said with reasonable assurance that the sentimental aspect of Gershwin's music was somewhat eclipsed during this, the early part of his mature period. After all, he had not yet written *Porgy and Bess*.

9 Concert Works

ike the stage works, Gershwin's concert music of the early 1930s displayed a technical growth that was distinct, deliberate, and generally underappreciated. In this category are two completely new compositions, *Second Rhapsody* and *Cuban Overture,* plus *George Gershwin's Song Book* and the *"I Got Rhythm" Variations.* Except for the new rhapsody, these were all written during the time when Gershwin took lessons with Joseph Schillinger, whose influence strengthened Gershwin's already considerable advancement in the areas of counterpoint and orchestration.[1]

The original incarnation of *Second Rhapsody* was an instrumental sequence in the 1931 film *Delicious,* starring Janet Gaynor and Charles Farrell.[2] The number, titled "New York Rhapsody," is introduced at the piano by its fictional composer via the following Russian-accented narrative: "It begins like we all see the city first: the great towers almost in the clouds [*vamp*]. Down below, in the long furrows, human seeds trying to grow to the light [*part 1, theme 1*]. And noise [*transition*]: riveters drumming your ear from every side [*sixteenth-note diminution of theme 1*]. And this is the night motif [*part 1, theme 2*]: night, silencing the rivets."[3] The composer's musings dissolve into the orchestral entrance of the lyrical main theme of part 2, at which point the scene shifts, with the rhapsody continuing as a backdrop for crowd noises and dialogue.[4] The film version of the rhapsody contains eight minutes of music, including all the main themes and transitions and an ending identical with that of the concert work.

There are two known manuscript sources for what was to become *Second Rhapsody*. The first, an informally written two-piano score with orchestral annotations,[5] bears Gershwin's signature, the title "2nd Rhapsody," and the designation "original manuscript," all in the composer's hand, albeit added after the fact at the bottom of a crossed-out page. Below that, in another handwriting, is "California, Jan. 1931." The title added by Gershwin ties this manuscript—hereafter referred to as "first manuscript" or "sketch"—to the concert version, and the place of origin, if identified correctly, would link it with the film score. Its shorter and less elaborate ending indicates that it preceded both versions. Clearly it is a working manuscript, as evidenced by the abundant changes that occurred between it and the final product. Most notable among these is a discarded ostinato-like secondary theme (ex. 104)

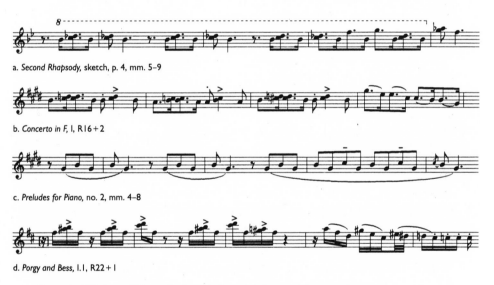

a. *Second Rhapsody*, sketch, p. 4, mm. 5–9

b. *Concerto in F*, I, R16 + 2

c. *Preludes for Piano*, no. 2, mm. 4–8

d. *Porgy and Bess*, I.1, R22 + 1

Example 104. *Second Rhapsody:* discarded second theme with comparisons

whose lineage extends back to a developmental theme in *Concerto in F* and to the second of the *Preludes for Piano*. One can also see a kinship to an important theme from *Porgy and Bess*.

The second source, an orchestral score in Gershwin's formal hand, bears the official title "2nd Rhapsody for Orchestra with Piano," followed by the date March 14, 1931—about two weeks after his return to New York from

Hollywood.[6] At the end is the declaration "Finished May 23, 1931." This score is the true representation of Gershwin's orchestration, which was for many years suppressed in favor of a supposedly "improved" version by Robert McBride, commissioned after Gershwin's death by the publisher's music editor Frank Campbell-Watson.[7] In this fair-copy manuscript we see, for the first time, the contrary-motion passage (cited earlier in ex. 23e) that dominates the piano introduction. Though certainly one of the striking moments of the piece, this passage originated as something of an afterthought, as can be seen from the first page of the manuscript (ex. 105).[8] Its role is expanded in the two-piano score published in 1932, where we find it reprised about one-third of the way through the piece as part of an extended solo passage in E♭ (at R10+12).[9] Yet this reprise is in neither the manuscript nor the recording of a run-through by Gershwin, with a hired orchestra, on June 26, 1931.[10] On the other hand, the latter has a solo cadenza, not in the manuscript, in the place where the reprise occurs in the published score.

The genesis of *Second Rhapsody* is atypical in several respects, including the length of time—over six months—between its completion and its first performance. This allowed time for the trial recording and no doubt contributed to the further changes that occurred after Gershwin had finished his fair copy. The relative lack of popularity of the work, so it seems, was a stamp placed on it almost from the beginning.

Second Rhapsody had its first public performance on January 29, 1932, at Symphony Hall in Boston—the first concert premiere of a Gershwin work to take place outside his native New York. Gershwin was the soloist, Serge Koussevitzky the conductor. Koussevitzky was a longtime champion of contemporary music, specifically that of the Russians and the French and of the Americans who were influenced by them. To be sure, Gershwin had the right lineage, both genealogically and artistically, to be included in this company. Still, his inclusion, through his most sophisticated concert work to date, was a significant milestone in his career.

The opening of *Second Rhapsody* confirms Gershwin's continuing passion for symmetry and contrapuntal layering. The first instance of the former comes with the newly added portion of the piano introduction in mm. 3–6. There, in the service of an extended $^6_4$–$^5_3$ resolution over a dominant pedal, the right and left hands fan outward in opposite directions. The inversional relationship between the hands is tempered, as it were, not only by the exclusively diatonic nature of the passage, but also by the setting of successive spans of a seventh in the left hand against the octaves in the right. The last iteration of this pattern unites the left hand's lowest note with the pedal C in

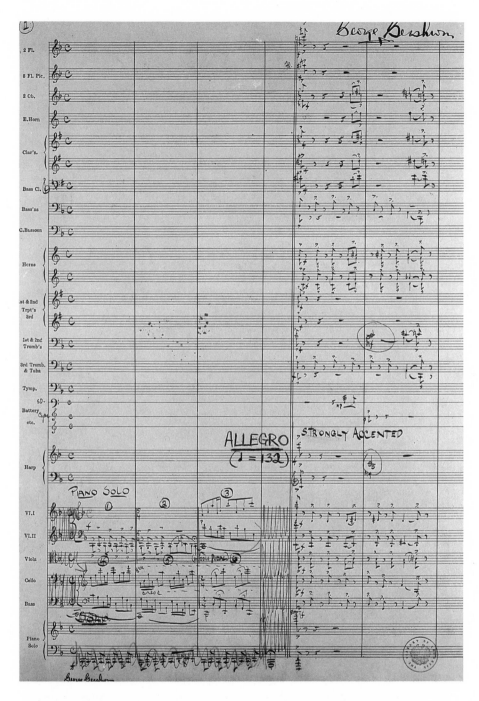

Example 105. *Second Rhapsody,* orchestral manuscript (Gershwin Collection, bound ms. 25), p. 1

a. vamp   b. flourish

c. theme A1 with counterpoints (R1–R3 + 2)

Example 106. *Second Rhapsody,* opening material (from orchestral manuscript)

the bass, while the two hands together contain the dominant seventh chord. This leads conveniently to the tonic on the downbeat of m. 7, at which point the rhapsody begins as originally sketched and as heard in the film.

It is here that the technique of contrapuntal layering comes to the fore. First a two-measure vamp is followed by a one-measure flourish in contrary motion (ex. 106).[11] The vamp and flourish are then restated, with the flourish transposed up a fourth. Eight measures later, over the vamp (minus the flourish), the main theme of the work (henceforth theme A1, that is, the first theme of section A), previously announced at the start of the piano introduction, enters in the oboes and first trumpet (ex. 106c). Accents in the pattern 3 + 2 + 3 followed by 3 + 3 + 2 are reinforced by the second trumpet and, additionally, by parallel triads in the flutes.[12]

Counterpointing theme A1 (in addition to the vamp) is a pattern of sustained dyads in the clarinets that alternates measure by measure between the

Example 106. (*continued*)

major second C–D (the top two voices of the added-sixth chord that begins the vamp) and B♭–C. This figure is followed (beginning in the ninth measure, or R1+8), by a countermelody in the horns, violas, and cellos whose main notes alternate between A and G. At the same time, the accentual material in the flutes is expanded and doubled at the lower octave by the oboes. In addition, there are what might be called incidental counterpoints in the bassoons (R1+6) and trumpets (R2+5). The two $\frac{6}{4}$ measures at R3, which exist in

CROSSED OUT

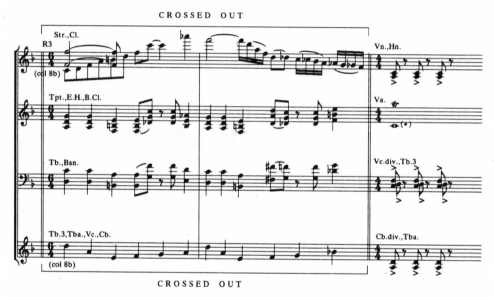

CROSSED OUT

Example 106. (*continued*)

simpler form in the sketch, are crossed out in the fair copy and omitted from both the recorded run-through and the published score (in which R3 falls at the following measure). In addition to allowing theme A1 to close explicitly on F, these measures introduce three new ideas—a soaring melody of linked arpeggiations, a walking bass, and a chordal figure in the winds and brasses that continues, with modification, the rhythm of the vamp—of which only the last has any apparent relevance to the rest of the piece. The result is a passage that, while in itself interesting, detracts from the logical progression of events; thus, from a compositional standpoint, Gershwin was wise to cut it.

Example 107. *Second Rhapsody:* introduction and theme A I

The foregoing details remain in the service of theme A1, whose structure, analyzed in example 107 along with the introductory material, is both clear and closed. The note C, or scale degree $\hat{5}$, is represented in a wide range of registers in the introduction, usually together with its upper neighbor D (highlighted by brackets in ex. 107), thus preparing its emergence as the primary melodic tone of the theme. Just as plainly, the melodic line is heading downward to scale degree $\hat{1}$ at the end of the theme. Closure first occurs implicitly, with the inverted tonic added-sixth chord that begins the transition at R3 (as published, minus the deleted $\frac{6}{4}$ measures),[13] then explicitly, with the abbreviated transposition of theme A1 that starts with scale degree $\hat{1}$ five measures later, at R4, and acts simultaneously as a transition to a new theme in the subdominant.

Transitions are surprisingly economical in *Second Rhapsody;* indeed, the generic passages so abundant in *Rhapsody in Blue* and *Concerto in F* are virtually absent here. In their stead are extensions of the main themes or corollaries to those themes. The concept of the corollary theme (introduced in connection with the opening bars of *Rhapsody in Blue*) is explored further in *Second Rhapsody*. A case in point is the theme in the subdominant, which is reached, not by means of a distinct transitional passage, but by an extension of theme A1; like each of the themes to follow, it has a corollary, or consequent. The main portion, theme A2a, begins in the solo piano with the upbeat to R5 (ex. 108a)

a. theme A2a (piano part only)

b. theme A2b (piano part only)

c. tonic reprise of theme A1 (orchestra)

Example 108. *Second Rhapsody*

and pits syncopated triads in the right hand against a quarter-note ostinato in the left. In the corollary, theme A2b, the right hand continues the quarter-note motion while the left is syncopated. The pitch material also represents a reversal in that the right hand has, on the surface, a single line, whereas the left has the verticals. The latter, three-note chords in fourths and tritones moving in descending chromatic steps, hint at what will eventually be an important inner-voice motive—one that makes its first appearance with the return of theme A1 in the tonic at R17 (ex. 108c)[14] and comes to the fore in the closing measures of the piece.

This technique of thematic foreshadowing, which would serve Gershwin well in *Porgy and Bess,* can also be found at work beginning at R13, where a corollary—which we can call theme A1a—is appended to theme A1 (ex. 109a). This figure, identifiable both rhythmically (eighth, two sixteenths,

a. R13–R13+3

b. R15–R15+3

c. R34–R34+6

Example 109. *Second Rhapsody:* theme A1a and transformations

dotted half) and melodically (the reversed skip of a third), changes and grows with each recurrence. It takes the lead at R15 (ex. 109b), with the reversed skip occurring in both directions. Another variant at R34 (ex. 109c), heard previously in the orchestra just before the cadenza leading to the slow movement (compare at R19+9), is yet more prominent due to the sparse texture, which pits it alone in the solo piano against a repeated quarter-note C (to be registrally specific, C_1) in the bass. The latter can be seen as a rhythmic augmentation of the repeated bass C of the introduction, where the solo piano states the motivic essence of theme A1. This last incarnation of theme A1a initiates the final section of the work, which can be seen as either a lengthy coda or a modified and abbreviated return of the A section—one that lacks, among other things, the second pair of themes (A2a and A2b).

The so-called slow movement or B section of *Second Rhapsody* invites com-

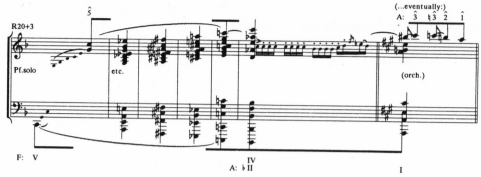

a. transition to B section

b. theme B1

Example 110. *Second Rhapsody*

parison with its counterpart in *Rhapsody in Blue*. Although it in no way matches the Andantino of the earlier work in popularity, it has its own strengths. In at least one respect, the inner-voice counterpoint, it bears a striking similarity to its predecessor, taking over where the latter (and, by way of association, "Funny Face") left off.

The B section of *Second Rhapsody* illustrates the work's most extensive application of the corollary-theme idea. The section, preceded by the cadenza (ex. 110a), begins at R21 with a sequential theme in quarter notes, here labeled B1 (ex. 110b). Theme B1 comes to rest on the downbeat of the ninth measure, at which point the two-measure nucleus of the corollary theme B_2 (cited

c. themes B2 (extended) and B3

Example 110. (*continued*)

earlier in ex. 32) makes its entrance. A second statement of theme B1 follows at R22 with an altered ending, shown in the insert in example 110b that shifts the key from A to Db (the enharmonic equivalent of a major third higher). There as before, theme B$_2$ follows, now doubled in size, with changes of position in the upper voices bringing to the fore successively the root, third, and fifth of the Db-major triad (ex. 110c). The closing figure, approached via the chromatic passing note G♮ and identified here as theme B3, completes the thematic cycle.

All three phases of this cycle are of interest rhythmically. Themes B1 and B3 share the attribute of even notes in the descant accompanied by even notes of longer duration in the lower voices. (The resulting texture hints strongly at species counterpoint, a subject Gershwin would later tackle under Schillinger's tutelage.) This idea is particularly well developed in theme B3 (see 110c), where the note values grow from eighths to quarters to halves. The halves move in descending parallel thirds, the quarter notes (actually syncopated halves with repeated instead of tied notes) forming a series of 7–6 suspensions against them. This is more or less reciprocal to the pattern of the lower voices supporting theme B1, whose salient motion is ascending parallel tenths.

In contrast to the even note values of themes B1 and B3 is theme B2, with its distinctive rhythmic scheme comprising a $^4_4$ plus an $^8_4$ measure. As shown previously (ex. 32), the latter is divided into a pattern of 2 + 4 + 2, thereby reflecting in quadruple augmentation the eighth-quarter-eighth rhythm that precedes it. Quite naturally, the middle 4 falls into focus, and it is there that we find the contrapuntal link with *Rhapsody in Blue*—the inner voice, initially played by clarinets and bass clarinet in unison, whose rhythm and contour evoke, albeit diatonically, the inner-voice counterpoint in the Andantino of the earlier work (cf. ex. 45f). The metric change clarifies the role of these four beats, which Gershwin plainly did not want to be interrupted by a barline, as the expressive centerpiece of theme B2—a role mirrored by the relationship of theme B2 to the slow movement, and of the slow movement to the rhapsody as a whole.

A comparison with *Rhapsody in Blue* can also be drawn in terms of macro-structure. In the earlier work, the slow movement's E major is a tritone above the tonic Bb,[15] whereas in *Second Rhapsody* the operative interval is a major third. Though there is a kinship between the two intervals (both, for example, are subsets of the whole-tone scale and of the dominant seventh chord), the major third, because it does not immediately reproduce itself, allows more extended, potentially more coherent, applications. In *Second Rhapsody* these occur not only in the interval between the respective tonics of the A and B sections (F and A) but at two conspicuous places within the B section itself. First, there is the shift from A to Db described above, where Db supports the first extended treatment of theme B2. This change is balanced by an equal progression in the opposite direction when themes B2 and B1 are presented in reverse order by the solo piano, in the local keys of A and F (R25+3, R27).

Melodically there is less ground for comparison. In *Rhapsody in Blue* the two main themes are distinct and largely disparate entities; in *Second Rhapsody* there is an explicit connection—the repeated C of theme A1, in a reminder in the solo piano that dovetails with the orchestra's initial B♯ of theme B1. In a remarkable though by no means unique show of symmetry, the pitch class C/B♯ links the slow movement with the finale, in the form of a C-major reprise of theme B1 in the orchestra that yields to the repeated bass C in the piano (see ex. 109c).[16]

More can be said about the connection between the A and B sections, whose context is shown in condensed form in example 110. The reminder of theme A1 comes at the end of a transitional cadenza—one of only two such passages (the other comes before the reprise of theme A1 at R17) that can be classed as "generic": that is, lacking in any clear identification with one of the themes of the work. This passage, which begins at R20+3, takes C as its point of departure in both outer voices—this on the heels of more than twenty measures of music in which C is present, almost continuously, in a variety of registers. Bass and descant then proceed in contrary motion through an entire octave in successive minor thirds, with the bass notes functioning as harmonic roots. This is a retrograde form of the progression G–B♭–D♭–E–G that opens part 2 of *Rhapsody in Blue* and forecasts that would soon be known to Gershwin, via Schillinger, as the system of four tonics.[17] In contrast with the earlier work, this sequence is a singular occurrence in *Second Rhapsody*. It ends where it begins—save for the differences in register—on C, then proceeds down to A via the passing note B♭. This progression, too, is reminiscent of *Rhapsody in Blue*—specifically, of the sequence leading to the closing theme of part 1 (ex. 50).

Gershwin's next orchestral work, *Cuban Overture*, was completed in August 1932, some months after he had begun his Schillinger studies.[18] It was his second orchestral score to exclude his own instrument, the piano; like its predecessor in this regard, *An American in Paris*, it aspired to an idiom indigenous to a place where he had sojourned, in this case Havana.[19] Its first performance, under the title *Rumba*, took place soon after its completion, at an outdoor concert at New York's Lewisohn Stadium under the direction of the English conductor Albert Coates. On its second airing in November 1932, in the more formal setting of the Metropolitan Opera House, Gershwin gave it the more formal title under which it was published and by which it is generally known today. As with Gershwin's other orchestrations, the manuscript score is an impeccable fair copy, with scrupulous documentation of starting and completion dates (August 1 and 9, respectively) and, in this instance, locale as well (Gershwin's apartment at 33 Riverside Drive).[20] Also on the title page are the date of the Lewisohn Stadium premiere and a diagram placing the Latin percussion instruments—claves, bongos, guiro, maracas—in front of the orchestra, in a semicircle facing the conductor.

Like *An American in Paris, Cuban Overture* opens busily with layer upon layer of material—indeed, more than can be grasped in a first hearing. This aspect of the work is immediately evident in the five introductory measures shown in example 111. The first measure, essentially an upbeat, contains the only unaccompanied figure in the entire piece; its identifying feature is a triplet combined with the reversed skip of a third (motive *a*). Within the next four measures we have: a neighbor note and a descending fourth (motive *b*) set against its mirror image (motive *b'*), moving in even sixteenths; a syncopated fanfare in parallel ⁶₃ and ⁶₄ chords (motive *c*), whose durations range

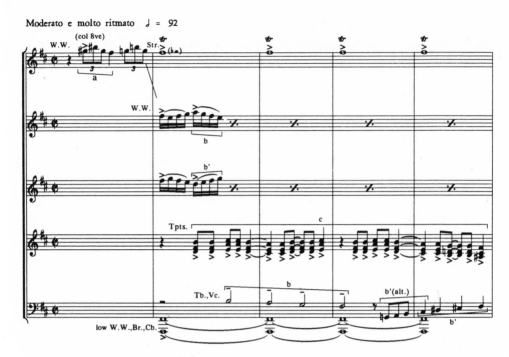

Example 111. *Cuban Overture*, mm. 1–5

from one to three eighth notes; and a stepwise descent in half notes spanning a fourth (motive *b* again), followed by an ascending scale comprising
two conjunct representations of motive *b′* (the first altered into a tritone) in
eighths and quarters respectively. All this occurs over a pedal F♯, which can
be seen as a functional intersection between the rival keys of D and D♭, that
is, as the mediant of one and the subdominant of the other.

Following these introductory measures are two false starts, in D♭ and E♭,
respectively, in which the long notes of the main theme emerge from beneath
an eighth-note ostinato based on motive *b* accompanied by a vamp whose
alternation between D♭ and D (at its initial pitch level) helps to reinforce the
D–D♭ dualism (ex. 112). Both the ostinato and the vamp are of interest rhythmically: the former in its superposition of a length of ten eighth notes on
the prevailing meter of $\frac{2}{2}$ meter (see the bracketed segments in example 112);
the latter in the simultaneous division of the measure into 2 + 3 + 3 and 3 +
3 + 2 (first cited in ex. 29).

The theme proper first appears "warmly," preceded and accompanied by
the vamp alone in mm. 32–48,[21] where the local key is C rather than D♭. The
latter, however, makes a prompt return with the theme's next statement ("fer-
vently"), where theme and vamp are joined by a brief reminder of the osti-

Example 112. *Cuban Overture*, mm. 16–19

nato and where the main melody is enhanced by a doubling, mostly in parallel thirds, that is joined by a third upper part midway through the twelfth measure. The three upper parts then come together, two bars later, to form the parallel ⁶₃ chords of the descending or consequent portion of the theme.

This is the definitive statement of the main theme of *Cuban Overture* profiled in example 113. The lower system, in rhythmic notation, presents the upper parts intact (minus octave doublings) over a simplified version of the vamp. Above is an analytic graph of the melody, with salient portions of the inner parts and bass (the latter transposed to the treble staff). Among its features are strong linear progressions both upward and downward: an ascent from Ab to Db emphasizing a conflict between Cb and C (a melodic reflection, perhaps, of the chromatic dualism that governs the piece harmonically) followed by a descent to Gb, which in turn resolves to an implied F underneath the reassertion of the primary tone Ab (m. 66). A chromatic ascent ensues in the inner voice, echoing the Ab–Db path of the opening portion of the theme. The close, meanwhile, shifts into whole-tone mode with an altered version of the descending fifth. This descent, marked with scale-degree numbers, is aborted just before its expected arrival on the tonic—an arrival that is nonetheless strongly implied and indeed is made explicit in the preceding statement of the theme in C major.

This truncated ending of the main theme gives way to the fragmentary development of its component parts, a process that occupies most of the re-

Example 113. *Cuban Overture,* main theme: analysis and condensed score

mainder of the work. The measures that follow (ex. 114), beginning with the
pervasive filled-in fourth—this time in its ascending form, motive *b'*—initi-
ate a unison figure in two horns, set to a rhythmic pattern extracted from the
main theme (compare m. 64 in ex. 113, also the segment here marked "N.B.").
Over an A♭ pedal sustained by the first horn at the close of this figure, the
seventh through tenth measures of the main theme (English horn) are set

Example 114. *Cuban Overture, mm. 72–76*

against simultaneous upper and lower counterpoints (flute and bass clarinet), of which the former begins as an approximate duplication at the fourth—in quarters rather than eighths and quarters. The same setting, rearranged, follows in the next four bars (not shown), with the thematic excerpt an octave higher (flute) and both counterpoints below (oboe and clarinet), and with the horn pedal up a twelfth.

Another instance of fragmentary development results in the expressive subtheme that first appears in the flutes and oboes (mm. 94–97), then in the flutes, clarinets, and upper strings (mm. 106–9). As shown in example 115,

Example 115. *Cuban Overture, mm. 94–97*

this newly derived melody joins motive *b'* as antecedent with a figure drawn from motive *c* (see ex. 111) as consequent.

A different juxtaposition initiates the sequence beginning in m. 122 (ex. 116), where the ascending fourth of motive *b'* is answered by a reprise of the ostinato from the opening measures of the work featuring motive *b*—the ascending fourth, or, in other words, the inversion of motive *b'*. Motive *b'* can

Concert Works 167

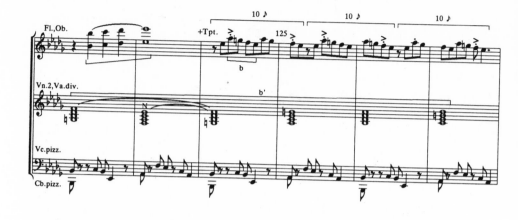

Example 116. *Cuban Overture,* mm. 122–44

also be found in the parallel seventh chords that form the nucleus of the accompaniment. Measures 122–127 are repeated a whole step higher beginning at m. 128, where the top voice of the accompaniment breaks into half notes. This rhythmic diminution is matched by an intervallic diminution, resulting in what can be seen as a chromatic variant of motive *b'* (motive *b"*).

The sequence begins its second phase at m. 134 with a dialogue between the chromatic and diatonic versions of the ascending four-step motive. The successive statements of motive *b'* in the top line form, with their goal notes, an expanded version of the same motive (see, in ex. 116, the beam connecting the notes a², b², c#³, and d³), joining with a recapitulation of mm. 7–10 of the main theme (the portion treated canonically in ex. 114). The chromatic motive *b"*, meanwhile, is taken downward through successive statements a major third apart, with starting points spanning the descending octave from c#² to d♭¹ and coming to rest on the major third below that (a).

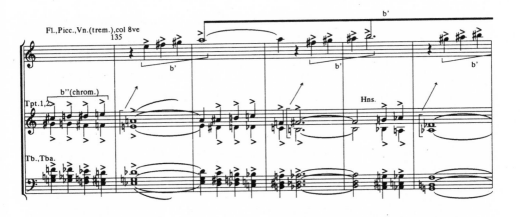

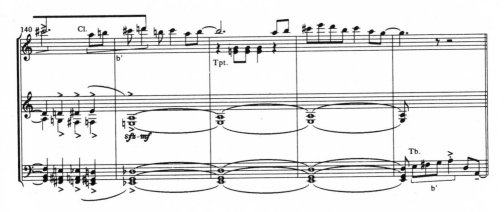

Example 116. (*continued*)

This sequence, played by the first trumpet, is counterpointed in the second trumpet by a descending chromatic scale, resulting in a series of chromatic wedges (shifting to the horns in m. 138 and doubled by divided violas beginning at m. 140), each expanding from a perfect fourth to a major seventh and coming to rest on a perfect fourth.[22] Three lower parts form a series of chromatically descending verticals consisting, from the bottom upward, of a major third and diminished fifth—in other words, the dominant seventh.

The accompanying trumpet (later horn) duet complements rather than negates this interpretation, as does the quasi-imitative ascending sequence in the flutes and violins. The latter, at each point of rest in the lower five parts, fills in the interval contained in the top two of those parts. Thus, in mm. 135–36, the vertical fourth e^1–a^1 is answered by the horizontal fourth e^2–a^2. The same relationship exists in mm. 37–38 between the vertical fifth b–f♯^{1} and the stepwise line f♯^{2}–b^2, except that the vertical interval is in its inverted form.

Finally, in mm. 139–40 the vertical fourth a♭–d♭¹ is replicated two octaves higher by the filled-in fourth g♯²–c♯³. This symbiosis is all the more remarkable—and more likely to be a deliberate design of the composer—because the two sequences move not only in different directions but by different intervals of both pitch and time; indeed, the points of rest in the lower parts, each five quarters in duration except for the last, are not in phase with the pitch sequence.

The lower parts land in m. 141, an octave below their first point of rest, on the chord E♭–G–D♭–A. Tantamount to what in jazz terminology would be called an E♭7 with a flat fifth, this collection combines the essential notes of both the dominants of A♭ and of D; it functions here in the latter context. This comes just as the melody takes up the main theme in the key of D and precedes the trombone entrance (m. 144) articulating the fourths e–a and d–A. The latter is a transposition, a semitone higher, of the horn part in m. 72, and it ushers in a reprise of the subsequent music (see ex. 114) at the same interval of transposition—in D as opposed to D♭—thus recalling the tonal dualism manifested in various ways earlier in the work.

The key of D remains in force through the end of the A section, which includes a reprise of the main theme in its entirety (beginning at m. 164, with an extended pickup in mm. 162–63). This is preceded by an eight-measure block of sound (ex. 117) that features a canonic treatment of the descending-fourth ostinato accompanied, in the middle register, by repeated chords in the rhythm of motive *c*. The canon pits the original form of the ostinato (labeled P for prime) against its inversion at the lower octave (labeled I) over a rhythmically augmented hybrid in the bass (a complete P plus a partial I). The pitch field, an unadulterated D major for the first four bars, is then altered beginning in the fifth measure to accommodate Gershwin's familiar lowered seventh and sixth scale degrees, in this case C♮ and B♭. The role of this passage parallels that of the busy music that opens the work (ex. 111), whose motivic material it shares.

The one motive absent since the beginning is the first (*a* in ex. 111). It returns in the clarinet cadenza (ex. 118) that simultaneously closes the A section and leads into the slow movement or B section. This is appropriate, as motive *a* is the ingredient common to the B section's two most identifiable themes. The first of these, entering at m. 194 (ex. 119), is particularly interesting, as it joins a variant of part of the main theme of the A section with first the pitches, then the rhythm, of motive *a*. The same motive, now with pitch and rhythm in phase, concludes the second melody seven bars later (ex. 120). These two melodies are supported, respectively, by the tonic and the domi-

Example 117. *Cuban Overture,* mm. 154–61

Example 118. *Cuban Overture,* mm. 190–91

nant of G. The latter, the local key for the first thirty-two measures of the slow movement, is next replaced by B and then by E (all in the free mixture of mode that, for Gershwin, signified what he would call the blues), leading to the dominant of D in the second half of m. 256. The finale, or second A section, begins on the following downbeat.

Subtitled "stretto" in the manuscript, the finale recapitulates all the ele-

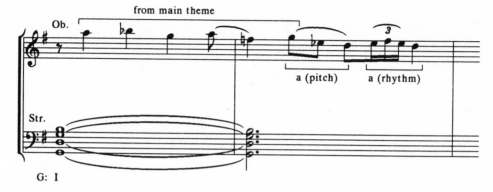

from main theme

a (pitch)   a (rhythm)

G: I

Example 119. *Cuban Overture,* mm. 194–95

G: V

Example 120. *Cuban Overture,* mm. 201–2

ments of the original A section, beginning with bits and pieces—vamp, ostinato, portions of the main theme—and culminating, in mm. 329–54, with a
literal repeat of the passage shown in example 117 (to which the term *stretto*
most aptly applies) and the subsequent reprise of the main theme in its entirety.[23] The final measures of the piece build to an expansive chord combin-
ing the tonic of D and the dominant of Db, which resolves to an unambigu-
ous D-major triad.[24]

Gershwin was right in giving his *Rumba* its definitive identity as *Cuban*

Overture. It is not a piece for dance band but an orchestral work of substance, whose technical complexity exceeds that of, say, Aaron Copland's *El Salon Mexico,* a work of similar character that it predates by about four years. As the first finished product of the Schillinger years it deserves to be regarded seriously. Gershwin had a distinct penchant for counterpoint: for turning themes into countermelodies, and vice versa. This tendency was clear as far back as *Concerto in F;* it continues in *Second Rhapsody,* more so in *Cuban Overture.* Where the last work differs is in the explicit use of polyphonic imitation and of devices such as inversion and rhythmic augmentation. This is a direct result of the composer's lessons with Schillinger.

Another staple of the art of canon, the retrograde, would come later, in *Porgy and Bess,* where we first find it used in an incontrovertibly conscious way.[25] One can also see the process at work, if only subconsciously, in the refrain of "I Got Rhythm," where mm. 3 and 4 echo, in reverse order, the four pitches in mm. 1 and 2. This relationship is enhanced by the internal symmetry of the four pitches themselves. The resulting motive, comprising two major seconds separated by a minor third, can be found in other Gershwin melodies as well.[26] Nonetheless, the "I Got Rhythm" context remains the one in which it is most readily identified.

The "I Got Rhythm" motive plays a substantial role in *The Schillinger System of Musical Composition,* published posthumously in two volumes containing twelve "books," the second of which is titled "Theory of Pitch-Scales."[27] One such scale, the scale of "three tonics," consists of three successive statements of this motive separated by major thirds; another, with "four tonics," comprises four such statements at successive minor thirds.[28] Both scales (exx. 121a–b) contain all twelve notes of the chromatic scale (the first with no repetitions). A rhythmicized version of the four-tonic scale is the basis of the "application derived from a well-known motif" (ex. 121c), where Schillinger mentions the song by name. The first setting applies the four-tonic scale straightforwardly; the second has the segments in reverse order, each permuted to start with a different note.

This intersection between one of Gershwin's most popular songs and the work of Joseph Schillinger was a likely starting point for the *"I Got Rhythm" Variations,* which Gershwin composed for a concert tour that began on January 14, 1934, just eight days after he finished the full score. Like *Rhapsody in Blue,* the *Variations* were conceived not for a standard symphony orchestra but for a smaller, more specialized ensemble — in this case, a touring orchestra of about thirty pieces (the Leo Reisman Orchestra), to be conducted by Charles Previn (uncle of André Previn), whose association with Gershwin extended

a. three tonics, four units (fig. 36, 1: 156)   b. four tonics, four units (fig. 36, 1: 157)

c. "Application derived from a well-known motif" (fig. 41, 1: 164): George Gershwin's "I Got Rhythm"

theme

four-tonic setting (without permutations)

four-tonic setting (with circular permutations)

Example 121. *The Schillinger System of Musical Composition:* "Theory of Pitch-Scales"

back to 1919 and *La-La-Lucille!,* the composer's first full-length show.[29] Also like *Rhapsody,* the piece opens with a clarinet solo.[30]

This solo, six measures in length, and the two bars in the solo piano that follow it, comprise the first phase of the introduction that precedes the variation theme. This eight-measure span is identical to a passage cited by Schillinger to illustrate "geometrical expansion" (bk. 3, chap. 2), by which Schillinger means the process of multiplying the intervals in a melody by a constant greater than one—a process that he likens to the selective stretching of a visual image in one of its dimensions.[31] Schillinger was evidently intrigued by the capacity of this process to change the stylistic character of a given melody without changing its inherent proportions, a quality that he demonstrates by transforming several themes of Bach (from the Two-Part Inventions and the *Well-Tempered Clavier*) by doubling the intervals between consecutive notes (ex. 122).

A corollary principle involves the successive expansion of a motive by successively larger coefficients; in this regard Schillinger cites the passage shown in example 123, which successively multiplies the note-to-note intervals of the "I Got Rhythm" motive by coefficients of 1, 2, and 3 in the original rhythm, then by 5, 3, 2, and 1 in even sixteenths. This illustration of intervallic expansion followed by contraction is identical to the piano-to-clarinet solo that opens the *"I Got Rhythm" Variations.*[32]

That Schillinger labels the passage "Geometric expansions of George

Example 122. *The Schillinger System of Musical Composition:* "Geometric expansion of Bach WTCI, theme from fugue 2" (excerpt from fig. 42, 1: 216)

pitch interval:	2 - 3 - 2	4 - 6 - 4	6 - 9 - 6	10 - 15 -10	6 - 9 - 6	4 - 6 - 4	2 - 3 - 2
multiplier:	1	2	3	5	3	2	1

Example 123. *"I Got Rhythm" Variations,* introduction (same as *The Schillinger System of Musical Composition,* fig. 43, 1: 217; annotations mine)

Gershwin's 'I Got Rhythm'" (and not, say, "Introduction to George Gershwin's *'I Got Rhythm' Variations*") suggests that perhaps he, not Gershwin, was its author. Suffice it to say that Schillinger and Gershwin were equally drawn to the symmetry and versatility of the seminal four-note motive, which constitutes four-fifths of the pentatonic scale, to which Gershwin had often turned in the past. As a result, the *"I Got Rhythm" Variations* are an exemplary, if lighthearted, reflection of the conflict between the new techniques that Gershwin endeavored to absorb during his mature period and the tonal procedures to which he still owed allegiance.

The permuted, four-tonic setting of the "I Got Rhythm" motive (ex. 121c, bottom staff) is the subject of another of Schillinger's examples (ex. 124) in

Example 124. *The Schillinger System of Musical Composition:* four-tonic scale, segments permuted and verticalized (fig. 61, 1: 177)

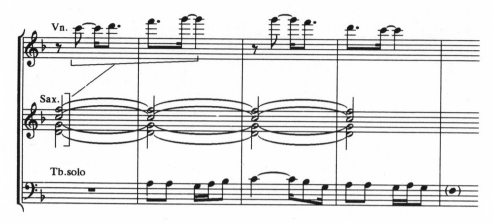

Example 125. *"I Got Rhythm" Variations,* introduction (R1 + 7)

which the reordered segments are each harmonized by chords containing the same four notes (more precisely, pitch classes). The horizontal and vertical dimensions are similarly integrated in a passage from *Variations* (ex. 125), where the notes of the descant (C, D, F, and G) form a sustained chord in the inner voices while a lower counterpoint has the closing portion of the refrain.[33]

Also demonstrated within the course of the introduction is the extent to which Gershwin had absorbed Schillinger's concept of pitch-scales. Just prior to the close of the introduction on the dominant of F is a melodic sequence alternating major seconds and minor thirds (ex. 126), which can be interpreted either as three interlocking statements of the "I Got Rhythm" motive or as two disjunct statements a minor seventh apart, separated by a minor third. The latter is the best guess as to how Gershwin saw it, inasmuch as the upper counterpoint takes four notes at a time and presents them in reverse order (or inverts them at the upper fifth, which yields the same result). The four notes that follow reverse the process on the notes G, F, D, C, producing, in the upper counterpoint, the "I Got Rhythm" motive in its original order and home key. The harmony also returns to the orbit of F major at that point, with the added-sixth chord on B♭ (or II$^6_5$) in preparation for the sustained dominant that heralds the variation theme.

The theme proper, in the solo piano, reveals in some subtle ways how Gershwin thought about the song. Not the least of these is the additional emphasis given the ambiguous note C, which competes with A for the role of primary melodic tone (cf. chap. 6). In the variation-theme setting (analyzed in ex. 127), C anchors a countermelody that migrates from the tenor to an elevated bass in the first two statements of the A section, then to an upper counterpoint in the reprise, where c^2, as an upper-voice pedal point or cover

Example 126. *"I Got Rhythm" Variations,* introduction (R1 + 12)

tone, foreshadows the high C of the coda. Meanwhile, in the B section, the original bass pattern of fifths (cf. ex. 66) is replaced by a chromatic descent from g, whose goal, the bass note C, is deflected an octave downward via the arpeggiation d♭–G♭–C. (The latter, shown in the analysis as a registrally expanded upper neighbor, emphasizes C still further.) Another chromatically descending line a tritone higher can be traced in the tenor voice beginning with c#[1].

The inventive spirit of the introduction returns with the ensuing transition and first variation. The expected close of the theme on the tonic (shown in parentheses in ex. 127) is replaced by a pentatonic passage that merely alludes to it. In this passage (see ex. 128, first three measures) an ostinato based on C–D–F–G is supported below by a homophonic setting of the same motive, extended to include the transposition G–A–C–D. All four voices of this setting use the same pitch material, the pentatonic scale C–D–F–G–A. But

Example 127. *"I Got Rhythm" Variations:* analysis of theme (piano solo)

Example 128. *"I Got Rhythm" Variations,* transition to variation 1

Example 129. *"I Got Rhythm" Variations,* finale: canonic use of motive

there is one additional feature: every vertical but one (the fourth), if put in close position, contains one of the two transpositions of the "I Got Rhythm" motive cited above.

The remainder of the transition uses chromatic material: first the chromatic wedge, introduced at R3+5; next the major sevenths in alternating directions, introduced at R4+3 over a dominant pedal. These two ideas are the mainstay of the counterpoint in variation 1, which begins at R5. The contrast of this chromatic counterpoint to the restatement of the song below it extends to rhythm as well as pitch in that its attack points occur on points of rest in the theme. This feature is traceable to another Schillinger technique, the "coordination of time structures".[34]

The second variation, a *valse triste,* takes its inspiration from the triple durations embedded in the rhythmic motive that runs throughout the song.[35] Like the ensuing "Chinese" variation, it lacks any reference to the song's middle section. Though the exaggerated gestures of these variations place them in the realm of entertainment music, the fact remains that each one addresses a central structural feature of the theme. The pentatonic focus of the Chinese variation continues in what Gershwin called the "modal variation," which therefore is heard more as a continuation and less as a distinct entity. It sports the novelty feature of two simultaneous key signatures in the piano part, in which the two hands play a pentatonic counterpoint in parallel minor seconds.[36]

These central variations (variations 2–4) make an orderly tonal excursion away from the tonic F: to D (the waltz), to a quasi–B major (the Chinese variation), to G (the modal variation). The tonic key returns in what Gershwin originally designated the "hot variation finale," which in its finished form turned into a languid, bluesy (and presumably hot) variation followed by a lengthy Allegro, the latter comprising yet another variation (in D♭) leading to a rousing peroration in F. (The two keys D♭ and F are employed the same way in the arrangement of "I Got Rhythm" in *George Gershwin's Song Book*, written two years earlier.) The portion in D♭ has a bass ostinato comprising two interlocked representations of the "I Got Rhythm" motive in eighth notes, over which the piano plays the same motive in its original durational pattern, with the left hand in contrary motion.[37] Twelve measures after the piano's entrance, a rhythmic complement to the piano part is supplied by a quartet of trumpets and trombone, using a technique that recalls variation 1. The result (ex. 129) is a complete contrapuntal matrix based solely on that all-pervasive, symmetrical motive of seemingly endless possibilities.

10 *Porgy and Bess*

t was Gershwin's crowning achievement: a grand coalescence of inspired melodies and intellectual sophistication. It was the best of Gershwin past and present. It was an idea that had preoccupied Gershwin for some time—even longer if one considers *Blue Monday,* his first attempt at African-American folk opera, a precursor. He had received a copy of DuBose Heyward's *Porgy* from Ira's sister-in-law Emily Paley and her husband Lou in 1926 and wrote to Heyward about doing an opera immediately upon finishing the book. Though receptive to the proposal, Heyward deferred for the time being to his wife Dorothy's nonmusical dramatization, which the Theatre Guild produced in 1927. Gershwin, meanwhile, bided his time, aware that he was not yet up to the task technically. He remained in contact with the Heywards in the intervening years, eventually signing a contract with the Theatre Guild in October 1933.[1] The idea of adding Bess's name to the title was Heyward's.[2] Gershwin, on the other hand, introducing a recorded rehearsal on July 19, 1935, still referred to his opera as "Porgy."[3]

Porgy and Bess, with book by Heyward and lyrics by Heyward and Ira Gershwin, opened on Broadway on October 10, 1935, just a month after the completion of the orchestral score.[4] Gershwin had written an opera, not a Broadway show, however, and it would be four decades before a truly complete production would take place.[5] Though defenses can be made for the cuts in the Broadway version, which, obviously, were made with the composer's knowledge,[6] there is the equally obvious fact that Gershwin never altered his score. The score stands, therefore, as the best representation of what Gershwin ultimately wanted to hear.

Heyward's story, gleaned from his orphaned childhood on the streets of Charleston, centers on the courtyards of Catfish Row, a neighborhood of mansions-turned-tenements not unlike an actual part of the city known as Cabbage Row.[7] The relief locale, Kittiwah Island, also has its basis in fact.[8] Porgy, loosely modeled on a person known in the community as Goat Sammy (Sammy Smalls), is steadfastly devoted to Bess, a woman whose virtue is alternately compromised by Crown, the villain of the piece, and by Sporting Life, who plies her with "happy dust" and promises of the good life in New York. Chief among the supporting characters are Robbins, killed by Crown in the first act; Serena, Robbins's widow ("My Man's Gone Now"); Jake, Catfish Row's model citizen and general commentator ("A Woman Is a Sometime Thing"); and Clara, whose "Summertime" puts the finish on the opening sequence.[9]

At the start of this sequence is an orchestral introduction whose initial run, trill, and ostinato comprise one of Gershwin's two all-time best beginnings (the other, that of *Rhapsody in Blue,* consists of a trill and a run). The run, covering a registrally expanded form of the sixth A♯–F♯, suggests the dominant of B. The latter is the dominant of E, the key suggested by the four-sharp signature and, in a broad sense, the home key of the opera. The introduction remains centered on this dominant, which is taken up by Jasbo Brown's piano solo and resolved to E minor. Midway through the Jasbo Brown section (at R8) the tonal center shifts from E to G, and in the transition to "Summertime" it moves to B. The result is a broad harmonic sweep—what Schenker would call a bass arpeggiation—that embraces an E-minor triad.

Despite the overall tonal platform, several themes, not to mention entire sections, invoke procedures that go beyond triadic tonality. A case in point is the introduction, where angular sixteenth notes in the treble are shortly joined below by a neighbor-note figure in fourth-chords (ex. 130). The latter is counterpointed in contrary motion by a two-voice layer (not shown in the published piano-vocal score) that moves from the tritone A–D♯ to the fifth A–E. Although the latter could be construed as implying a progression from V⁷ to IV, the fourth-chords are harmonically ambiguous. They do relate intervallically to the ostinato above, whose first three notes, F♯, G♯, and

Example 130. *Porgy and Bess,* introduction, mm. 8–9

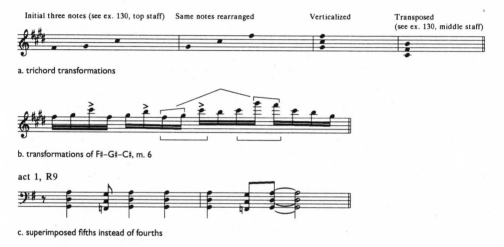

Example 131. *Porgy and Bess,* introduction

C♯, can be rearranged into the same vertical formation of two superimposed fourths (ex. 131a).

This three-note cell appears in several guises. For example, in m. 6, two measures before the entrance of the fourth-chords, a register change transforms a representation of this trichord as a major second plus perfect fourth into a perfect fourth plus major second—in other words, from a prime to an inverted form—without a change in pitch-class content (ex. 131b). Later, after Jasbo Brown and the chorus get under way, the vertical perfect fourths are expressed as vertical perfect fifths (ex. 131c).

The other significant trichord in the opening ostinato, F♯–G♯–B, combines with F♯–G♯–C♯ (and with its intervallic equivalent F♯–B–C♯) to form F♯–G♯–B–C♯, which is none other than a transposition of the "I Got Rhythm" tetrachord.[10] Yet its use here does not recall "I Got Rhythm" as much as it does the opening of Stravinsky's *Petroushka* (ex. 132).[11] There, as in *Porgy,* this

Example 132. Stravinsky, *Petroushka*, I, mm. 1–11

tetrachord (now at the transposition D–E–G–A) is the basis for a perpetual-motion ostinato in sixteenth notes, to which various elements are added as the scene progresses from the general to the specific. Though the scene is different, the function of the music is substantially the same.

Combined with this broad influence from Stravinsky is the more immediate presence of Joseph Schillinger, which can be seen in Gershwin's predilection for symmetry not only in matters of pitch but in certain rhythmic patterns. One such pattern exists in the way pitch and dynamic accents in the ostinato combine to form groups of three, three, and two sixteenths followed by two, three, and three—and vice versa. Thus, in the notation used by Schillinger and learned by Gershwin, the first measure of this pattern translates into (3 + 3 + 2) + (2 + 3 + 3); the second, (2 + 3 + 3) + (3 + 3 + 2). Each pattern is symmetrical within itself and with respect to the other (ex. 133). Analogously, the introduction as a whole is balanced by the reciprocal reprise which begins at m. 22 (ex. 134), in which the fourth-chords are on top, their supporting intervals in the middle, and the sixteenths on the bottom. The middle layer differs from its counterpart in the opening in that the fifth A–E is replaced by a second iteration of the tritone A–D♯.

Yet another change takes place in the same pair of chords with the be-

Example 133. *Porgy and Bess,* introduction: rhythmic analysis of ostinato

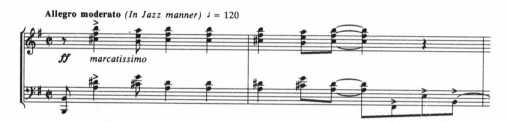

Example 134. *Porgy and Bess,* introduction, mm. 22–23

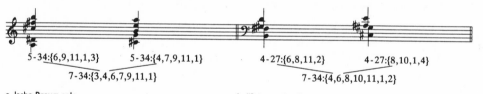

Example 135. *Porgy and Bess,* I.1, mm. 1–2 (Jasbo Brown solo)

5-34:{6,9,11,1,3} 5-34:{4,7,9,11,1}	4-27:{6,8,11,2} 4-27:{8,10,1,4}
7-34:{3,4,6,7,9,11,1}	7-34:{4,6,8,10,11,1,2}
a. Jasbo Brown solo	b. "Summertime"

Example 136. Comparison of chord pairs in *Porgy and Bess*

ginning of Jasbo Brown's piano solo (ex. 135): the replacement of C♯–F♯, in the lower stratum of the second chord, by C♯–G. Because of the inherent invertibility of the tritone, this effectively turns the second chord into a transposition of the first, despite the semblance of difference created by the contrary motion (ex. 136a). Closely related is the chordal ostinato that accompanies much of "Summertime" (ex. 136b). As with the Jasbo Brown chords, there are two strata representing the same two classes of interval— the tritone (now spelled as a diminished fifth) and the perfect fourth (now expressed as a fifth); moreover, the interval formed by the pitches B and F♯ continues to be central. The two "Summertime" chords are also identical intervallically—more clearly so, as the parallel motion is no longer masked by contrary voice leading. As shown in example 136, their combined content of seven notes (E,F♯,G♯,A♯,B,C♯,D) displays, in the opposite order, the same intervals as the content of the two chords in the Jasbo Brown section (D♯,E,F♯,G,A,B,C♯). The intersection of these seven-note sets (B,C♯,E,F♯) is yet another representation of the "I Got Rhythm" tetrachord featured in the opening ostinato.[12]

The music of the introduction has a twofold role in the rest of the opera. First, there are the literal recurrences, which are very selective. The chordal component in its initial rhythm, restated and developed in the Jasbo Brown music, makes no literal appearances thereafter. The sixteenth-note ostinato returns in its original form only four times: twice in the huge first scene (at R69 and R120) and twice in the last (at R128 and R176), always in association with Porgy and his themes. The last occurrence leads into Porgy's (and the opera's) final song, "Oh Lawd, I'm On My Way," in which the first measure of the ostinato returns twice in rhythmic augmentation as a countermelody.

In contrast, the various nonliteral spinoffs of the two components number a multitude. Fourth-chords, alternating a whole step apart but without their earlier rhythm, form an accompaniment ostinato in Jasbo Brown's solo shortly after the entrance of the voices (ex. 137a),[13] and at the close of act 1—the latter in the reiterated accent pattern 3 + 3 + 2 (ex. 137b). A triplet version of this ostinato closes the first scene of act 2, between and following reprises of "Bess, You Is My Woman Now" and "I Got Plenty o' Nuttin'" (ex. 137c).[14] A final incarnation joins the fourth-chords with a question-and-answer, mirror-image theme, whose pitches draw on a transposition of the four-note set featured in the sixteenth notes of the introduction (ex. 138). This last example, from the instrumental coda to "Good Mornin' Sistuh," the first song of the opera's final scene, prefaces Porgy's return and the first of that scene's two literal reprises of the opening sixteenths.

Allusions to the latter come in two other important themes. The first immediately follows "Summertime" as the action shifts from Clara and her baby to the men's crap game. This theme continues the earlier figure's sixteenth notes (the rests are filled by complementary sixteenth-note drumbeats) as well as its focus on the trichords F♯–G♯–C♯ and F♯–B–C♯ (ex. 139a).[15] Abandoned after five more bars, it returns later in the scene, transposed, as the crap game evolves into a fight, leading eventually to the fugue that accompanies Crown's murder of Robbins (and, in its reprise in the third act, Porgy's

a. I.I (Jasbo Brown solo)

b. I.2 ("Leavin' for the Promise' Lan'")

c. II.I (instrumental coda)

Example 137. *Porgy and Bess:* fourth-chord ostinati

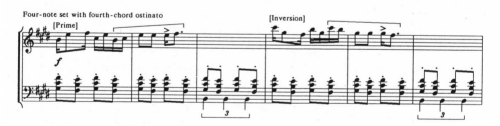

Example 138. *Porgy and Bess,* III.3: "Good Mornin', Sistuh," coda (R125 + 2)

(F#,G#,C#)
(G#,C#,D#)

a. *Porgy and Bess,* I.I, R22 + I (crap game theme)

Example 139.

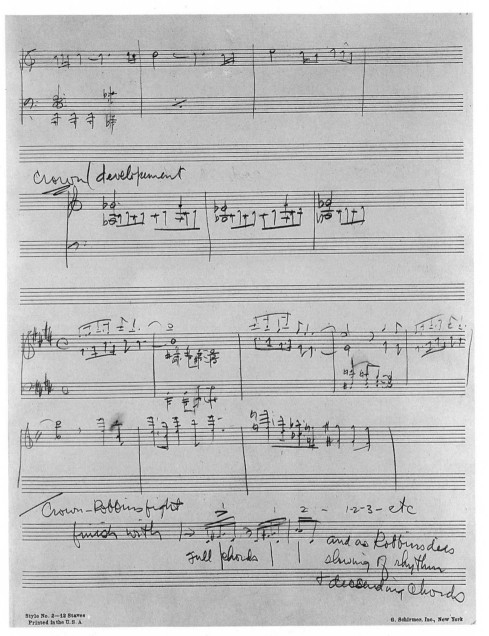

Example 139. (*continued*)

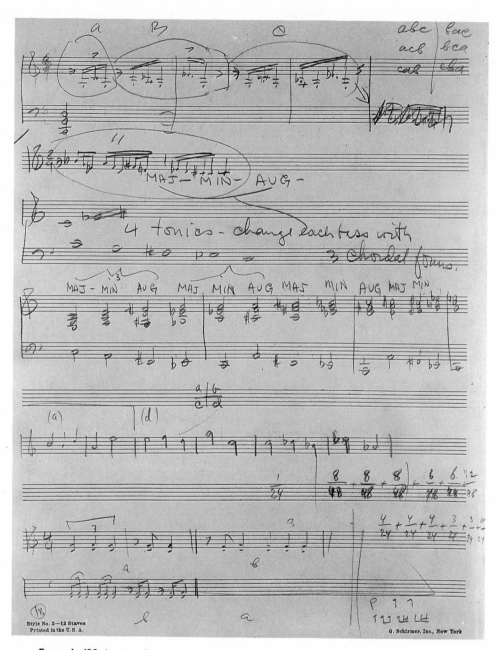

Example 139. (continued)

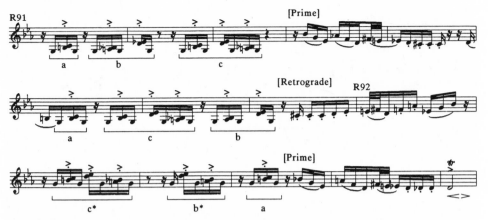

c. *Porgy and Bess*, I.1, R91–R92+5 (crap game continues; permutations of a, b, c)

Example 139. (*continued*)

killing of Crown). A telling view of how Gershwin saw this theme appears on two consecutive pages in the *Tune Book* of 1933–37 (ex. 139b),[16] where it is marked, first, by the number of accents in each group of notes (1, 2, and 3), then by letters denoting each group (*a*, *b*, and *c*). Gershwin follows this with the various possible permutations of these letters, some of which occur in the development of the theme prior to the fugue (ex. 139c), though not in the fugue itself. (Notice, in ex. 139c, that in their last ordering, *cba*, the segments marked by asterisks are retrograded as well, except for segment *a*, which is symmetrical. The consequent portion of the crap game theme, though not included in the permutation process, is retrograded in its second statement.) At the climactic moment where Crown kills Robbins (and later, when Porgy kills Crown), the low brasses and bass drum sound out groups of one, two, and three eighth notes, in direct correspondence to the pattern of accents in the crap game theme (ex. 139d).

Also reminiscent of the opening are the perpetual sixteenths, closely allied in tempo, pitch, and interval content, that follow the "Roll dem Bones" chorus at R29 (ex. 140, motive *a*). Entering below this three-voice counterpoint is a preview of "A Woman Is a Sometime Thing" (motive *b*), which leads into a marchlike tune spanning the tritone F♯–C (motive *c*) accompanied by alternating chords related by the same tritone both horizontally and vertically (motive *d*).[17] The F♯–C relation also serves, via C as dominant, to connect this basically F♯-minor music to F, the initial key of the ensuing humoresque (ex. 141a),[18] the final theme in the group.

This collection of generalized Catfish Row themes reappears intact, at

Example 140. *Porgy and Bess*, I.1, R29: transitional music, components identified

original pitch levels, at the start of act 3, scene 2, whereas elsewhere its constituent parts recur individually. Of these, the humoresque emerges most consistently as having a life of its own. At both its first appearance and its tranquil recasting in act 2, scene 3 (ex. 141b) it accompanies sung dialogue or arioso (a major component of the opera), mainly by Jake, the de facto voice of Catfish Row. At the opening curtain of the latter scene, after the chimes of St. Michael's sound the half-hour (represented by a repeated, six-note fourth-chord, as befits the return of the locale from Kittiwah Island to Catfish Row), a solo English horn plays the initial phrase three times, its intervals progressively larger with each repetition (ex. 141c).

Allegretto ♩ = 108   R35

p espressivo

a. initial appearance under vocal (I.1, R34)

Larghetto ♩. = 60

mp calmato e semplice

b. "Calmato" setting (II.3, R172)

Adagio ♩ = 56   R171

mp

c. interval expansion (II.3, R171–4)

Example 141. *Porgy and Bess:* humoresque theme and variants

This last represents another use of the process of interval expansion, seen earlier in the *"I Got Rhythm" Variations* (ex. 123); here, however, the technique is applied only approximately. It can be argued that its dramatic role as a reflection of Bess's state of confusion following her capitulation to Crown is better served by such an approximation than by anything precise (its second appearance shortly afterward, at R181, is as an accompaniment to Maria's observation that all is not right with Bess). It is also apparent, here and elsewhere in *Porgy and Bess,* that Gershwin had absorbed Schillinger's technical repertory to an extent that allowed him to adapt it to his own needs.

"My Man's Gone Now," the celebrated aria from the first act, is another case in point. Cast in a traditional AABA form, it builds on what is sure to have been Gershwin's favorite melodic interval, the minor third, with the simple palindrome E–G–G–E. The inherent immobility of this motive, appropriate to the song's expression of abject grief, is reflected on another plane by a rhythmic pattern (established in the introduction and continuing in the accompaniment) of reversed durations of one and four eighth notes alternating with eighth-note downbeats (ex. 142). This pattern, expressible in eighth-note units as 1 + (1 + 4) + 1 + (4 + 1), is stated completely in the introduction's first two measures, followed by the first half of the pattern in the third. The fourth measure has a little palindromic pattern of its own, (1 + 2) + (2 + 1), which also underlies the odd-numbered measures of the B section (ex. 143). Yet, a lament needs to be simple, and so these rhythmic patterns remain confined to the accompaniment. Moreover, Gershwin made it a point to revert to a straight three quarters per measure at the cadences.

Example 142. *Porgy and Bess:* "My Man's Gone Now," introduction and mm. 1–4

Example 143. *Porgy and Bess:* "My Man's Gone Now," mm. 29–32

Although Gershwin's long-standing fascination with rhythm was obviously sparked by what he had learned from Schillinger, another Gershwin hallmark in *Porgy and Bess* of a more personal nature most likely would have come through whether Schillinger was around or not: the later emergence of motives and themes from material stated early in the opera. These motives and themes not only recur; they *precur*. The premier example of this from Gershwin's earlier work is *Rhapsody in Blue,* where the technique was no doubt applied intuitively. The additional element of drama, with its attendant nonmusical associations, makes the field infinitely more fertile—to say nothing of the sheer size of *Porgy and Bess* and the amount of time that went into its execution. These factors combine to form a vast web of connections, with numerous glances forward and back.

One instance was already observed in example 140, where one component of a recurring, generalized Catfish Row sequence (motive *b*) previews the refrain of "A Woman Is a Sometime Thing," sung shortly thereafter by Jake—the chief exemplar among the generalized Catfish Row characters—to Clara's baby (the same baby to whom Clara sings "Summertime," the exemplary Catfish Row song). But this is not all: the same melodic profile returns in Sporting Life's "It Ain't Necessarily So," introduced in act 2, scene 2. As if to reinforce this connection, both "A Woman is a Sometime Thing" and "It Ain't Necessarily So" are in the same key, G minor, in a range that overlaps Jake's baritone and Sporting Life's tenor (ex. 144).

a. "A Woman Is a Sometime Thing," refrain, mm. 1–4

b. "It Ain't Necessarily So," mm. 1–8

Example 144. *Porgy and Bess:* melodic comparisons

Other examples involve parts of themes. The consequent portion of the Catfish Row humoresque (ex. 141a, last four measures) reappears later in the first scene of act 1 as a consequent to Porgy's entrance theme (see 149). It can also be found in a two-measure transitional passage in Jasbo Brown's solo (ex. 145 at "N.B."). An inkling of Crown's theme comes five measures earlier, where a riff in the treble reiterates a filled-in minor third descending from B♭ (ex. 146a). The same figure returns, first to confirm G as an intermediate harmonic goal (ex. 146b), later as an ingredient in the crap game fugue (ex. 146c). Its association with Crown, established in the fugue, is confirmed by another extended treatment in act 2, scene 2, which includes a juxtaposition of inverted and prime forms as well as a reminder of the rhythmic motive—the repeated chord with increasing attack points—that accompanies the murder at the climax of the fugue (ex. 147).

Example 145. *Porgy and Bess*, I.1, R2 + 5: transitional passage in Jasbo Brown solo

a. Jasbo Brown solo (I.1, R2)

b. Jasbo Brown solo (I.1, R8 – 1)

c. fugue theme (I.1, R127)

Example 146. *Porgy and Bess*: Crown's theme and its precursors

Not surprisingly, it is Porgy's material that gets the most glances forward and back. His entrace, heralded by a reprise of the opening of the introduction (whose run, trill, and sixteenth-note ostinato can be said, in retrospect, to denote Porgy himself as well as Catfish Row), is represented by a theme whose horizontal and vertical dimensions combine to symbolize the E–major-minor complex that dominates the opera as a whole (ex. 148). Ten bars later (ex. 149), Porgy's line "Luck been ridin' high with Porgy today," accompanied by his entrance theme in its home key, is framed by a retrograde inversion of the opening pitches (B–G♯–B–E as opposed to B–E–G–E) that

Example 147. *Porgy and Bess,* II.2, R153: Crown advances and threatens Bess

preserves the fifth E–B while replacing G♮ with G♯; in so doing, it takes the theme's major-minor duality one step further. The consequent portion of the entrance theme, which occurs here for the first time (ex. 149, fourth measure), is—like the consequent portion of the humoresque (see the last four measures of ex. 141a)—a variant of the passage from Jasbo Brown's solo cited in example 145. Much later, following Porgy's return in the last scene of the opera, his entrance theme and its supporting verticals appear in inverted and retrograde forms under his sung dialogue (ex. 150).

Example 148. *Porgy and Bess*, I.1, R70: Porgy's entrance theme

Example 149. *Porgy and Bess*, I.1, R71 + 4: "Luck Been Ridin' High with Porgy Today"

Example 150. *Porgy and Bess*, III.3, R131 + 4: inversion and retrograde of Porgy's entrance theme

Night time, day time, he got to trab- ble dat lone- some road,____

a. Porgy, I.1 ("They Pass By Singin'," mm. 12–15)

I ain' go- in'! You hear me say-in', if you ain' go- in', wid you I'm stay- in'.

b. Bess, II.2 ("Bess, You Is My Woman Now," mm. 33–36)

Example 151. *Porgy and Bess:* melodic recurrence

Another instance of partial recurrence involves what first appears as the setting of the words "Night time, day time, he got to trabble dat lonesome road," in Porgy's arioso "They Pass By Singin'" (ex. 151a), whose orchestral reprise, a fourth higher, closes the first scene of act 1. The same melody returns in act 2 just prior to "Bess, You Is My Woman Now," and within the song we hear it yet again, with a slight rhythmic shift, in Bess's line that begins "I ain' goin'!" (ex. 151b). This relationship is justified dramatically in that the words sung by Bess in effect answer the loneliness earlier expressed by Porgy; musically, it is unmistakable.

Porgy's alternative main theme, of at least comparable stature to the theme that marks his entrance, is "I Got Plenty o' Nuttin'," whose working title, as evidenced by a sketch in Gershwin's *Tune Book,* was simply "Porgy," with "Plenty O' Nuthin'" added in parentheses and initialed by Ira Gershwin.[19] Although the song does not appear until the second act, its harmonic and melodic components occur, separately but unmistakably, in the first. The chord changes—in G major, the key Gershwin will eventually use for the song—accompany the recitative "Oh Little Stars," which Porgy incants as he shoots the dice in the first scene of act 1 (ex. 152). When he wins the pot for the

Example 152. *Porgy and Bess,* I.1, R81: recitative, "Oh Little Stars"

second time, we hear the first line of the "Plenty o' Nuttin'" melody—also in G—over an ongoing restatement of the Catfish Row sixteenths (ex. 153).[20] Preceding this is a combination of the opera's opening material with Porgy's entrance theme, which Porgy himself counterpoints (at "Turn me loose!") with a major variant.

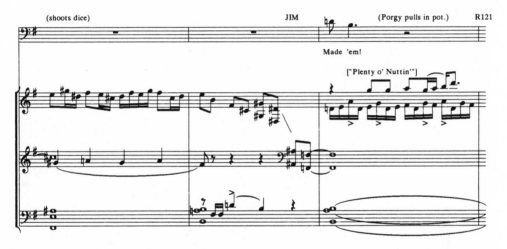

Example 153. *Porgy and Bess,* I.1, R120: themes in counterpoint

The first phrase of "I Got Plenty o' Nuttin'" resumes its role as an adjunct to Porgy's entrance theme on his return in act 3, where it is hard as a countermelody in the horns (ex. 154a).[21] As if to confirm its special status, a final reference occurs in the course of a running counterpoint to "Oh Lawd, I'm On My Way," where the reference is followed by the first line of "Bess, You Is My Woman Now" and by the opening Catfish Row sixteenths in augmentation (ex. 154b).[22] Thus, summarily and symbolically, Porgy's last song is united with his main arias from the two preceding acts as well as with the very beginning of the opera. The orchestral close completes the circle by linking "Bess, You Is My Woman Now" with Porgy's entrance theme.

In light of such compatibility, it should come as no surprise that these

a. III.3, R130 (small notes not in piano-vocal score): "I Got Plenty o' Nuttin'" as counterpoint (orchestral manuscript, p. 30)

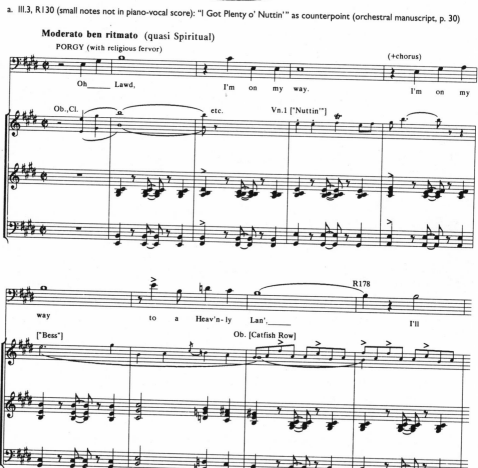

b. III.3, R177 (small notes not in piano-vocal score): "Oh Lawd, I'm on My Way" (orchestral manuscript, pp. 65–66)

Example 154. *Porgy and Bess*

melodies share a set of common characteristics. Porgy's entrance theme and "Oh Lawd, I'm On My Way" (his exit theme) both emphasize the fifth of the triad while differing in the quality of the third. Moreover, the conflict of the thirds within the entrance theme has multiple significance. The vertical major third, which may denote Porgy's tireless optimism, also lays the foundation for the major thirds in "Bess, You Is My Woman Now," whose sentiments are likewise. The latter song, whose full presentation in act 2, scene 1 begins in the tritone-related key of B♭, favors the major third melodically; the same interval also separates the successive choruses and, if taken in a descending direction—from B♭ to G♭ (the enharmonic equivalent of B♭–F♯)—separates the song's beginning and end. Connecting these starting and ending points is the overall melodic progression D–C♯, interpreted in example 155 as $\hat{3}$–flat $\hat{3}$

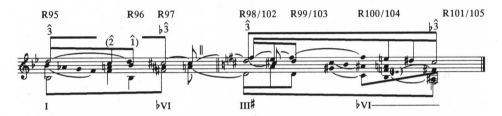

Example 155. *Porgy and Bess*, II.1: "Bess, You Is My Woman Now," schematic

in the background key of B♭. The enharmonic common tone (B♭–A♯) shared by the opening and closing chords provides yet another connection, which is strengthened by the dual attribute of B♭ as Porgy's first note and A♯ as Bess's highest.

Both species of third play a role in "I Got Plenty o' Nuttin," which is analyzed in example 156. In the outer sections the melody traces the major third from G to and from B, while the local harmonic progression spans the minor third to and from E—the same interval that separates the key of the song from that of the opera as a whole. The middle section prolongs F♯ by means of the major third F♯–D over a progression of a minor third to D from B, which is a major third away from the tonic G. Interestingly, it is the other third from G, E♭, that is the tonal center of the reprise at the end of act 2, scene 1.

The structural framework of *Porgy and Bess* remains tonal despite its flirtations with other procedures. One can therefore discuss the work in broad terms of keys and tonal functions, as summarized in example 157.[23] From this table one can see at a glance the bass arpeggiation spelling an E-minor triad that governs the opening sequence, as well as the predominance of E

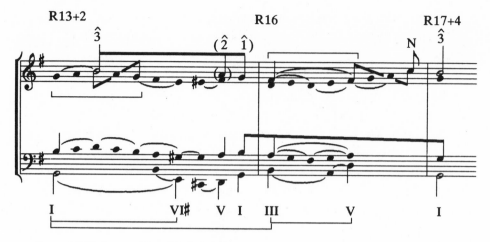

Example 156. *Porgy and Bess*, II.1: "I Got Plenty o' Nuttin'," schematic

Scene		Song/Aria/Theme	Key	Page
1.1	Catfish Row:	Introduction	E: V	1
	A Summer	Jasbo Brown Blues	e: I;	4
	Evening		g–G (flat 7)	15
		Summertime	b	18
		Roll Dem Bones	f♯	21
		Catfish Row music	f♯	23
		Humoresque: Seems Like These Bones (Jake)	F–D♭–F	36
		A Woman Is a Sometime Thing	g	42
		Here Come de Honey Man	G	50
		They Pass By Singin'	C	75
		Oh Little Stars [Plenty o' Nuttin changes]	G	81
		Fugue [Crown kills Robbins]	g	106
		Instrumental coda: They Pass By Singin'	F	
1.2	Serena's Room:	Gone, Gone, Gone	g	108
	The Following	Overflow	g	121
	Night	My Man's Gone Now	e	154
		Leavin' for the Promise' Lan'	F	166
II.1	Catfish Row:	Reprise: Catfish Row music	g	189
	A Month Later	It Take a Long Pull to Get There	G–g	190
		I Got Plenty o' Nuttin'	G	197
		Buzzard Song	a	235
		Bess, You Is My Woman Now	B♭–D–F♯	252

Example 157. *Porgy and Bess*: scenes, songs, and keys

Example 157. (*continued*)

major at the end of the opera. The most frequently occurring tonal center, G, has two functions: in some contexts, as in the Jasbo Brown section and in the sequence ending with "My Man's Gone Now," it is a third away from E; in others, as in the fugue (in both the first-act and third-act versions), it occurs as a point on the circle of fifths leading to either C or to F by way of C. Among the secondary keys in the opera, F and B♭ emerge as the most important. Both scenes of act 1 end in F; in act 2, a reintroduction of that key sets the stage for Porgy's portion of "Bess, You Is My Woman Now" in B♭. There, in the emotional centerpiece of act 2, B♭ initiates a large-scale progression of major thirds to F♯. This contrasts with its earlier role in the Jasbo Brown section as the third of G minor, which in turn is a minor third above E.

More could be said about the various connections, musical and dramatic, motivic and tonal, that comprise the opera *Porgy and Bess.* But no matter how coherent the whole, it is the eloquence of the various parts that ultimately makes the work worthwhile. This is especially so with *Porgy and Bess,* which for more than forty years survived on the basis of individual songs and abridged performances—presentations that only added fuel to the misconception that Gershwin, talented songwriter though he may have been, was incapable of producing anything that could pass analytical muster as a large work.

Another hindrance to a full appreciation of *Porgy and Bess* has, ironically, been Gershwin's greatest strength: his overwhelming presence as an American original. There is a tendency to equate "original" with "primitive": apply the latter label and one no longer needs to examine the matter of artistic influence. But Gershwin knew and admired much in the works of others, and it stands to reason that such admiration would occasionally translate itself into a tangible musical presence—as, for example, that of Stravinsky, here and in *An American in Paris.*

There is another affinity, on the surface less likely but potentially more profound, with a composer whose very soul was opera. Gershwin met Alban Berg in Vienna on May 3, 1928; two days later he was invited to the apartment of Rudolf Kolisch, whose string quartet played Berg's *Lyric Suite* with the composer present. Gershwin, deeply moved by the work, came away with an autographed page and a pocket score, in addition to a signed photograph that he later had framed.[24] Impressed though he was, Gershwin was probably unaware of Berg's deep-seated love of numbers and symmetry, which would not be reflected in Gershwin's work for another few years and would come to him by way of Schillinger rather than Berg. Still, the rhythmic motive that is stated so starkly when Crown kills Robbins in the first scene of the first act, and which returns with fearful symmetry when Porgy kills Crown at the same point in the third, displays an uncanny parallel to Berg's second opera *Lulu,* whose first-to-third-act symmetry is also framed by a rhythmic fate motive. Berg had barely finished his masterpiece at the time of his death in December 1935, two months after Gershwin had completed *Porgy and Bess.* Not long thereafter, in Hollywood, Gershwin would come to know Berg's teacher, Arnold Schoenberg.

The song is ended, but as the songwriter wrote,
The melody lingers on.

"They Can't Take That Away from Me"
(*Shall We Dance,* 1937)

11 The Final Period

With his masterpiece now completed, Gershwin had to face the question of what to do next. The lack of instant box-office success for *Porgy and Bess,* combined with normal postpartum blues, led him into a profound retreat: a destructive encounter with psychotherapy; a disappointing Mexican vacation; and, in August 1936, a move to California, which entailed a separation from his longtime friend and confidant Kay Swift.[1] Once George, Ira, and Leonore Gershwin were settled in Beverly Hills, the two brothers returned to the work in which they were acknowledged masters: writing songs.

The products of this, the last year of George Gershwin's life, communicate style, grace, and consummate craftsmanship. Some songs, such as "Love Is Here to Stay" and "Love Walked In," are distinguished by sheer melodic eloquence; both were cited in chapter 2 (exs. 4–5) for clarity of linear progression and, in "Love Is Here to Stay," first-order arpeggiation. In others, among them "I've Got Beginner's Luck" and "Things Are Looking Up," Gershwin used unconventional phrase and period lengths, along with permutational devices attributable to Schillinger. Still others crossed into the realm of the art song in one or more aspects: the satirical waltz "By Strauss"; the madrigals "The Jolly Tar and the Milkmaid" and "Sing of Spring"; and "Hi-Ho!" and "Just Another Rhumba," both cast in large musical forms in which the piano has its own themes separate from the voice.[2] All but one were written for films: *Shall We Dance* (1937), starring Fred Astaire and Ginger Rogers and *A Damsel in Distress* (1937), starring Fred Astaire and Joan Fontaine, both produced by Pandro S. Berman for RKO Radio Pictures; and the posthumous *Goldwyn Follies* (1938).

"By Strauss" owes its existence to a request from Vincente Minnelli, who was putting together a new Broadway revue, and who had heard the Gershwins at the piano parodying the style of the Viennese waltz.[3] Minnelli's revue *The Show Is On,* with songs by various composers (including Richard Rodgers, Arthur Schwartz, and Gershwin intimates Harold Arlen and Vernon Duke), opened on Christmas 1936 and ran for 237 performances.[4] The song was revived in 1951 in Minnelli's film *An American in Paris.*[5]

As a piece of verbal and musical satire, "By Strauss" is a direct descendant of "Dancing in the Streets" from *Pardon My English,* specifically the *Tempo di Ländler* bridge (ex. 102). Musically it is, if anything, more subtle. With the setting of the phrase "Swinging to three-quarter time" (refrain, mm. 13–14), two bars of $\frac{3}{4}$ are effectively combined into one bar of $\frac{3}{2}$ through their accent pattern; the resumption of a true $\frac{3}{4}$ (mm. 15–16) coincides with the resolution to the dominant via the so-called German-sixth chord, a nineteenth-century cliché, whose emphasis is heightened by the registral transfer on the bass note D♭. At the close, following "Just give me an oom-pah-pah" (refrain, mm. 33–34), we hear, in a pair of inner voices, more than a hint of Wagner's "Tristan" motive—that hallmark of nineteenth-century Teutonism—counterpointed by its mirror image.

The song as a whole is in F major, with a strong presence of A minor in the verse. The balance between these two keys—I and III in the home key of F—is summarized by the eight-measure introduction, which returns intact as the second eight-measure period of the verse. The verse, analyzed in example 158, is distinguished by strong linear progressions that balance one another either by direction or by local key. In the first eight measures ("Away with the music of Broadway! / Be off with your Irving Berlin!") a descending fifth is answered by a descending fourth, both in A minor. In the second ("I'd give no quarter / To Kern or Cole Porter, / And Gershwin keeps pounding on tin."), a partial descent from the fifth of A minor is coupled with a complete one from the fifth of F. The note c^2, functioning doubly as

Example 158. "By Strauss": analysis of verse

$\hat{3}$ of A minor and $\hat{5}$ of the home key of F, is here judged to be the primary melodic tone, at least temporarily. (The main emphasis is on a^1 for most of the refrain, with c^2 reasserted toward the end.)

The second portion of the verse is characterized by broader strokes both harmonically and melodically. The f^1 reached in m. 15 is now taken back to c^2 in a large, ascending fifth-progression, supported by pedal points on I, V of

V, and V, with intermediate steps asserted on the downbeats of m. 17 ("How can I be civil . . . ?"), m. 23 (". . . souses"), and m. 25 ("Oh, give me the free 'n' easy . . ."); the goal note C (scale degree $\hat{5}$) is dramatized by the octave leap on "Strauss's" in m. 35. The concluding couplet ("Ya, ya, ya! / Give me oom-pah-pah!") bears the final descent of the verse, $\hat{5}$–$\hat{4}$–$\hat{3}$–$\hat{2}$, whose last step links with the refrain's initial emphasized note, f^1. This descending line is preceded by the upper neighbor to $\hat{5}$, which, with the intervening chromatic step, produces d^2–db^2–c^2, a motive which is echoed a fourth lower, four measures later, in the notes a^1–ab^1–g^1.

This is the same motive whose ascending form, with the accent on the chromatic passing note, produces the *Tristan* echo. Another manifestation can be seen in the liberal use of chromatic scale segments throughout the accompaniment. This is especially so in the verse, as witness the ascending chromatic dyads in mm. 1–2 (marked "N.B." in ex. 158), the descending dyads imitated in two inner voices in mm. 9–13, the inner voice d–db–c in mm. 22–23, and the bass A–Ab–G in mm. 30–31, to name a few. In mm. 5–7 of the refrain (analyzed in ex. 159), the melody note g^1 leads structurally to a^1 (ostensibly an inner voice) via the chromatic passing note $g\#^1$; next, in the accompaniment (beginning at m. 8), that chromatic path is reversed. Chromatics in the inner voices enrich each recurrence of the refrain's main theme, and the first and second endings make multiple references to the chromatic dyads, each in a different way, and to the thematically significant augmented ("German") sixth.

The core of Gershwin's final period is represented by the two Fred Astaire films *Shall We Dance* (whose initial working title was *Watch Your Step*) and *A Damsel in Distress*. Gershwin's association with Astaire extended back to the twenties—notably to the stage shows *Lady, Be Good!* (1924) and *Funny Face* (1927)—and he welcomed the opportunity to write for him in this different medium. The score of *Shall We Dance* ranks with the best of the Gershwin stage musicals; its songs include the standards "They All Laughed," "Let's Call the Whole Thing Off," and "They Can't Take That Away From Me." Gershwin also composed several of the dance and instrumental numbers, among them "Walking the Dog," subsequently published as "Promenade."

What would have been Astaire's first song in *Shall We Dance* was dropped from production.[6] "Hi-Ho!," an elaborate number about "at last" having "found" but not yet having met "her" (the Ginger Rogers character), is one of the longest songs Gershwin ever wrote. The refrain, sans verse (a rarity for Gershwin), comprises 118 measures, without repeat signs (a recapitulation of mm. 1–38 occurs in mm. 69–106 with new lyrics) plus a four-measure

Example 159. "By Strauss": analysis of refrain

introduction. The sections of the large ABA form (so labeled in Gershwin's manuscript) stand in the harmonic relationship I–♭VI–I.

The differences between the manuscript of "Hi-Ho!" and what came out in print thirty years later are similar to those in songs published within Gershwin's lifetime: First, the song is transposed from G to F, evidently in consideration of range (in other instances the published key has fewer acciden-

Example 160. "Hi-Ho!" introduction and mm. 1–10

tals). Second are various concessions to playability; four-note chords in the right hand with doubled soprano are reduced to three by omitting the doubling. An obvious capitulation to convention drops the first two measures of the introduction down an octave.

The A section of "Hi-Ho!" is through-composed, comprising four periods of varying lengths (ten, eight, eight, and sixteen measures, respectively) each initiated by the greeting that is the title of the song, set to a descending semitone and accompanied by the piano theme (marked *a* in ex. 160),[7] which is first heard in the introduction. At the end of the first ten measures is a new little theme in the piano (*b*), which returns at the close of the A section and continues through the B section, or bridge, as a cadential punctuation. The vocal melody, which is not stated again until m. 69,[8] features an ascent to scale degree $\hat{5}$ (d²).

This hint at word-painting—an ascending figure in an insouciantly optimistic lyric—acquires added strength in the retransition linking the B section with the recapitulation. A rising sequence of descending broken triads takes the voice to a heady g², and each step in the sequence is doubled—actually anticipated an eighth note earlier—by the right hand of the piano. The passage as Gershwin originally wrote it (ex. 161) exaggerates the climb by having the

Example 161. "Hi-Ho!" mm. 61–68 (retransition)

piano doubling an octave above the voice; since the voice is a tenor, the doubling is actually two octaves higher. In the published score, the right hand is brought down an octave and the syncopations on the high notes eliminated.[9] The climactic interval in the voice, the major third, returns at the end with the final "Hi-Ho!"

The first song in the finished picture, "I've Got Beginner's Luck,"[10] is faster-paced and more manageable in length. Its treatment in the film, symptomatic of what bothered Gershwin about working for the movies in general,[11] may have contributed to its relative (and undeserved) obscurity: Astaire and Rogers meet on the promenade deck, walking their dogs; Astaire sings the song to Rogers; the dogs howl.

The four-measure introduction to "Beginner's Luck," omitted in the film, illustrates one of the most interesting differences between a Gershwin manuscript and the same passage in the published score (ex. 162). The key is the

Example 162. "(I've Got) Beginner's Luck"

same in both, as is the top voice, which states the refrain theme a fifth higher. The verse, in D, prolongs the dominant of the refrain, which is in G; the introduction, prolonging A, functions as the dominant of that dominant. As published, the left hand is almost entirely diatonic, and its beginning on the fourth E–A, combined with the right hand's C♯, makes its harmonic role as V of D major clear from the start.

This is not so in the manuscript, where the left hand begins with E♭–A♭ instead of E–A, and where the ensuing parallel fourths descend chromatically rather than diatonically, arriving at G♯–C♯ instead of A–D on the down-beat of m. 3. The contents of m. 4 are the same in both versions (save for the minor detail of the location of the double bar, which Gershwin originally put after the pickup to the verse); what differs is the approach, which in the manuscript version is exclusively contrapuntal, connecting only with the tritone G–C♯ rather than a combination of this tritone with its harmonic root A, as in the published version. Along with the verse to "Blue Blue Blue" (ex. 103), this is the closest Gershwin ever came to atonality in his showtunes.

As for the song itself, the accompaniment to the syncopated, repeated notes of the verse, with bass D–D♯–E counterpointed by D–C♯–B in the bottom voice of the right hand (ex. 163), reaffirms Gershwin's continuing affinity

Example 163. "(I've Got) Beginner's Luck," verse, mm. 1–4

for inversional balance. The refrain, though in the AABA form of the standard thirty-two-measure chorus, allots only six measures each to the first two A sections, reducing the total number of measures to twenty-eight. But the six-measure stanzas occupy the same verbal space—four lines—as those of the eight-measure periods. This is accomplished by running the second and third lines together into a patter of syncopated eighths and quarters, with a breathless whole note at the end (see ex. 35). The corresponding whole notes in the first two stanzas (mm. 5 and 11) form the only rhyme ("you" / "blue") in the first twelve measures of the song.

The use of permutation comes with the fourth line in each of the first two stanzas, which is set apart both verbally and rhythmically. The line in question in stanza 1, "Gosh, I'm lucky!," uses the pitches D♯, E, A♯, and B; that of stanza 2, the synonymous "Gosh, I'm fortunate!," has A♯, B, and E—the same pitches minus one. As shown in example 164, the verticals supporting these pitches follow suit. Thus, if we assign the "Gosh, I'm lucky!" chords the numbers 1–2–3–4, then the ordering for "Gosh, I'm fortunate!" is

Example 164. "(I've Got) Beginner's Luck," refrain, mm. 1–12 (manuscript variants in small notes)

3–4–2.[12] Holding the two stanzas together through these disparate melodic and rhythmic shifts is an inner voice centered on the note b, whose progress is traced in example 164. The small note c^1 (mm. 2, 8) is part of this voice, as is the b on the downbeat of m. 13 (the beginning of the bridge). These notes are physically present in Gershwin's manuscript, and no doubt would appear in the published score if it were not for the need to eliminate stretches of more than an octave.

"Beginner's Luck" is not unique. One finds a similar situation with "They All Laughed" (ex. 165), whose manuscript and published versions are virtually identical in the right-hand part, which uses the opening melody of the refrain (whose pitches, D, E, G, A, B, are a strong reminder that Gershwin never quite abandoned the plagal pentatonicism that characterized the road to "I Got Rhythm"). The published version replaces the manuscript's alternating fourth-chords in mm. 1–2 (cf. ex. 137a) with 7–6 and 6–5 suspensions resolving to the triads I^6 and VI, respectively. The original introduction to each song holds functional harmony at bay until the fourth and last measure; the published version, in contrast, establishes a clear harmonic identification from the start.

Another companion piece is "Things Are Looking Up," whose strains accompany the opening credits in the next film, *A Damsel in Distress*. As with "Beginner's Luck," the verse is in D, the refrain in G. The beginning of the verse, with the vocal melody on a repeated A, reveals another point in com-

a. as published

b. as in manuscript

Example 165. "They All Laughed," introduction

mon. Parallel fourths are present also—not as baldly as in the original introductions of "Beginner's Luck" and "They All Laughed," but submerged, as it were, in a pair of inner voices, where they remain in the service of triadically-based harmonic progression (ex. 166). The appearance of C♮–F♮ within the context of the A7 chord in the second half of m. 1 gives the verse its initial "lift" and anticipates the actual harmonic shift to F♮ at m. 11.

Somewhat analogously, the period lengths established in the verse—ten and nine measures, respectively—forecast those used in the first half of the refrain (cf. 36). Just as the first two A sections of "Beginner's Luck" are shorter than normal, those in "Things are Looking Up" are longer: ten measures each, rather than eight. (In both cases, the B and the concluding A sections revert to eight-measure lengths.)

Evidence of permutational thinking, though less compelling than in "Beginner's Luck," may be found here as well. The title phrase "Things are looking up," with its five syllables, is initially set to the five notes G, A, F♯, D, and E. It returns at m. 7 as the beginning of the closing sentence, "Things are looking up since love looked up at me," with the same five pitches in a different order, G, A, E, F♯, and D, followed by an octave shift and a close on

Example 166. "Things Are Looking Up," verse, mm. 1–14 (text omitted)

the tonic (ex. 167a). The same sentence closes the second A section, leading upward rather than downward, with a field of four pitches rather than five (ex. 167b). The end of the final A section completes the transformation, with "Things are looking up" replaced by "Oh, I'm happy as a pup" and a melodic profile that moves directly to the fifth of the scale and descends linearly to $\hat{1}$ (ex. 167c). The accompaniment to this closing passage also represents a departure for this song; its chromatically descending major thirds and tritones hark back to parts of *Rhapsody* and the early songs.

This dualism is not an isolated instance. There is an autumnal quality to Gershwin's final period that extends to his brother's lyrics as well. The echoes of songs past are one aspect of this. "Nice Work If You Can Get It," from *A Damsel in Distress,* contains a well-known example at the end of the bridge, which asks the famous question, "Who could ask for anything more?"[13] An even stronger plug comes in "Slap That Bass," from *Shall We Dance,* whose bridge ends with a reference to "I Got Rhythm" that is both verbal and musical (ex. 168).

a. refrain, mm. 1–10

b. mm. 17–20

c. mm. 33–36 (second ending)

Example 167. "Things Are Looking Up," settings of title phrase

Example 168. "Slap That Bass," refrain, mm. 22–25

Although Gershwin, in the end, preferred writing for the stage than for films, the latter have the obvious advantage of being viewable in their original forms. Of the late films, *Shall We Dance* has a well-integrated score that comes through despite Gershwin's misgivings about the treatment of his material. That the picture showcased Hollywood's premiere song-and-dance couple also did not hurt. In this respect, *A Damsel in Distress,* which cast Astaire opposite the non-singing and mostly non-dancing Joan Fontaine, suffered by comparison. From the standpoint of musical style, however, *Damsel* was the more adventurous of the two. The presence of a madrigal group within the cast allowed for two very un-Hollywood-like period pieces, "The Jolly Tar and the Milkmaid" and "Sing of Spring." Moreover, Astaire's superb rendition of "A Foggy Day," with its atmospheric backdrop, made a welcome contrast to the way in which "I've Got Beginner's Luck" was literally thrown to the dogs in *Shall We Dance.*

The Goldwyn Follies (1938) was the last film on which the two brothers worked together. In keeping with the retrospective aspect of this final period, the film's revue format and catch-all cast recalled musical comedy's earlier days, when a show was nothing more than a vehicle for a collection of songs. George Gershwin's death in July 1937 left some work unfinished, and Ira called in Vernon Duke to complete the score.[14] Two more songs resulted from this collaboration, "Spring Again" and "I'm Not Complaining" (of which only the first was used), along with some ballet music. It is generally assumed that Duke also composed the verses to "I Was Doing All Right," "Love Walked In," and "Love Is Here to Stay," though this is not completely certain.[15] All three are general enough in appeal to be potential standards; the last two, of course, are actual ones.

Of all the songs written for *The Goldwyn Follies,* the one that least fits the "retro" mold was among those not used. "Just Another Rhumba" resembles "Hi-Ho!" in length, form, and pianistic scope; it was first published in 1959 and was included in a 1973 anthology.[16] Setting aside its extremely tongue-in-cheek lyric, which rhymes "rhumba" with the likes of "numbah," "slumbah," "dumbah," and the pièce de resistance, "Septumbah," the song is, at times, a work of grandeur. Its length, roughly the same as that of "Hi-Ho!," encompasses verse, refrain, and trio. The latter, a throwback to "Swanee"—the only other Gershwin song with this feature—has basically the same formal role as the large B section of "Hi-Ho!" As in "Hi-Ho!," the retransition at the end of this section is the high point, leading to a resumption of the opening music (ex. 169). The climactic chord, which resolves tonally as a dominant seventh with suspended fourth, is extended, accompanied by a fourth-rich

Example 169. "Just Another Rhumba" (unpublished 1937 version), trio, mm. 19–25 (retransition)

right hand, to a point where it begins to have a life of its own, alluding once again to the forays into quartal harmony cited earlier in this chapter. The recapitulation and the conclusion (not shown) further illustrate the degree to which "Just Another Rhumba," like "Hi-Ho!," is as much a concert piece as it is a song.

Ultimately, Gershwin's life in music made sense as it was. One can only speculate how much further and in what directions he might have continued; still, his achievements were sufficiently monumental to bring about, in the brief final chapter of his short life, a kind of summing-up. Ira Gershwin, devastated by his brother's death, would continue in this retrospective vein for decades to come. In addition to his work with other composers (which took place not only after but during the years of his collaboration with George),[17] Ira, who could both play the piano and read music, managed to fashion new songs from his brother's unfinished tunes. In this manner he produced scores for two films, *The Shocking Miss Pilgrim* (1946; released January 1947) and *Kiss Me, Stupid* (1964). The first, which benefited from the involvement of Kay Swift,[18] is by far the more memorable of the two, with more and better songs. Its principal ballad, "For You, For Me, For Evermore," stands fittingly with "They Can't Take That Away from Me"—and with "Love Is Here to Stay," the last song on which both Gershwins worked together—as a closing tribute to and by one of the great musical geniuses of all time.

Notes

1: The Music of Gershwin

1 *George Gershwin's Song Book* (New York: Simon & Schuster, 1932) contains eighteen songs, each in its original format followed by a piano solo based on the refrain, with illustrations by Constantin Alajalov. A limited edition of three hundred, signed by Gershwin and Alajalov, was published earlier in 1932 by Random House and included, in a separate folio, the song "Mischa, Yascha, Toscha, Sascha," written ten years earlier. The latter is included in the anthology *Gershwin on Broadway (from 1919 to 1933)*, ed. Jeff Sultanof (Secaucus, N.J.: Warner Brothers Publications, 1987), pp. 365–68. The piano solos are reprinted as *Gershwin at the Keyboard: Eighteen Song Hits Arranged by the Composer* (New York: Warner Brothers Publications, n.d.). Charles Schwartz, *Gershwin: His Life and Music* (New York: Bobbs-Merrill, 1973; reprint, New York: Da Capo Press, 1979), pp. 187–88, takes a dim view of the piano solos and cites critic Olin Downes to support his reservations about their authenticity. Nonetheless, the entire *Song Book* exists in manuscript and every note is in Gershwin's hand. This and other Gershwin manuscripts cited in this study are in the Gershwin Collection of the Library of Congress. Manuscripts whose citations here lack call numbers were in the process of being re-boxed at the time of writing.

2 Schwartz, *Gershwin,* p. 24.

3 Although George never finished high school, Ira's education included two years at the College of the City of New York, where he contributed (together with another eventually well-known lyricist E. Y. Harburg) to the college's literary magazine. See especially Isaac Goldberg, *George Gershwin: A Study in American Music* (New York: Simon & Schuster, 1931; reprint, New York: Frederick Ungar, 1958), p. 171. Goldberg, a Harvard professor, came to be friendly with the Gershwins in the course of his work, and his book is especially enlightening regarding the early music, Ira Gershwin, and the George-Ira partnership. His plans to update his biography after George's death were interrupted by his own, almost exactly one year later. A more up-to-date source is Edward Jablonski, *Gershwin: A Biography* (New York: Doubleday, 1987).

4 The notebook, henceforth referred to as *Kilenyi,* was originally titled "Studies." It was given to Kilenyi, inscribed to "George's Harmony Teacher" by Ira Gershwin in 1950, and purchased by the Library of Congress in 1963 (Gershwin Collection, Microfilm Music 1346).

5 *Kilenyi,* pp. [27–28].

6 *Kilenyi,* p. [15]. The first six measures appear in a preliminary version at the bottom of the preceding page, with a different flute obbligato begun and evidently discarded after two measures.

7 *Kilenyi,* p. [11]. There Kilenyi writes, "Law of propinquity / ('Stufenreichtum' [lit-

erally, richness of steps] / (Stepwise)"—and Gershwin, "Stufenreichun [*sic*] = stepwise" followed by three figure eights or ampersands. Significantly, Gershwin then prints "Stepwise," underscored, at the bottom of the page.

8 *Kilenyi,* p. [16], also bottom of p. [23] and top of p. [24]. Kilenyi advises (top of p. [24]), "Modulate with *sequences* [underscored] (rigid & free)."

9 Ira Gershwin, "My Brother's Manuscript," preface to the first published edition of *Lullaby for String Quartet* (New York: New World Music Corporation, 1968), p. 2.

10 Jablonski, *Gershwin,* p. 42.

11 *Blue Monday* was first presented in an orchestration by Will H. Vodery as part of *George White's Scandals of 1922;* its full title there was *Blue Monday: Opera Ala Afro-American.* Vodery (1885–1951), a black arranger, was a friend of Gershwin's who helped him enter the musical-comedy field after he left Remick's in 1917 (Schwartz, *Gershwin,* p. 32). Withdrawn after its first New York performance (though it did well in New Haven), *Blue Monday* was reorchestrated by Ferde Grofé, the orchestrator of *Rhapsody in Blue,* and reintroduced by the Paul White-man Orchestra (with the alternate title *One Hundred Thirty-Fifth Street*) in December 1925. Parts of the work can be seen in the 1945 film *Rhapsody in Blue,* from which it is possible to form a kinder opinion than that expressed by Schwartz, *Gershwin* pp. 60–62. Balanced accounts of the opera's reception are given in Gold-berg, *George Gershwin,* pp. 120–23; Edward Jablonski and Lawrence D. Stewart, *The Gershwin Years* (New York: Doubleday, 1973), pp. 72–74; and Jablonski, *Gershwin,* pp. 51–53.

12 "My Brother's Manuscript," p. 2.

13 The 1930 version of *Strike Up the Band* was a revision, with many new songs, of an unsuccessful 1927 production. The book, originally by George S. Kaufman, was revised for the 1930 production by Morrie Ryskind (together, the two authors later wrote *Of Thee I Sing* and *Let 'Em Eat Cake*).

14 The role of *Second Rhapsody* in the film is detailed in Irene Kahn Atkins, *Source Music in Motion Pictures* (Rutherford, N.J.: Fairleigh Dickinson University Press, 1983), pp. 101–7.

15 Vernon Duke, who wrote concert music under his original name Vladimir Dukel-sky, is the composer of such tunes as "April in Paris" and "I Can't Get Started," the latter with lyrics by Ira Gershwin. Anonymously, Duke wrote or at least com-pleted the verses to Gershwin's last songs (for the 1938 film *The Goldwyn Follies*), including "Love Walked In" and "Love Is Here to Stay." Duke writes about his and Gershwin's studies with Schillinger in "Gershwin, Schillinger, and Dukel-sky," *The Musical Quarterly* 33 (1947): 102–15; he also reminisces about the Gersh-wins generally in his autobiography *Passport to Paris* (Boston: Little, Brown, 1955).

16 The genesis of the *Preludes* is addressed in Jablonski, *Gershwin,* pp. 136–37, and in Robert Wyatt, "The Seven Jazz Preludes of George Gershwin: A Historical Nar-rative," *American Music,* 7 (1989): 68–85.

2: An Analytic Approach

1 The central source for Schenker's definitive analytic language is his *Free Composition (Der freie Satz): Volume III of New Musical Theories and Fantasies,* trans. and ed. Ernst Oster (New York: Longman, 1979). For a textbook based on Schenkerian concepts, see Allen Forte and Steven E. Gilbert, *Introduction to Schenkerian Analysis* (New York: Norton, 1982).

2 Forte and Gilbert, *Introduction,* pp. 223, 235–37.

3 Forte and Gilbert, *Introduction,* pp. 154–55.

4 The unfolding is also used to clarify voice leading. In the present example the unfolded interval C–Gb voice-leads to Db–F in m. 14, where the Db, since it does not occur in precisely that register, is represented as an implied note (shown by parentheses). For a systematic discussion of unfoldings, see Forte and Gilbert, *Introduction,* pp. 251–60.

5 Schenker, *Free Composition,* 1: 43–45 (vol. 2, figs. 33–36); see also Forte and Gilbert, *Introduction,* pp. 237–38.

6 The concept of prolongation is basic to Schenkerian analysis. It refers essentially to a melody note or a harmony that remains in control, so to speak, for a span of time beyond its sounding duration. Linear progressions are themselves prolongational: they normally prolong their highest structural note—whether it be the head note (beginning) of a descending progression or the goal note (end) of one that ascends.

7 The register designations in this book follow Schenker. The scale starting with middle C is c^1–b^1; the next higher octave, c^2–b^2; the one after that, c^3–b^3; etc. The octave below middle C is c–b; the one below that, C–B; below that, C_1–B_1. (The lowest note on the piano keyboard is thus A_2, the highest c^5.) Uppercase letters alone are used in describing pitch patterns that occur in more than one register and where register is not of immediate concern. Elsewhere, when uppercase letters refer specifically to bass notes, the word "bass" is added if this fact is not otherwise apparent.

8 An early copyright deposit with the Library of Congress has the initial G9 chord changed to a root-position tonic—incorrect as per Gershwin's manuscript. See "Tune Book (1933–37)," p. 7 (Gershwin Collection). According to Wayne Shirley (letter to the author, November 13, 1985), the proper harmony was restored after Oscar Levant had seen the change and protested to the Goldwyn studio.

9 Linear intervallic patterns are normally highlighted in Schenker's graphs in this fashion, though it was Allen Forte who coined the term. A detailed summary of the various linear intervallic patterns, with examples, is in Forte and Gilbert, *Introduction,* pp. 83–100.

10 See Forte and Gilbert, *Introduction,* pp. 131–33.

11 One might argue that d^2, with its rhythmically weak position, is merely an embellishment to the Bb, and that the main thread of the melody ought to be Bb–C and not D–C. A larger view of the song would tend to refute this reading, however,

as the note D (along with its leading tone C#) is the link between Porgy's chorus in B♭ and Bess's in D. (The final statement of the melody, in F#, concludes on C#.)

12 As with other tenor parts cited in this book, references to register-specific pitches in this song are to those as written; technically, however, though the effect may be treble, the tenor voice in treble clef is written an octave higher than actual pitch.

13 Also highlighted in example 9b are the rhythmic articulations in the bass, with notes in successive groups of 4, 3, 2, and 1. Devices such as this, which reflect the teachings of Schillinger, occur at various points throughout the opera and are discussed at greater length in chap. 10.

14 The opening measures are also the source of most melodic and rhythmic material for the remainder of the piece. See Schwartz, *Gershwin*, pp. 328–31, and discussions of *Rhapsody* in chap. 3 and 5 below.

15 The history of the verse-refrain or verse-chorus form in American popular song goes back to the mid-nineteenth century, when the main content of a song was presented in a series of verses that alternated with repetitions of a brief chorus. Gradually the two portions switched roles, to the point where the verse was a mere preface and the refrain (or chorus, or burthen—an antiquated expression that Ira Gershwin liked) the main body of the song. See Charles Hamm, *Yesterdays: Popular Song in America* (New York: Norton, 1979), especially pp. 254–56, 291–93, and 358–61. Gershwin's practice was to repeat the refrain but usually not the verse. His piano introductions would often use the main theme of the refrain, thus tying the whole package together.

16 References to the accompaniments of the earlier songs are made with caution, as the writing may not be Gershwin's alone. In cases such as the present one, however, the accompaniment is stylistically consistent with what we find in the manuscripts.

17 This is a second meaning to the term *refrain*, whereby it denotes the recurring first portion of a rondo form.

18 Schenker called this phenomenon *obligatory register*.

3: Fascinating Rhythm

1 Charles Hamm, *Yesterdays*, pp. 319–21, 330–33.

2 "Rialto Ripples," written by Gershwin in collaboration with Will Donaldson (a colleague at Remick's, not to be confused with the songwriter Walter Donaldson), was recorded on piano roll by Gershwin in 1916 and published by Remick the next year.

3 Schwartz, *Gershwin*, p. 44.

4 B. G. ("Buddy") DeSylva (1895–1950), Gershwin's main lyricist in the early years, was also a friend and associate of Al Jolson. This connection led to Jolson's landmark performance of "Swanee" (lyrics by Irving Caesar), which gave Gershwin his first major success. See Jablonski, *Gershwin*, pp. 37–39 and elsewhere.

5 Jablonski, *Gershwin*, p. 78.

6 References to rehearsal numbers are based on the published two-piano and orchestral scores; these numbers differ from those in the manuscript.

7 See Schwartz, *Gershwin,* pp. 329–31.

8 An essay by the pianist and conductor Henry Levine, "An Explanation of the Characteristic Rhythmic Figures in the 'Rhapsody in Blue,'" published as a preface to the two-piano score (New York: New World Music Corporation, 1924), enumerates in detail the variants of this pattern, citing in addition a similar figure in Bach's *Chromatic Fantasia.*

9 On deposit in the Library of Congress (Gershwin Collection, ML 30.25a.G or ML30.25a.G47 R5, microfilm Music 1036), evidently for the purpose of securing copyright, is a manuscript copy of *Rhapsody in Blue* for piano solo, dated June 12, 1924, and not in Gershwin's hand, which ends with a two-measure C-major chord at what would be R11 in the published two-piano score. In this manuscript, the measure corresponding to our ex. 21b (R5+16 in the published score) is presented as a $^6_4$, *più mosso* measure of eighth-note triplets. The same change is made for the measures corresponding to R5+20–23.

10 Gershwin's junior by seven years, Confrey was given equal billing with Gershwin on the Paul Whiteman program that included *Rhapsody in Blue* (and Confrey's "Kitten on the Keys"). Gershwin also cites Confrey as an important contributor to contemporary piano style in his preface to *George Gershwin's Song Book,* reprinted on the inside front cover of *Gershwin at the Keyboard.*

11 See Alec Wilder, *American Popular Song: The Great Innovators, 1900–1950* (New York: Oxford University Press, 1972), pp. 457–58.

12 Hans Keller, "Rhythm: Gershwin and Stravinsky," *The Score and I.M.A. Magazine,* no. 20 (June 1957), p. 21.

13 Gershwin did not number the variations.

14 The metronome setting 108 is from Gershwin's orchestral manuscript, as opposed to 120 in the published two-piano score.

15 Palindromic rhythms, whereby a pattern achieves symmetry by being followed by its retrograde, were an important part of Joseph Schillinger's theory of rhythm, as developed in *The Schillinger System of Musical Composition* (New York: Carl Fischer, 1941; reprint, New York: Da Capo Press, 1978), 1: 1–95. That Gershwin had become familiar with the main aspects of this theory is documented in his notebooks of study with Schillinger (1932–36) and in notes for *Porgy and Bess* in "Tune Book (1933–37)." Only the first part of the canon is shown in the two-piano score, hence the condensed orchestral score in ex. 27b. The upward stems on the first six pitches of staff 2 are Gershwin's own notation.

16 Schillinger used the term *converse* as a synonym for *retrograde;* his figure 85 (*The Schillinger System,* 1: 49) is germane.

17 The source for this example and for ex. 169 (chap. 11) is the copyright deposit in the Library of Congress (M1508 — Goldwyn Follies). The published score, in *The Great Songs of George Gershwin: Thirty Songs Celebrating the Genius of Gershwin on the*

75th Anniversary of His Birth (New York: Chappell, 1973), pp. 58–65, is in G rather than Bb, and the accompaniment for the first two lines of the refrain has the right hand doubling the vocal line in quarter notes instead of complementing the 3 + 3 + 2 rhythm of the bass. The notation of the bass in ex. 30 (as in ex. 29, from *Cuban Overture*), with what would normally be a quarter rest written as two eighths, confirms that Gershwin was indeed thinking in terms of the eighth-note multiples used in this discussion.

4: The Early Period

1 The only substantive discussion of this song in the existing literature is in Wilder, *American Popular Song,* pp. 123–24. Though he declares it to be "for the most part a product of the pop music mill," Wilder nonetheless finds "a few measures untypical of a ground-out tune." Two such measures are mm. 13–14, where at a climactic point the melody has a skip of a seventh, f#¹–e²–f#¹, using the third and ninth of the dominant of V.

2 About Will Donaldson (not to be confused with the songwriter Walter Donaldson), little is known except that he had worked with Gershwin at Remick's (Jablonski, *Gershwin,* p. 21).

3 In an effort to escape the stigma of riding on his brother's coattails, Ira Gershwin coined his pseudonym from the names of his youngest brother Arthur and his sister Frances, herself a singer. He used his own name beginning in 1924, first with the show *Primrose,* for which he wrote half the lyrics, then with *Lady Be Good,* for which he wrote them all.

4 See Ira Gershwin's comments in *Lyrics on Several Occasions* (New York: Alfred A. Knopf, 1959; reprint, New York: Viking Press, 1973), p. 180.

5 *The Best of George Gershwin,* pp. 6–10. A facsimile of the sheet music cover appears on p. 5. In the absence of an extant or available manuscript, this published version was my only source. The long hiatus between the song's composition and its first publication could have permitted considerable editing—perhaps even by Ira Gershwin, who oversaw its publication. The piano writing in the accompaniment is typical of Gershwin's style, though it seems somewhat more sophisticated than what might be expected of him in 1918.

6 In *Crazy for You: Vocal Selection* (Secaucus, N.J.: Warner-Chappell Music, 1992). *Crazy for You* is but the latest in what has been a series of posthumous musicals written around preexisting Gershwin songs and the first to have been done without the presence of Ira Gershwin. Its closest predecessor was *My One and Only* (1983).

7 In his preface to the *Lullaby* score, Ira Gershwin observes that his brother never mentioned the piece in later years—either because he had borrowed upon it for the other work, or because he came to think of it "as merely an exercise."

8 These sixteen measures are later reprised a half step higher (at R44), with a new verse beginning "I love but you my Joe." The source for the *Blue Monday* examples is a handwritten piano-vocal score available on rental from Warner Brothers.

Credit for "adaptation" is given to George Bassman, composer of "I'm Getting Sentimental Over You," the song that would later become Tommy Dorsey's signature.

9 The autograph of *Blue Monday* no longer exists; according to Goldberg, *George Gershwin*, p. 122, it disappeared shortly after its first performance (*Scandals of 1922*). The Bassman vocal score used here is based on the orchestration done by Grofé for the Carnegie Hall revival of 1925. The lower staff of ex. 39 has what is given in the score, the upper the vocal line plus inner voices where necessary. Though one may doubt the authenticity of every detail of the accompaniment (including the misspelled C♮ in the fourth measure), the assumption here is that the essential choices of bass and harmony were Gershwin's

10 Jablonski and Stewart, *The Gershwin Years*, p. 72.

11 The main body of this song was a conscious emulation of the style of the Negro spiritual: Gershwin's thematic synopsis (one of several pages in the composer's hand, evidently written specifically for the book), in Goldberg, *George Gershwin*, p. 219, lists as its title "Spiritual ('I'm gonna see my mother')."

12 B. G. DeSylva (1895–1950), who contributed to the lyrics of many early Gershwin songs, was closely involved in the career of Al Jolson and owned proprietary interest in several hit songs (Jablonski, *Gershwin* p. 37). On his role in "Stairway," Goldberg writes (p. 177): "It [was] to Buddy [B. G.] DeSylva that Ira [owed] the success of the lyrics to 'I'll Build a Stairway to Paradise.' Originally the song, by 'Arthur Francis' [i.e., Ira Gershwin], was called 'New Step Every Day.' DeSylva, hearing it, pointed out that the lyric itself was but fair; it had one line, however, that could produce a hit. Accordingly that one line was salvaged from the stanzas, a new lyric written around it, with the result as already chronicled."

13 "Stairway to Paradise," in an elaborate staging, closed the first act; *Blue Monday*, which "to the pleasure-loving *Scandals* devotee came as a jolt," opened the second (Jablonski and Stewart, *The Gershwin Years*, p. 72).

14 This was no doubt facilitated by Jolson's connection with B. G. DeSylva (Jablonski, *Gershwin*, p. 37).

15 Wilder, *American Popular Song*, p. 125.

16 *The Gershwin Years*, p. 67.

17 See Schwartz, *Gershwin*, pp. 322–23.

18 This song, which is rhythmically quite interesting, appears in *Gershwin on Broadway*, pp. 12–15.

19 Pointed out by Wilder, *American Popular Song*, pp. 124–25.

20 Reprinted in *Gershwin on Broadway*, pp. 21–25 and 104–7.

21 *Kilenyi*, p. [26], reproduced in Jablonski and Stewart, *The Gershwin Years*, p. 84 (upper left).

5: *Rhapsody in Blue*

1 Herbert, the one composer of "classical" stature on the program, heard *Rhapsody* in rehearsal and suggested to Gershwin that he expand the transition to the slow

theme, which he did. See Goldberg, *George Gershwin,* pp. 160–61; also Jablonski and Stewart, *The Gershwin Years,* p. 96.

2 Jablonski and Stewart, *The Gershwin Years,* p. 94.

3 Goldberg, *George Gershwin,* p. 157.

4 Schwartz, *Gershwin,* p. 328.

5 Schwartz, *Gershwin,* p. 329.

6 In this and similar descriptions, scale degree numbers refer to the key of the theme, not that of the piece as a whole. The opposite will be true in discussions pertaining to macrostructure—i.e., in Schenkerian terms, the background and deeper levels of middleground.

7 Structures such as this illustrate how Gershwin's thinking, even in an early work like *Rhapsody,* tended toward the ideas promulgated by Joseph Schillinger, with whom he would be studying a decade hence. Harmonic progression by successive minor thirds is tantamount to Schillinger's system of four tonics, as set forth in *The Schillinger System,* 1: 399.

8 A crossed-out portion of the manuscript has a bravura upbeat in the piano leading to an up-tempo orchestral version of main theme 1 (initially labeled "Marked and Jazzy"), such as eventually occurs at R6. Gershwin evidently considered this too abrupt, and so we have the two A-major statements, each with the same attendant transition and corollary themes. These are represented only once in the schematic shown in ex. 48.

9 Another Schenkerian view of *Rhapsody,* differing from and independent of the present study, is offered by Arthur Maisel in his dissertation, "Talent and Technique: George Gershwin's *Rhapsody in Blue*" (Ph.D., City University of New York, 1990), whose salient content has been excerpted in an essay of the same title in Alan Cadwallader (ed.), *Trends in Schenkerian Research* (New York: Schirmer Books, 1990), pp. 51–69. Though he gives local importance to the initial descent from $\hat{8}$, Maisel reads the primary melodic tone of the entire work as $\hat{3}$.

10 Gershwin—and others; the notations in the manuscripts are not always in the composer's hand—tended to add tempo directions as afterthoughts. As a result, it is often virtually impossible to discern the precise history of the various labels and directions that appear in print. Conversely, there are annotations in Gershwin's hand that do not get published. One such example is the label *Finale* appended to the two-piano score (below rather than above the staff lines) at the point where the F#-minor music begins. This appellation invites the interpretation of *Rhapsody* as being in three parts rather than two. However, as this would-be finale begins with a sequence based on main theme 2, justification remains for regarding it as a continuation of part 2. The putative finale was initially prefaced by sixteen additional measures in the solo part (labeled "faster"): three statements, in different registers, of a variant of the inner-voice ostinato of main theme 2 supported by two measures of C#7 and two of A7 in succession, followed by four measures of a high C# tremolo in the right hand against a trill of C and D natural in the left. These measures appear in both the Gershwin

and Grofé manuscripts, although in the former there are already marks indicating that they were to be cut—and they were, following the first performance. Another eight measures were cut from the Misterioso itself—again in the piano solo, between the four measures of *sognando* and the *a tempo*. These and other cuts, totaling forty-four measures, of which all but four are piano solo, were made by the composer following the first performance (see Schwartz, *Gershwin,* pp. 92 and 317 nn. 36–37).

11 The first of the optional cuts indicated in the published score extends from the first statement of transition 1 through the first statement of transition 2. With this cut, the second statement of transition 1 (at R5+24) effectively becomes the first, likewise the return of transition 2 at R37.

6: The Road to "I Got Rhythm"

1 Wayne D. Shirley, "Scoring the Concerto in F: George Gershwin's First Orchestration," *American Music* 3/3 (Fall 1985): 297–98 n. 13. The manuscript of "Oh, Lady Be Good!" is in the Gershwin Collection of the Library of Congress.

2 In a note dated September 2, 1964, on file with the manuscript in the Library of Congress, Ira Gershwin offers the possibility that this leadsheet could have been "sketched for a rehearsal pianist or for a principal—or even later for George's 1934 radio show." In other words, this leadsheet may well have been written following the writing (even publication) of the score.

3 Plagal melodies operate generally in the range from the fourth below to the tonic to the fifth above; the contrasting type, the authentic, has a basic range extending from tonic to tonic an octave above. The pentatonic scale may be used in either type: in the key of C, for example, the authentic arrangement would be C, D, E, G, A; the plagal, G, A, C, D, E. Gershwin favored the latter by an overwhelming margin.

4 Points of resemblance between Gershwin melodies are a favored topic in Deena Rosenberg, *Fascinating Rhythm: The Collaboration of George and Ira Gershwin* (New York: Dutton, 1991). Her discussion of pentatonicism throughout the score of *Oh, Kay!* (pp. 134–41) includes the parallelism between "Maybe" and "Clap Yo' Hands."

5 *Show Girl* was the second show that George and Ira Gershwin wrote for Ziegfeld. Ziegfeld, who blamed the Gershwins for the show's failure, never paid them their royalties for its one hundred eleven performances (Jablonski, *Gershwin,* p. 192).

6 The diagonal lines in ex. 61 are Gershwin's; the brackets highlighting the left-hand doublings are mine. For another instance of overlapping, recall the refrain opening of "Love is Here to Stay," which was analyzed in chapter 2, example 4. There the resultant pattern was an ascending arpeggiation, as contrasted with the partially linear ascent in "Liza."

7 Ira Gershwin, *Lyrics on Several Occasions,* p. 4.

8 Schwartz, *Gershwin,* p. 322.

9 Consider, for example, the respective first movements of Mozart's "easy" sonata

in C, K. 545, and Beethoven's Fifth Symphony. Schenker's own bias is toward $\hat{3}$ in both instances.

10 The often cited history of this song is related by Ira Gershwin in *Lyrics on Several Occasions,* pp. 4–7.

11 The key of F, chosen here, is used for the first statement of the song in *Girl Crazy;* it is also the key Gershwin uses in the *"I Got Rhythm" Variations.* The choral reprise and the published song sheet are in B♭, however.

7: *Concerto in F* and *An American in Paris*

1 The title page of the orchestral manuscript (Gershwin Collection, Library of Congress, microfilm Music 1338) reads, "'An American in Paris.' / a Tone Poem for Orchestra. / Composed and Orchestrated by George Gershwin. / Begun early in 1928. / Finished November 18, 1928." (This is quoted in Jablonski, *Gershwin,* p. 176 and also known to this author first-hand: the punctuation and capitalization are the composer's.) The deliberateness with which Gershwin announced the genre of the work, the authorship of its orchestration, and the chronology of its composition indicates that these matters weighed on his own mind no less than those of his critics. An intermediate stage in the genesis of the work is represented by a two-piano manuscript score dated January 1928 (Gershwin Collection), which is marked in various places with notes on instrumentation, along with various cuts, splices, and changes of mind.

2 Jablonski, *Gershwin,* pp. 176–77. *Les Six* were a group of composers of a decidedly anti-Romantic bent comprising Darius Milhaud, Francis Poulenc, Arthur Honegger (stylistically an anomaly, being more Romantic and less "French"), Georges Auric (whose most famous work was the score to the film *Moulin Rouge*), Louis Durey, and Germaine Tailleferre. Born between the years 1888 and 1899, all could be considered contemporaries of one another—and of Gershwin. Erik Satie (1866–1925) held the unofficial position of father-figure to the group; he was of an earlier generation, close in years to Debussy (1862–1918) though of a decidedly different aesthetic.

3 Gershwin's orchestral manuscript lacks the tenuto marks and the slurs over the barlines.

4 A change in the bass clarifies the harmonic shift to III, shown with a question mark in ex. 67.

5 The meter, cut-time in the published two-piano and orchestral scores, is given as $\frac{4}{4}$ in the orchestral manuscript, which, except for the piano part, is entirely in Gershwin's hand.

6 Jablonski, *Gershwin,* p. 170.

7 The rehearsal number appears in the published orchestral score but is missing from the two-piano version. This may be due to the forty-four-measure cut from the manuscript (see Shirley, "Scoring the Concerto in F," p. 286), which resulted in a net loss of three rehearsal numbers—i.e., ms. no. 10 is published no. 7.

8 Gershwin may have seen the balancing of the first and fourth chairs as an addi-

tional element of symmetry; more mundanely, he may simply have wanted to give the fourth player a chance to prove himself.

9 These intervals comprise a specific representation of the trichord listed as 3-7 in Allen Forte, *The Structure of Atonal Music* (New Haven and London: Yale University Press, 1973), p. 179.

10 Robert Payne, *Gershwin* (New York: Pyramid Books, 1960), p. 68.

11 Jablonski and Stewart, *The Gershwin Years,* p. 106.

12 Cited in Jablonski, *Gershwin,* p. 170.

13 Payne, *Gershwin,* p. 67.

14 G minor is also the key of the original version of this theme: a piano prelude dated January 1925 that was abandoned after eleven measures. See Robert Wyatt, "The Seven Piano Preludes of George Gershwin," pp. 72–73.

15 Speculation about the work's program comes from two sources: Gershwin's own description, and Deems Taylor's program notes for the first performance. These are cited in Jablonski, *Gershwin,* pp. 176–78.

16 Jablonski, *Gershwin,* p. 176.

17 This passage also appears in rhythmic diminution as part of an extended transition to the coda that was cut from the published score. It is found on p. 57 of the two-piano manuscript.

18 By this I mean the more specific sense of the term, namely a twelve-bar, three-phrase structure whose basic version comprises four measures of I, two of IV, two of I, two of V, and two of I.

19 Jablonski, *Gershwin,* p. 177.

20 See the orchestral music that first appears in act 1 at R30. It is perhaps not coincidental that the specific pitches in the tritone relationship—initially in *An American in Paris* and repeatedly in *Porgy and Bess*—are C and F♯.

21 In ex. 91, as is typical for a graph of this scope, bass notes are frequently shown an octave higher and octave doublings are not shown at all. Upper voices, also, may not be in the same register as in the score, and in this case, too, octave doublings are normally omitted. Since specific register is not usually an issue at this level, the letter names of pitches in the accompanying discussion are mostly given in capitals.

8: New Musicals

1 An indispensable secondary source is Wayne Schneider's dissertation, "George Gershwin's Political Operettas *Of Thee I Sing* (1931) and *Let 'Em Eat Cake* (1933), and Their Role in Gershwin's Musical and Emotional Maturing" (Ph.D., Cornell University, 1985). In particular, the reader is referred to the detailed analyses of the subject operettas, pp. 218–466 and 571–797, respectively. On Kaufman and Ryskind, see pp. 112–17.

2 As noted by Schneider, "George Gershwin's Political Operettas," p. 125, there is no extant manuscript of the unpublished 1927 score, and one can only speculate about how much of it was retained in the 1930 revision.

3 Jablonski, *Gershwin,* p. 171; see also pp. 172–74.

4 "Union Square," a scene rather than a song, was published on its own in abridged form, yet there is no evidence of any separate success. The title song is still in print, in *Gershwin on Broadway,* pp. 355–59. Also in the same anthology is "Blue Blue Blue," whose unusual verse is discussed at the end of this chapter. Another song from *Let 'Em Eat Cake,* "On and On and On"—like the title song, a satirical march—is included in *Rediscovered Gershwin* (Secaucus, N.J.: Warner Brothers, 1991), pp. 248–51.

5 *Gershwin on Broadway,* pp. 350–54, 336–39, and 360–64. "Isn't It a Pity" also appears in *The Great Songs of George Gershwin* (Secaucus, N.J.: Warner Brothers, ca. 1986).

6 Jablonski, *Gershwin,* p. 220; Schwartz, *Gershwin,* pp. 217–18.

7 The acknowledged orchestrators *Of Thee I Sing* were William Daly (Gershwin's close friend and musical associate) and Robert Russell Bennett. Gershwin, however, left specific requests as to who should orchestrate what (Daly, the overture and opening of act 1; Bennett, the opening of scene 3 of the same act); in addition, he did some of it himself. Notes on these matters from Ira Gershwin (dated March 5, 1962, and May 18, 1965) accompany twenty-two pages of orchestral score headed "Opening Act II / (orch. by) George Gershwin" (Gershwin Collection, Library of Congress). These pages contain all of the published "Opening Act II," plus a dance sequence that was not used.

8 This first broadcast of February 19, 1934, along with another from April 10, can be heard on a private-label record album, *Gershwin Conducts Gershwin* (Mark56 M60173). "Music by Gershwin" was aired in fifteen-minute segments on Monday and Friday evenings and ran from February 19 until May 31. A second series, broadcast as a half-hour show on Sunday nights, ran from September 30 to December 23 of the same year (Jablonski, *Gershwin,* pp. 260–62). The announcer was Don Wilson, best known for his long association with Jack Benny.

9 The version of the overture used in the Gershwin radio broadcast, abridged and arranged for the house orchestra, begins at this point.

10 Deena Rosenberg, *Fascinating Rhythm,* p. 232, cites a parallel use of the same motive at the lines, "He's the man the people choose; / Loves the Irish and the Jews," in "Wintergreen for President."

11 There is an incomplete piano-vocal score in the Library of Congress (Gershwin Collection, bound ms. no. 15, microfilm Music 3073), which was pieced together by Ira Gershwin from finished manuscript, sketches, and some of the separately published songs. The orchestral score, which had been lost completely, was reconstructed in the 1970s at the request of the Gershwin family by Don Rose, an arranger for Warner Brothers Music (see Schneider, "George Gershwin's Political Operettas," pp. 42–43). This arrangement of *Let 'Em Eat Cake* was produced together with *Of Thee I Sing* by the Brooklyn Academy of Music in 1987. The CBS recording of this double bill (catalog no. S2-M42522) was released the same year.

12 From "Wintergreen": "He's the man the people choose; / Loves the Irish and the Jews!" The corresponding lines from "Tweedledee" are: "He's the man the coun-

try seeks; / Loves the Turks and Greeks!" Each is followed by a repeated "ta ta ta" set to a quote from a pre-existing tune that features an arpeggiation on an Ab-major triad: "There'll Be a Hot Time in the Old Town Tonight" (written by Theodore Metz putatively in 1886, published 1896) in the first instance; "Over There" (written by George M. Cohan in 1917 and published the following year) in the second.

13 For a complete analysis of this opening scene, see Schneider, "George Gershwin's Political Operettas," pp. 574–83.

14 Detailed analyses of these overtures are done by Schneider, "George Gershwin's Political Operettas," pp. 454–63 and 778–894.

15 *Schillinger A,* pp. 44–46. Schneider, "George Gershwin's Political Operettas," pp. 629–30, conjectures that the *Tune Book* sketch came first and that the Schillinger study was concerned only with matters of treatment. Schillinger's widow, on the other hand, maintains (letter of Frances Schillinger to the author, May 28, 1984), that the entire song was written as an exercise for Schillinger, who then suggested that lyrics be added (hence the working title in the *Tune Book*) and the song used in the show. (She goes on to say that Glenn Miller's "Moonlight Serenade" had similar origins and that it was upon her husband's advice that it became Miller's theme song.)

16 The harmonic roots of these chords form the familiar pattern I–VI–II–V. But Gershwin seemed to pay more attention to the closely spaced inner voices. In the sketch in *Schillinger A,* in fact, he leaves out the bass when the tune moves to the subdominant at m. 9, placing the inner voices in the bottom staff.

17 The concept of chorus as commentator, ancient though it may be, was evidently attractive to Gershwin in his mature and final periods. It is used extensively in one of his last scores, the film *A Damsel in Distress.*

18 This came with the dismantling of the so-called Secaucus Trunk, discovered in the Warner Bros. warehouse in Secaucus, New Jersey, in 1982. Among its contents, which included material by the Gershwins and others, were complete scores for *Pardon My English* and *Primrose* (one of whose songs, "Naughty Baby," was cited in chap. 3). All of the Gershwin music from the trunk is now housed in the Library of Congress.

19 The Polish accent owed itself more precisely to Lyda Roberti, for whom this song was expressly written (Jablonski, *Gershwin,* p. 240).

20 The technique of repeating a melodic segment with a different, presumably unexpected, harmonization is nothing new for Gershwin. As a case in point, see the early song "Nobody But You" (ex. 7); see also the refrain of "But Not for Me."

21 A sign of how little these pieces were known is Wilder's observation that "By Strauss" (1936; discussed in chap. 11) was "the only Gershwin waltz [he had] come across" (*American Popular Song,* p. 155).

22 This version, edited by Ira Gershwin and adapted by Saul Chaplin, is in the anthology *Music by Gershwin* (Midland Park, N.J.: University Society, 1975), pp. 131–38. This is the only number from the show released by Ira Gershwin, who report-

edly felt that songs from failed shows were best left forgotten. With this song he had the further concern that its original title would lead to confusion with the far better-known "Tonight" from *West Side Story* (Jablonski, *Gershwin,* p. 241).

23 My source for the vocal version, "Tonight," is a copyist's manuscript prepared for a 1987 concert performance of *Pardon My English* at the Library of Congress. In places where "Tonight" and *Two Waltzes in C* differ, the former is given preference.

24 Such a sequence relates to the system of multiple "tonics" as defined by Schillinger. These tonics are derived from the equal division of the octave. A harmonic series moving in minor thirds, such as occurs in mm. 6–7, would be called a progression of four tonics (see, for example, *The Schillinger System of Musical Composition* [New York: Carl Fischer, 1946; reprint, New York: Da Capo, 1978], 1: 425). Although this song was written during Gershwin's period of study with Schillinger, and could thus be ascribed to his influence at least in part, one can also point to the opening of part 2 of *Rhapsody in Blue,* which moves sequentially through G, Bb, Db, and E, as demonstrating that Gershwin was thinking in this way long before he and Schillinger met.

25 Available in *Gershwin on Broadway,* pp. 347–49.

26 A more precise term for these numbers is *pitch-class integers*. The term *pitch class* is as a way of referring to a note without specifying its register or duration.

27 Were this study to go further into atonal theory than it does, we would at this point introduce the concept of normal order, as in Allen Forte, *The Structure of Atonal Music,* pp. 3–5. The notation 0,2,5,7,9 does not represent the best normal order, or prime form, of the set under discussion. However, this ordering has the advantage of starting with pitch-class zero. (It also recalls the basic shape of "I Got Rhythm," bringing it into line with the main thrust of chap. 6.)

28 This technique can also be seen as a direct outgrowth of Gershwin's studies with Schillinger; cf. *The Schillinger System,* 1: 164 (fig. 41), where Schillinger takes the first four notes of "I Got Rhythm" (which are the same as the first four notes of the first of the pentatonic scales isolated in ex. 103) and transposes them by successive minor thirds to form a sixteen-note continuum containing all twelve pitches.

29 Wilder, *American Popular Song,* p. 154.

9: Concert Works

1 This view of Schillinger's role is generally in line with Ira Gershwin's assessment, quoted by Schwartz, *Gershwin,* p. 113, that "lessons like these unquestionably broaden musical horizons, but they don't inspire an opera like *Porgy*." As chronicled by Jablonski, *Gershwin,* pp. 231–33, Gershwin probably came to Schillinger on the recommendation of the pianist-composer Vladimir Drozdoff and the violinist-composer Joseph Achron, both Russian emigres living in the United States. Drozdoff was a former colleague of the Russian composer Alexander Glazounov, who was living in Paris at the time of Gershwin's sojourn there and with whom Gershwin had wanted to study orchestration. Glazounov, however, on hearing *Rhapsody in Blue* in 1928, reportedly declared, "He wants to study

orchestration but hasn't the slightest knowledge of counterpoint" (Jablonski, *Gershwin,* p. 232). Glazounov's remarks, obsolete given such pieces as *Second Rhapsody, An American in Paris,* and even *Concerto in F,* were nonetheless taken to heart by Gershwin, who turned to Schillinger to remedy the situation.

2 As the context for the Gershwins' first film score, *Delicious* deserves more than the obscurity to which it has been relegated. An account of the film and its reception is in Schneider, "George Gershwin's Political Operettas," pp. 90–93. A good summary of the plot, including the scenario for the rhapsody, appears in Jablonski, *Gershwin,* pp. 206–7. Two songs from the picture, "Delishious" and "Blah, Blah, Blah," are in *The Great Songs of George Gershwin,* pp. 46–49 and 166–69, respectively.

3 This narrative was transcribed from a private-label recording of movie soundtrack excerpts, *The Gershwins in Hollywood: A Box-Office Production* (JJA/Music Masters, no number). The references to rivets in the narrative coincide with the work's alternate title, "Rhapsody in Rivets" (Jablonski, *Gershwin,* pp. 206, 212), and with the characterization of the first theme as the "rivet motif" (ibid., p. 222). A new rendition of "New York Rhapsody" minus the narrative, by Wayne Marshall and the Hollywood Bowl Orchestra (John Mauceri, conductor), can be heard on a compact disk of the same title (*The Gershwins in Hollywood,* Philips 434274-2).

4 Jablonski, *Gershwin,* p. 207, describes the scenario for this material.

5 Gershwin Collection, bound ms. 27 (microfilm Music 1354).

6 Jablonski, *Gershwin,* p. 211. Gershwin Collection, bound ms. 25 (microfilm Music 1353).

7 On McBride, see the entries by the present author in *The New Grove Dictionary of Music* (London: Macmillan, 1980), 11: 410, and in *The New Grove Dictionary of Music in the United States* (London: Macmillan, 1986), 3: 135. The McBride orchestration of *Second Rhapsody* was one of a number of "fixes" ordered by Campbell-Watson, as chronicled in Jablonski, *Gershwin,* pp. 223–26.

8 For his orchestral scores, Gershwin favored manuscript paper with preprinted instrumental layouts, which he often had made to order, as indicated in the present case by the reproduction of his signature in the lower left corner. The same paper was used earlier in his scores for *Concerto in F* and *An American in Paris.* In the latter instance the unused system for solo piano remains blank, albeit with key signatures dutifully noted.

9 Unlike the McBride orchestration, the two-piano score (New York: New World Music, 1932) was produced during Gershwin's lifetime and, presumably, with his approval. Its rehearsal numbers correspond to those in the fair-copy orchestral score.

10 The recording is included in a collection titled *Gershwin Conducts Gershwin* (Mark56 M60173). Despite obvious deficiencies in ensemble and sound quality, this recording provides a rare opportunity to hear the work as Gershwin intended it. For details about the session, see Schwartz, *Gershwin,* p. 202.

11 This passage is more complicated than the published two-piano score would sug-

gest. The descending scale in the bass (cellos and second bassoon) is doubled at the tritone above (violas and first bassoon), and there is also a descending chromatic scale in thirds in two clarinets. The latter, in sixteenth notes, is the only component of the passage not in triplets.

12 There is an increase in tempo at this point, from quarter equals 132 (Allegro) to 144 (Allegro assai), in both the published two-piano score and the orchestral manuscript. In the sketch, which lacks metronome markings, the corresponding indications are "Moderato e rhythmato [*sic*]" and "Marcato." The second trumpet's unison accents are present in the sketch as well, and the accent pattern of the first measure of the theme (3 + 2 + 3) is already an essential component of the contrary-motion passage in the piano introduction.

13 The rehearsal numbers in the orchestral manuscript and in the published score are in agreement except where there is a cut or altered passage.

14 The measures cited here (R17 through R17+3) are condensed from Gershwin's orchestral manuscript. His sketch, likewise, has them in the orchestra, as does (even) the Campbell-Watson/Robert McBride revision. However, they are transferred to the first piano (presumably the solo piano) part in the two-piano score, with the second piano (presumably, that is, the orchestra) taking over at R17+4. Although the two-piano score was published in Gershwin's lifetime, his performance follows the orchestral score, which has the piano complementing the new, chordal countertheme with bravura flourishes.

15 A second tritone occurs between the F♯ minor of the Misterioso and the ensuing retransition, which begins in C.

16 In the sketch, the orchestral statement of theme B1, starting on B♯, is preceded by three measures of quarter-note Cs in successively higher octaves, also in the orchestra. The original start of the finale had the piano enter with a variant of theme A1, with C as both melody and harmony. This was abandoned and crossed out in favor of theme A1a, as in the score.

17 *The Schillinger System,* 1: 399.

18 It is not exactly known when he began these studies, but it is generally conceded that he did so in spring 1932 (Jablonski, *Gershwin,* p. 232; Schwartz, *Gershwin,* p. 222).

19 Another parallel with *An American in Paris* is that Gershwin produced piano scores for both works: a two-piano score for *An American in Paris* (which remains in manuscript) and a one-piano, four-hand score for *Cuban Overture* published in 1933. Transcriptions by Gregory Stone were published also: a solo-piano arrangement of *An American in Paris* and a two-piano adaptation of *Cuban Overture.* Local color in *Cuban Overture* (the counterpart of the taxi horns in *An American in Paris*) came by way of Ignacio Piñero, a singer-composer of *son* (a general term for Latin-American folksong) whose *Echale salsita* ("Pour On the Sauce"), a *son pregon* (street-call *son*) found its way into Gershwin's thematic material.

20 This manuscript (Gershwin Collection, bound ms. no. 8, microfilm Music 1344)

has been published in facsimile (Secaucus, N.J.: Warner Brothers, 1987), with background material and editorial commentary by Jeff Sultanof and with Gershwin's program notes.

21 Although the orchestral score has rehearsal numbers, the published two-piano score, transcribed by Gregory Stone (New York: New World Music, 1934) does not. Since it is the latter to which the reader is more likely to have access, references here will be to measure numbers alone.

22 The perfect fourth was originally to have been a tritone, the lower part descending a whole step to e♭ (thus doubling the bass—and, tonally, the root of the chord, an altered E♭7). However, the e♭ was distinctly changed in the manuscript to e♮ in the horn parts, making the final interval consistent with the sequence. Gershwin's solo piano score reads e♮, though e♭ remains in Stone's two-piano transcription.

23 The manuscript of these measures is only partially written out, with the direction to copy from R15 to R18 (mm. 154–79).

24 In the manuscript, this portion of the piece is labeled a coda and begins with percussion alone. Both the coda designation and the percussion passage are deleted in the published score. The penultimate measure, with its rhythmic articulation of the cadential chord, has the direction "3 TIMES" above it in the manuscript. This direction is lost in the published orchestral score and parts, but not in either of the published piano scores, where the rhythmically articulated measure is stated three times as directed and the number of preceding measures (in which the chord is sustained) is cut by two. In both instances the cadential chord is built up and sustained (and/or repeated) over a span of seventeen measures, resolving in the eighteenth.

25 In the treatment of Porgy's entrance theme in act 3, one measure before R133.

26 As chronicled in chap. 6, this four-note pattern forms the nucleus of other Gershwin song melodies ("Clap Yo' Hands," "Maybe," "Liza") that predated "I Got Rhythm." Its preeminent role in the opening of *Porgy and Bess* is discussed in chap. 10.

27 *The Schillinger System,* 1: 98-178. The motive in question first appears as one of several possible divisions of the available space into "four units" (i.e., pitches). See *The Schillinger System,* 1: 156 (the second scale under "Four Units"), also pp. 161, 165.

28 *The Schillinger System,* 1: 157 (first scale under "Four Units").

29 The same can be said of *Lucille*'s producer Alex Aarons, who co-produced *Pardon My English*.

30 Gershwin made the following outline of the variations (manuscript in Gershwin Collection), which is quoted in both Jablonski, *Gershwin,* p. 259, and Schwartz, *Gershwin,* p. 316 n. 17. The annotations in brackets are mine:

1. Simple [variation theme, R2]
2. Orch[estra:] melody—piano[:] chromatic variation [variation 1, R5]
3. Orch[estra:] rich melody in ¾ piano[:] variation [dynamic] P [variation 2, R8]

4. Chinese variation interlude [variation 3, R11+3]

   5. Modal variation [variation 4, R14; B section, absent in previous two variations, returns at R15+13]

   6. Hot variation[;?] finale [variation 5, R19; finale, R21]

31 As examples, Schillinger shows vertically expanded pictures by El Greco and Modigliani (*The Schillinger System*, 1: 210).

32 Schillinger's fig. 40 (*The Schillinger System*, 1: 214–15) is also germane and is virtually identical to a page labeled "multiples of pitch coefficient of a theme" in Gershwin's Schillinger notebooks (*Schillinger B*, p. 12).

33 The concept of verticalizing a segment of melody to form a chord is a cornerstone of the twelve-tone system of Arnold Schoenberg. Gershwin was probably unaware of this at the time of the *Variations*, and his friendship with Schoenberg, which began later, was largely nontechnical in nature. See Jablonski, *Gershwin*, pp. 300–01, 309.

34 *The Schillinger System*, 1: 34–45).

35 In the first Schillinger notebook (*Schillinger A*, p. 41), as an illustration of "rhythm in its natural development," the first four notes of "I Got Rhythm" are analyzed durationally as 2 (opening rest), 3, 3, 3 (first three notes), 5 (fourth note).

36 No doubt this counterpoint is what Gershwin referred to as his imitation of "Chinese flutes, played out of tune, as they always are," in his introduction to his performance of the work on his radio broadcast of April 10, 1934. Evidently, he considered this "modal variation" to be of a piece with the preceding "Chinese variation interlude."

37 In Gershwin's words from the radio broadcast of April 10, 1934, "the piano plays the rhythmic variation in which the left hand plays the melody upside down and the right plays it straight, on the theory that you shouldn't let one hand know what the other is doing."

10: *Porgy and Bess*

1 The genesis of *Porgy* is covered by Jablonski, *Gershwin*, pp. 250–91; for a biographical sketch of Heyward, see pp. 252–55. Hollis Alpert, *The Life and Times of Porgy and Bess: The Story of An American Classic* (New York: Knopf, 1990), gives a complete history of the work, including accounts of all productions to date. Heyward recounts his collaboration with Gershwin in "Porgy and Bess Return on Wings of Song," *George Gershwin*, ed. Merle Armitage (London, New York, and Toronto: Longmans Green, 1938), pp. 34–42. The Armitage book, a collection of essays assembled just after Gershwin's death, contains numerous pertinent comments by others associated with the opera, including the vocal coach Alexander Steinert (pp. 43–46), the stage director Rouben Mamoulian (pp. 47–57), and the original Porgy, Todd Duncan (pp. 58–64). The opening paragraph of Gershwin's "Rhapsody in Catfish Row" (pp. 72–77) explains his view of the work as a folk opera.

2 Deena Rosenberg, *Fascinating Rhythm*, p. 274.

3 The recorded rehearsal, with Gershwin's introduction, can be heard on *Gershwin Conducts Gershwin* (Mark56 M60173).

4 The end of Gershwin's manuscript (Gershwin Collection, bound ms. no. 18, microfilm Music 1035, item 2) gives a completion date of August 23, 1935, whereas the title page indicates that the orchestration was begun in "late 1934" and finished September 2, 1935. The impeccable manuscript is unique among Gershwin's large scores in its use of staff paper without preprinted instrumentation. Still unpublished, it follows the published piano-vocal score (New York: Gershwin Publishing Corporation, 1935), though it contains numerous details that the piano score is unable to accommodate.

5 This was the production by Sherwin M. Goldman and the Houston Opera, conducted by John DeMain, which opened in 1976 (recording: RCA Red Seal ARL3-2109 [1977], reissued as RCD3-2109). This performance restored changes in the libretto made by Ira Gershwin at the behest of producer Goddard Lieberson in preparation for the Columbia recording of 1951 to exclude the word "nigger." In the previous year, Lorin Maazel conducted a complete concert version with the Cleveland Orchestra (recording: London OSA-13116 [1976], reissued as London 414559-2 LH3). See Alpert, *The Life and Times of "Porgy and Bess,"* pp. 139–40, 292–311.

6 Charles Hamm, "The Theatre Guild Production of *Porgy and Bess,*" *Journal of the American Musicological Society* 40 (1987): 495–532, contends that the cuts made for the original Broadway production improved the dramatic structure of the play. The pros and cons of Hamm's thesis are discussed in Alpert, *The Life and Times of "Porgy and Bess,"* pp. 309–10.

7 For a photo of Cabbage Row, see Alpert, *The Life and Times of "Porgy and Bess,"* p. 12.

8 For slightly over a month during June–July 1934), Gershwin lived with his cousin, artist Henry Botkin, in a rented cottage on Folly Island off the coast of Charleston, where he worked in near seclusion. On nearby James Island, with Heyward as his guide, he became steeped in the music and speech patterns of the indigenous Gullah blacks, whose language and customs remain close to their African roots (Jablonski, *Gershwin,* pp. 272–76; Alpert, *The Life and Times of "Porgy and Bess,"* pp. 87–89). The chanting in the introduction and the use of African drums at the opening of act 2, scene 2 reflect this influence.

9 Gershwin kept this sequence intact, sans voices, as the first movement of a promotional orchestral suite introduced in 1936. Shelved the next year after only a few performances, this suite, renamed *Catfish Row* by Ira Gershwin on its rediscovery in 1958 by his secretary Lawrence D. Stewart (coauthor with Jablonski of *The Gershwin Years*), was Gershwin's last orchestral work (Jablonski, *Gershwin,* pp. 294–96). The first movement, also titled "Catfish Row," includes the Jasbo Brown music that was excised from the Broadway production; this corroborates the view that the cuts were not what Gershwin ideally wanted.

10 See chaps. 6 and 10. Following the classification of pitch-class sets in Allen Forte,

The Structure of Atonal Music, the trichords F♯–G♯–C♯ and F♯–B–C♯ are of the form 3-9, while F♯–G♯–B represents the form 3-7. Their union, F♯–G♯–B–C♯, is set 4-23. Representations of set 4-23 are identified in exx. 130 and 132 with the numbers in curly brackets denoting steps of the chromatic scale, with C set at zero.

11 The ghost of Petroushka also loomed large over the "Dancing in the Streets" number in *Pardon My English* (ex. 101). The concrete connection between *Petroushka* and the latter work makes the association with *Porgy* that much more plausible.

12 In Forte's system of set classification, the respective set names and pitch-class contents in example 136 are as follows. In Jasbo Brown section, chord 1: 5-34 {6,9,11,1,3}; chord 2: 5-34 {4,7,9,11,1}; combined: 7-34 {3,4,6,7,9,11,1} in "Summertime," chord 1: 4-27 {6,8,11,2}; chord 2: 4-27 {8,10,1,4}; combined: 7-34 {4,6,8,10,11,1,2}; intersection of Jasbo Brown section and "Summertime": 4-23 {11,1,4,6}.

13 The voices sing in syllables described by Gershwin in a letter to Heyward (cited in Jablonski, *Gershwin,* p. 270) as "a sort of African chant."

14 "Bess, You Is My Woman Now" is the way to which the song is usually referred; the published title, which lacks the "now," seems stilted by comparison. An early manuscript version of "I Got Plenty o' Nuttin'" spells the last word "Nuthin'."

15 The crap game theme also foreshadows Porgy's entrance theme, as pointed out in Rosenberg, *Fascinating Rhythm,* p. 282. Pertinent to the discussion of this portion of the opera and to the influence of Joseph Schillinger is Paul Nauert, "Theory and Practice in *Porgy and Bess:* The Gershwin-Schillinger Connection," *Musical Quarterly* 78 (1994): 9–34.

16 The chord progression contiguous to the sketch in ex. 139b ("Tune Book," pp. 17-18) is closely related to a passage in the postmortem scene (I.2) beginning at R204.

17 The Gs on the bottom staff are clearly marked with natural signs in the orchestral manuscript, though not in the piano-vocal score.

18 "Occupational Humoresque" was the title Gershwin gave to the third-act incarnation of this music in the *Catfish Row* suite.

19 *Tune Book (1933–37),* p. 26. Ira Gershwin's inventory, compiled in 1971, lists the entry as "'Porgy'; probably 1st sketch of 'I Got Plenty O' Nuthin'.'" (Note his preference for *Nuthin'* over the score's *Nuttin'.*) Written in A major rather than the eventual G, the sketch gives the song melody in full, without lyrics, as was consistent with the Gershwins' normal procedure of doing the music first. Consistent as well with George's long-standing but newly enriched love of counterpoint, he indicates no chords but does write the chromatically descending inner voice at the start of the bridge.

20 The piano-vocal score has this material in small type.

21 These countermelodies do not appear in the published vocal score. Most likely they were added during the orchestration; otherwise they probably would have been published in small type, like similar counterpoints elsewhere.

22 A literal statement of the Catfish Row opening would have the note B on the fourth eighth note of each of the two measures beginning one before R178; in-

stead, Gershwin has C♯. There is no apparent reason for this change: B is part of the E-major triad that supports these measures and is otherwise used as expected.

23 This table takes as its point of departure the indices of scenes and of "songs, arias and themes" published on facing pages in the piano-vocal score. Salient reprises and transitions, overlooked in the published index, are added, along with the home key(s) of each musical number.

24 Jablonski, *Gershwin,* p. 167.

11: The Final Period

1 Jablonski, *Gershwin,* pp. 292–93, 297–98.

2 An anomaly from an earlier period is "In the Mandarin's Orchid Garden," composed in 1929 for *East is West* (a Ziegfeld revue that was never produced) and published on its own the following year (New York: New World Music, 1930). In the manner of a true art song, its piano part is complementary to the voice, with no doublings.

3 Ira Gershwin, *Lyrics on Several Occasions,* p. 170; see also Jablonski, *Gershwin,* p. 299.

4 Jablonski, *Gershwin,* pp. 299–300; Schwartz, *Gershwin,* p. 347.

5 Ira Gershwin wrote a substitute first quatrain for the film version of "By Strauss" that obviated the need to get clearances from Irving Berlin, Cole Porter, and the estate of Jerome Kern, all of whom were mentioned in the original (*Lyrics on Several Occasions,* p. 171).

6 "Hi-Ho!" was discarded before filming began, not because the director, Mark Sandrich, did not like it—he did—but because of the cost of staging it. See the account by Ira Gershwin in his preface to the posthumously published score (New York: Chappell, 1967), also Jablonski, *Gershwin,* p. 299.

7 This and other examples from "Hi-Ho!" are based on Gershwin's manuscript (Gershwin Collection, Library of Congress). The published score is in F rather than G and makes the usual pianistic compromises discussed in the text. The manuscript is musically complete in both the vocal and piano parts but lacks lyrics.

8 In the recapitulation, the text after the first "Hi-Ho!" (beginning at m. 73) was originally "For me there's none can top her; / Even if you offered Garbo, I wouldn't swap her." The published score substitutes "Venus" for "Garbo." Though the lyrics are mostly missing from the manuscript, they were recorded, presumably as first written, by Ira Gershwin himself at a party in 1938, with the Gershwins' friend Harold Arlen at the piano. This performance is among the rarities included in *Gershwin Conducts Gershwin* (Mark56 M60173).

9 This passage is immediately reminiscent of the Tin Man's song "If I Only Had a Brain" from *The Wizard of Oz* (1939), with lyrics by E. Y. Harburg and music by Harold Arlen. Harburg (born Isidore Hochberg) wrote a column with Ira Gershwin when both attended the City College of New York. Arlen accompanied Ira's singing of the song (see previous note) and might have been influenced by it.

10 The title in the published score has "I've Got" in parentheses.

11 For example, about "They Can't Take That Away" Gershwin felt that in the film it was "literally throw[n] . . . away without a plug" (Jablonski, *Gershwin,* p. 302).

12 A sketch for the refrain in "Tune Book 1933–37," p. 53, has the "Gosh, I'm lucky!" measure (the last two beats as an eighth plus dotted quarter instead of two quarters) but not "Gosh, I'm fortunate!" The latter was obviously added later, and it is only logical that it would have been derived from its counterpart in the first stanza. The melody for the bridge differs as well, chiefly in its use of B♭ where the final version has B♮.

13 In the manuscript to "Nice Work," written in A♭ (as opposed to the published score's "easier" key of G), this line is labeled "marcato" (Gershwin Collection). In addition, the first lines of the bridge, "Just imagine someone / Waiting at the cottage door," suggest imagery from two earlier songs, "Soon" (". . . a little cottage will find us / Safe . . .") and "I've Got a Crush On You" ("Could you care / For a cunning cottage we could share?"). Deena Rosenberg, *Fascinating Rhythm,* p. 357, notes the first of these, observing the correspondence between "Where two hearts become one" from "Nice Work" and "Soon—two hearts as one will be blended."

14 Ira Gershwin and Vernon Duke had previously worked together on the score for *Ziegfeld Follies of 1936,* which included "I Can't Get Started."

15 Though he worked anonymously at the time, Duke took credit for these verses in subsequent interviews. However, Jablonski, *Gershwin,* p. 326, asserts that Gershwin had played prospective verses for his brother and for Oscar Levant, both of whom would have remembered what they had heard. Ira Gershwin's recollection on the subject is that he and Duke "fixed up a couple of missing verses later" (*Lyrics on Several Occasions,* p. 284.)

16 It should be noted that the verse of "Just Another Rhumba" was copyrighted in a separate folio in a different copyist's hand and that Gershwin's pencil holograph (Gershwin Collection) contains only the refrain and trio. These facts strongly indicate that "Just Another Rhumba," like other songs from *The Goldwyn Follies,* had a verse that was completed by Duke. Still, the entire song, verse and all, was deposited for copyright in the Library of Congress on July 29, 1937, just over two weeks after Gershwin's death on July 11.

17 Jablonski, *Gershwin,* pp. 327–71.

18 The opening credits list "Miss Kay Swift" as "Musical Assistant to Ira Gershwin." Swift, herself a songwriter, is best known for "Fine and Dandy" (1930).

Select Bibliography

Alpert, Hollis. *The Life and Times of "Porgy and Bess": The Story of an American Classic.* New York: Alfred A. Knopf, 1990.

Atkins, Irene Kahn. *Source Music in Motion Pictures.* Rutherford, Madison, and Teaneck, N.J.: Fairleigh Dickinson University Press, 1983.

Crawford, Richard. "Gershwin's Reputation: A Note on *Porgy and Bess.*" *The Musical Quarterly* 65 (1979): 257–64.

Duke, Vernon. "Gershwin, Schillinger, and Dukelsky." *The Musical Quarterly* 33 (1947): 102–15.

Duke, Vernon. *Passport to Paris.* Boston: Little, Brown, 1955.

Ewen, David. *George Gershwin: His Journey to Greatness.* Englewood Cliffs, N.J.: Prentice-Hall, 1970. Earlier version published as *Journey to Greatness* (New York: Henry Holt, and London: W. H. Allen, 1956).

Forte, Allen. *The Structure of Atonal Music.* New Haven and London: Yale University Press, 1973.

Forte, Allen. *The American Popular Ballad of the Golden Era, 1924–1950.* Princeton: Princeton University Press, 1995.

Forte, Allen, and Steven E. Gilbert. *Introduction to Schenkerian Analysis.* New York: Norton, 1982.

Gershwin, Ira. "My Brother's Manuscript." Preface to the first published edition of *Lullaby for String Quartet.* New York: New World Music Corporation, 1968.

Gershwin, Ira. *Lyrics on Several Occasions: A Selection of Stage and Screen Lyrics Written for Sundry Situations; and Now Arranged in Arbitrary Categories. To Which Have Been Added Many Informative Annotations and Disquisitions on Their Why and Wherefore, Their Whom-For, Their How; and Matters Associative.* New York: Alfred A. Knopf, 1959. Reprint, New York: Viking Press, 1973.

Gilbert, Steven E. "Gershwin's Art of Counterpoint." *The Musical Quarterly* 70 (1984): 423–56.

Goldberg, Isaac. *George Gershwin: A Study in American Music.* New York: Simon & Schuster, 1931. Reprint. Supplemented by Edith Garson. Foreword and discography by Alan Dashiell. New York: Frederick Ungar, 1958.

Hamm, Charles. "The Theatre Guild Production of *Porgy and Bess.*" *Journal of the American Musicological Society* 40 (1987): 495–532.

——— . *Yesterdays: Popular Song in America.* New York: Norton, 1979.

Isacoff, Stuart. "Fascinatin' Gershwin." *Keyboard Classics* (January–February 1984), pp. 6–11.

Jablonski, Edward. *Gershwin: A Biography.* New York: Doubleday, 1987.

Jablonski, Edward, and Lawrence D. Stewart. *The Gershwin Years.* 2nd ed. Introduction by Carl Van Vechten. New York: Doubleday, 1973.

Keller, Hans. "Rhythm: Gershwin and Stravinsky." *The Score and I.M.A. Magazine,* no. 20 (June 1957): 19–31.

Kimball, Robert, ed. *The Complete Lyrics of Ira Gershwin.* New York: Alfred A. Knopf, 1993. Incorporates commentary from *Lyrics on Several Occasions.*

Maisel, Arthur. "Talent and Technique: George Gershwin's *Rhapsody in Blue.*" Ph.D. diss., City University of New York, 1989.

Maisel, Arthur. "Talent and Technique: George Gershwin's *Rhapsody in Blue.*" In *Trends in Schenkerian Research,* ed. Allen Cadwallader, pp. 51–69. New York: Schirmer Books, 1990.

Nauert, Paul. "Theory and Practice in *Porgy and Bess:* The Gershwin-Schillinger Connection." *Musical Quarterly* 78 (1994): 9–34.

Payne, Robert. *Gershwin.* New York: Pyramid Books, 1960.

Peyser, Joan. *The Memory of All That: The Life of George Gershwin.* New York: Simon & Schuster, 1993.

Rosenberg, Deena. *Fascinating Rhythm: The Collaboration of George and Ira Gershwin.* New York: Dutton, 1991.

Schenker, Heinrich. *Free Composition (Der freie Satz): Volume III of New Musical Theories and Fantasies.* Translated and edited by Ernst Oster. 2 vols. New York: Longman, 1979.

Schiff, David. "Composers on the Couch." *The Atlantic Monthly* 273/1 (January 1994): 106–122.

Schillinger, Joseph. *The Schillinger System of Musical Composition.* 2 vols. New York: Carl Fischer, 1941. Reprint, New York: Da Capo, 1978.

Schneider, Wayne J. "George Gershwin's Political Operettas *Of Thee I Sing* (1931) and *Let 'Em Eat Cake* (1933), and Their Role in Gershwin's Musical and Emotional Maturing." Ph.D. dissertation, Cornell University, 1985.

Schwartz, Charles. *Gershwin: His Life and Music.* With an appreciation by Leonard Bernstein. New York: Bobbs-Merrill, 1973. Reprint, New York: Da Capo Press, 1979.

Shirley, Wayne D. "George Gershwin Learns to Orchestrate." *The Sonneck Society Bulletin* 16/3 (Fall 1990): 101–2.

Shirley, Wayne D. "Scoring the Concerto in F: George Gershwin's First Orchestration." *American Music* 3/3 (Fall 1985): 277–98.

Starr, Lawrence. "Gershwin's 'Bess, You Is My Woman Now': The Sophistication and Subtlety of a Great Tune." *The Musical Quarterly* 72 (1986): 429–48.

Starr, Lawrence. "Toward a Reevaluation of Gershwin's *Porgy and Bess.*" *American Music* 2/2 (Summer 1984): 25–37.

Wilder, Alec. *American Popular Song: The Great Innovators, 1900–1950.* Edited with an introduction by James T. Maher. New York: Oxford University Press, 1972. See especially chapter 4, "George Gershwin (1898–1937)," pp. 121–62.

Wyatt, Robert. "The Seven Jazz Preludes of George Gershwin: A Historical Narrative." *American Music* 7/1 (1989): 68–85.

Credits

An American in Paris, by George Gershwin. © 1929 WB Music Corp. (Renewed). All Rights Reserved. Used by Permission. Warner Bros. Publications, Inc., Miami, Fla. 33014.

"Blue Blue Blue," by George Gershwin, Ira Gershwin. © 1933 (Renewed) WB Music Corp. (ASCAP). All Rights Reserved. Used by Permission. Warner Bros. Publications, Inc., Miami, Fla. 33014.

Blue Monday, by George Gershwin, B. G. DeSylva. © 1976 New World Music Corp. All Rights Reserved. Used by Permission. Warner Bros. Publications, Inc., Miami, Fla. 33014.

"By Strauss." Music and lyrics by George Gershwin and Ira Gershwin. © 1936 (Renewed 1963) George Gershwin Music and Ira Gershwin Music. All Rights Administered by WB Music Corp. All Rights Reserved. Used by Permission. Warner Bros. Publications, Inc., Miami, Fla. 33014.

"Clap Yo' Hands," by Ira Gershwin, George Gershwin. © 1926 WB Music Corp. (Renewed). All Rights Reserved. Used by Permission. Warner Bros. Publications, Inc., Miami, Fla. 33014.

Concerto in F, by George Gershwin. © 1927 WB Music Corp. (Renewed). All Rights Reserved. Used by Permission. Warner Bros. Publications, Inc., Miami, Fla. 33014.

Cuban Overture, by George Gershwin. © 1933 WB Music Corp. (Renewed). All Rights Reserved. Used by Permission. Warner Bros. Publications, Inc., Miami, Fla. 33014.

"Dancing in the Streets." Words by Ira Gershwin, music by George Gershwin. © 1932 WB Music Corp. (Renewed). All Rights Reserved. Used by Permission. Warner Bros. Publications, Inc., Miami, Fla. 33014.

"Do It Again!" by George Gershwin, B. G. DeSylva. © 1922 WB Music Corp. (Renewed). All Rights Reserved. Used by Permission. Warner Bros. Publications, Inc., Miami, Fla. 33014.

"Embraceable You," by Ira Gershwin, George Gershwin. © 1930 WB Music Corp. (Renewed). All Rights Reserved. Used by Permission. Warner Bros. Publications, Inc., Miami, Fla. 33014.

"Fascinating Rhythm," by Ira Gershwin, George Gershwin. © 1924 WB Music Corp. (Renewed). All Rights Reserved. Used by Permission. Warner Bros. Publications, Inc., Miami, Fla. 33014.

"Fidgety Feet," by George Gershwin, Ira Gershwin. © 1926 WB Music Corporation (Renewed). All Rights Reserved. Used by Permission. Warner Bros. Publications, Inc., Miami, Fla. 33014.

"Funny Face," by George Gershwin, Ira Gershwin. © 1927 WB Music Corp. (Renewed) (ASCAP). All Rights Reserved. Used by Permission. Warner Bros. Publications, Inc., Miami, Fla. 33014.

"Hi-Ho!" by George Gershwin, Ira Gershwin. © 1936 (Renewed) George Gershwin Music (ASCAP) and Ira Gershwin Music (ASCAP). All Rights Administered by WB Music Corp. All Rights Reserved. Used by Permission. Warner Bros. Publications, Inc., Miami, Fla. 33014.

"How Long Has This Been Going On?" by Ira Gershwin, George Gershwin. © 1927 WB Music Corp. (Renewed). All Rights Reserved. Used by Permission. Warner Bros. Publications, Inc., Miami, Fla. 33014.

"I Got Rhythm," by Ira Gershwin, George Gershwin. © 1930 WB Music Corp. (Renewed). All Rights Reserved. Used by Permission. Warner Bros. Publications, Inc., Miami, Fla. 33014.

"I'll Build a Stairway to Paradise," by George Gershwin, B. G. DeSylva, Ira Gershwin. © 1922 WB Music Corp. (Renewed). All Rights Reserved. Used by Permission. Warner Bros. Publications, Inc., Miami, Fla. 33014.

"Isn't It a Pity?" Music and lyrics by George Gershwin and Ira Gershwin. © 1932 WB Music Corp. (Renewed). All Rights Reserved. Used by Permission. Warner Bros. Publications, Inc., Miami, Fla. 33014.

"I've Got Beginner's Luck." Music and lyrics by George Gershwin and Ira Gershwin. © 1936 (Renewed) George Gershwin Music and Ira Gershwin Music. All Rights Administered by WB Music Corp. All Rights Reserved. Used by Permission. Warner Bros. Publications, Inc., Miami, Fla. 33014.

"Just Another Rhumba." Music and lyrics by George Gershwin and Ira Gershwin. © 1937 (Renewed 1964) George Gershwin Music and Ira Gershwin Music. All Rights Administered by WB Music Corp. All Rights Reserved. Used by Permission. Warner Bros. Publications, Inc., Miami, Fla. 33014.

"Liza," by George Gershwin, Gus Kahn, Ira Gershwin. © 1929 WB Music Corp. (Renewed). All Rights Reserved. Used by Permission. Warner Bros. Publications, Inc., Miami, Fla. 33014.

"Love Is Here to Stay." Music and lyrics by George Gershwin and Ira Gershwin. © 1938 (Renewed 1965) George Gershwin Music and Ira Gershwin Music. All Rights Administered by WB Music Corp. All Rights Reserved. Used by Permission. Warner Bros. Publications, Inc., Miami, Fla. 33014.

"Love Walked In." Music and lyrics by George Gershwin and Ira Gershwin. © 1937, 1938 (Renewed 1964, 1965) George Gershwin Music and Ira Gershwin Music. All Rights Administered by WB Music Corp. All Rights Reserved. Used by Permission. Warner Bros. Publications, Inc., Miami, Fla. 33014.

Lullaby for String Quartet, by George Gershwin. © 1963, 1968 New World Music Co., Ltd. All Rights Reserved. Used by Permission. Warner Bros. Publications, Inc., Miami, Fla. 33014.

"The Man I Love," by Ira Gershwin, George Gershwin. © 1924 WB Music Corp. (Renewed). All Rights Reserved. Used by Permission. Warner Bros. Publications, Inc., Miami, Fla. 33014.

"Maybe," by Ira Gershwin, George Gershwin. © 1926 WB Music Corp. (Renewed).

Index